Bridal Durries of India

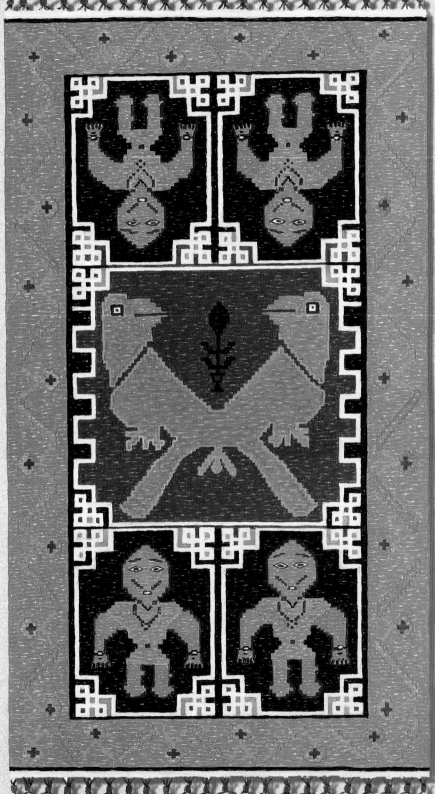

Bridal Durries of India

Ann Shankar

Jenny Housego

Mapin Publishing Pvt. Ltd.
Ahmedabad

First published in the United States of America
in 1997 by
Grantha Corporation
80 Cliffedgeway, Middletown, NJ 07701

in association with
Mapin Publishing Pvt. Ltd.
Chidambaram, Ahmedabad 380013 India

Distributed in North America by
Antique Collectors' Club
Market Street, Industrial Park
Wappingers' Falls, NY 12590
Tel: 800-252-5231 • Fax: 914-297-0068

Distributed in the United Kingdom
& Europe by
Antique Collectors' Club
5 Church Street, Woodbridge
Suffolk IP12 1DS
Tel: 1394 385-501 • Fax: 1394 384-434

ISBN: 0-944142-79-6
ISBN: 81-85822-44-1
LC: 96-77162

Edited by Shernaz Cama
Designed by Paulomi Shah/Mapin Design Studio
Typeset by Swift Graphics Pvt. Ltd
Processed by Reproscan
Printed in Singapore

All illustrations are based on author's photographs
and are illustrated by:

Ashok Bhavsar: 5, 34, 53(bottom), 55, 57, 58, 60,
61, 62(top), 64, 70, 76, 78, 82(top), 83, 85, 86, 88,
89, 92, 93, 98, 102, 105, 109(left), 113(left), 117,
128, 131, 134, 142, 143, 146, 154, 155, 156, 158,
159.

Jalp Lakhia: 6, 16, 30, 38, 40, 50, 53(top), 63, 69,
73, 74, 81, 99,103, 111, 130, 138.

Pankaj Mohan: 2, 54, 72, 75, 77, 79, 112,
113(right), 114, 118, 119, 120, 126, 129, 150, 151,
166.

Sunil Parmar: 18

Umesh Soni: 45, 46, 47, 48, 62(bottom), 65, 66, 71,
80, 82(bottom), 84, 91, 97, 101, 104, 106,
109(right), 115, 116, 121, 123, 124, 125, 135, 136,
140, 144, 148.

....

The corporations concerned with
the preservation of India's heritage, who
have made this book possible are:

Air India
Arvind Mills
Reliance Industries
(Textile Division)
Tiger Tops Mountain Travel,
India and Nepal
Rajshree Group of Companies,
Coimbatore

....

Dedication

To the women of North India
who so generously took us into their homes
and shared their traditions with us

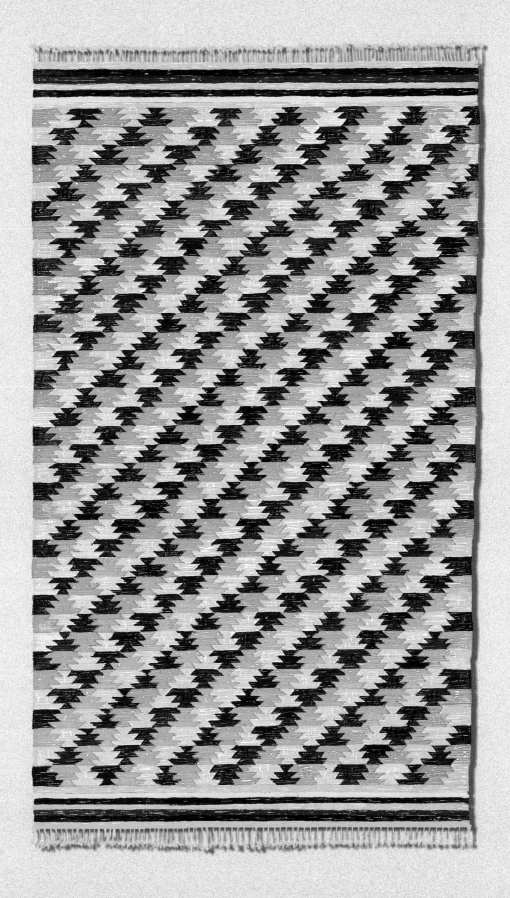

Contents

Acknowledgements   8

Preface   10

Map   12

The World of the Weavers   14
    The Women
    The Setting
    Dowry
    The Bridal or Dowry Durrie
    Other Durries

The Web of Tradition:
Myth & History   24
    Myth
    Historical Roots
    Durrie Weaving
    The *Charpoi*

Warp and Weft   42
    Yarn Preparation
    Spinning
    Dyeing
    Weaving Techniques
    Warp Finishes
    Printing Techniques
    The Loom
    Jail Weaving

Designs for Dowry   52
    Durrie Names and Symbols
    A Naturalistic Canvas
    Dolls
    The *Pipal* Tree
    Animals
    Lions
    Horses
    Deer
    Hare
    Squirrels
    Snakes

    Fish
    Peacocks
    Roseringed Parakeets
    Domestic Fowl
    Ducks
    Sparrows

The Geometry of Design   96
    Phul
    Half Lozenges
    Serrated Rectangles and Rhomboids
    Serrated Bands
    Intersecting Circles
    Three Plant Forms
    Cross and Triangle
    Eight Pointed Stars
    Diagonal Crosses
    The "S" Forms
    Combs and Drums
    Rows of Triangles
    Lozenges in a Lattice
    Earth and Sky
    Boxes
    Crenellated Borders
    Boats
    Teasets

Spun Tales:
Legends and Couplets   162
    Mirza-Sahiban
    Hir-Ranjha
    Jeona Maur

Postscript/Appendix   169
    Natural Dyes

Endnotes   172

Bibliography   184

Glossary   195

Acknowledgements

Our thanks go first to Mr. Iqbal Singh, then editor of *Advance*, a magazine on Punjab affairs, who in 1988 suggested an article on Punjab durries and, as the material grew, encouraged us to write a complete book. Our work was given its initial impetus through the help of Mr. S. K. Sinha, at the time Director of the Department of Information and Public Relations, Government of Punjab, and members of its staff in various parts of the state. Without this support the study could not have been undertaken and no village door would have been opened to us.

Through Mr. Julio Ribeiro, formerly Advisor to the Governor of Punjab, we visited jails in the state, and saw the weaving there at first hand. Through Mrs. Melba Ribeiro we met Mrs. Gurshi Aulakh, whose great interest in Punjab durries and personal kindness led us to a great deal of information never duplicated in later field work. To them, our warmest thanks.

The greatest proportion of our field work was accomplished with the help of Mr. Prem Singh, a farmer living at the village of Khuda Ali Sher in the Union Territory of Chandigarh and working with the *Tribune* newspaper in Chandigarh. For months he accompanied us to villages in the Chandigarh area where his friends and family showed us their durries and patiently answered our questions. Through him the realities of life for the smallholding farmer of Punjab gradually came alive for us. We are deeply grateful to everyone who made time for us to see their durries but our chief thanks are to Mr. Prem Singh, for it is his contribution that forms the backbone of this book.

Research into the history of the durrie designs would scarcely have been possible without the archaeology and art history collections of the library of the University of Bombay.

Mr. Kulbashan Rishi and Mr. Kuldeep Singh of the Department of Cultural Affairs, Archaeology and Museums of the Government of Punjab, gave most valuable help and suggestions, and we were made welcome in the library of this department.

Professor Devendra Handa of the Department of Ancient Indian History, Culture and Archaeology, Punjab University, gave constant encouragement and advice. He kindly read through much of the manuscript. Mr. Lalman of Punjab University, accompanied us on tours of the Kangra Valley and extended to us his knowledge of the area and the warm hospitality of his family and friends.

Our thanks also go to Dr. Irving Finkel, Dr. Elizabeth Savage, Dr. Lovelina Sidhu and Mr. Iqbal Singh, who read through earlier versions of the manuscript and whose suggestions we have tried to incorporate.

Our research in Haryana was largely due to the unstinted energy and enthusiasm of Vijneshu Mohan, who took us into villages where he had carried out his own archaeological field work. Our most grateful thanks are due also to his family, who welcomed us into their home at Kurukshetra. Through his father, Professor Chandra Mohan, we were able to explore Western Haryana. We thank members of the staff at the Haryana Agricultural University at Hissar for their help and in particular Dr. O.P. Parik and Dr. Shamsher Narwal. Through Mr. K.K. Sharma we were made welcome in villages in the Gurgaon region of Southern Haryana.

We would also like to thank members of the Department of Archaeology at Kurukshetra University, and in particular Dr. Suraj Bhan.

Dr. Harjeet Singh Gill of the Jawaharlal Nehru University, New Delhi, provided a forum for discussion of our work. Dr. B.M. Pande of the Archaeological Survey of India most kindly devoted time to reading part of the manuscript. We would also like to thank Dr. Jyotindra Jain of the Crafts Museum, New Delhi, Ms. Madhu Bala of the Archaeological Survey as well as members of the Staff in the library of the Archaeological Survey of India and in that of the National Museum in New Delhi, in particular Mr. Jitendra Nath of the Central Asian Department of the National Museum.

Dr. Oliver Guillaume of the Centre des Sciences Humaines in New Delhi generously read another part of the manuscript. We are indebted to him and also to Dr. Lotika Varadarajan and to Mr. Simon Digby, both of whom gave invaluable comments on further sections. Dr. Varadarajan was a constant source of support throughout the project, and we should like to offer our special thanks to her, as also to Dr. Chhahya Haesner. Of course no-one who read the manuscript and offered suggestions is in any way responsible for any of the views expressed in the book. We are also extremely grateful for the help and encouragement of Ms. Laila Tyabji, Ms. Bunny Page, Ms. Jasleen Dhamija, Dr. Yolande Crowe, Mr. Manmohan Singh, Mr. M.S. Gill, Dr. Surjeet Singh and Dr. Geet Oberio, and Ms. Clara Shroff and Ms. Smita Lahiri who did much of the early typing and checking.

We thank our publishers Mallika Sarabhai and Bipin Shah of Mapin for the skill and taste with which they have created a book in perfect harmony with its subject; Paulomi Shah worked with tireless efficiency and good humour to design and prepare the manuscript for the printers while our sympathetic and professional editor Shernaz Cama re-organized and improved the text in countless ways. We deeply appreciate all their effort.

Finally, we offer our most grateful thanks to Gowri Shankar and David Housego for their support and forbearance throughout the course of this study.

Preface

The Indian durrie, a flat-woven cotton rug, varies in size from a 1m x 1m *asan*, seat, on which a person sits cross-legged to a 4m x 6m *farshi*, for a large room or tent. Durries are woven by men and women for personal or commercial use all over the subcontinent. The bridal durries are however strictly personal, woven by women and carried to their new homes as part of their dowry. These have a standard size, roughly 1m x 2m and are placed on the *charpoi*, the traditional Indian bed, never on the floor.

This study was initially begun for a short article on the durries of Punjab, which soon expanded into this book. Since this was the first systematic study of these bridal durries almost everything about them was a discovery. The great variety of their designs came as a surprise, as well as the fact that they were woven not only in Punjab but throughout Haryana, the lower parts of Himachal Pradesh, northern Rajasthan and western Uttar Pradesh, approximately the region comprising the earlier state of Punjab before its division into three states in 1966. A study of durrie designs is of interest for two reasons. Firstly, a picture of contemporary rural life emerges from the names and stories attached to the durries by the weavers and, secondly, they record an ancient tradition common to the entire area. It is thus possible to draw comparisons with motifs found in very early times in India, and trace some of them over several millennia up to the present day. Here we may perhaps best recall the thoughts of Heinrich Zimmer, who says:

> "The life strength of symbols and symbolic figures is inexhaustible, especially when carried forward by a highly conservative traditional civilization such as that of India.... The vista of <u>duration</u> that they open...... suggests spiritual continuities persisting through immense reaches of time."[1]

Comparisons are also made in this study with designs found on material from ancient sites in West and Central Asia, to show the remote ancestry of these motifs and to point out parallels from cultures with which India had ancient links.

The survey began in November, 1988 and continued until February, 1991, with occasional trips as late as 1992. It is as thorough as circumstances and opportunities would allow. Every bridal durrie is a prized personal possession; our visits had to be through personal introductions and, as we were guests in busy households, there were limits to the demands that could be made on families. Most weavers could spare an hour at the most for exploring dowry chests and answering questions. Ninety-four villages of the bridal durrie region were visited and 1365 durries, woven in 249 villages belonging to 32 disctricts, were recorded. A total survey would mean visiting every village house – clearly an impossibility. The scale of the task may be gauged from the figures for the village of Khuda Ali Sher where the highest number of durries were seen. In this village of about 500 families, almost all of whose members sleep on *charpoi* covered with handwoven durries, 102 durries woven by 19 women in 10 households were examined. In the text the names of the durrie designs have been used in the original Hindi and Punjabi.

We were fortunate in being able to visit jails in Punjab to see in addition the durrie weaving done by prisoners. Though related by technique to the village weaving, jail durries proved to be distinct in function, size and design, warranting an independent study. We were not in a position to undertake this but have included a short section on the jail weaving and have used it for comparison in several cases.

Pakistani Punjab could not be included. A study of bridal durrie weaving there would take several years and might be more easily undertaken by people living in that area.

In the study durrie weaving is seen both in its village as well as in its historical context. The technicalities of the process of manufacture are also described in order to give as complete a picture as possible of this ancient yet vigorous craft.

---

1. Zimmer, H. *Myths and Symbols in Indian Art and Civilization*, New York, Pantheon, 1962; 169-170.

Durrie Weaving Regions

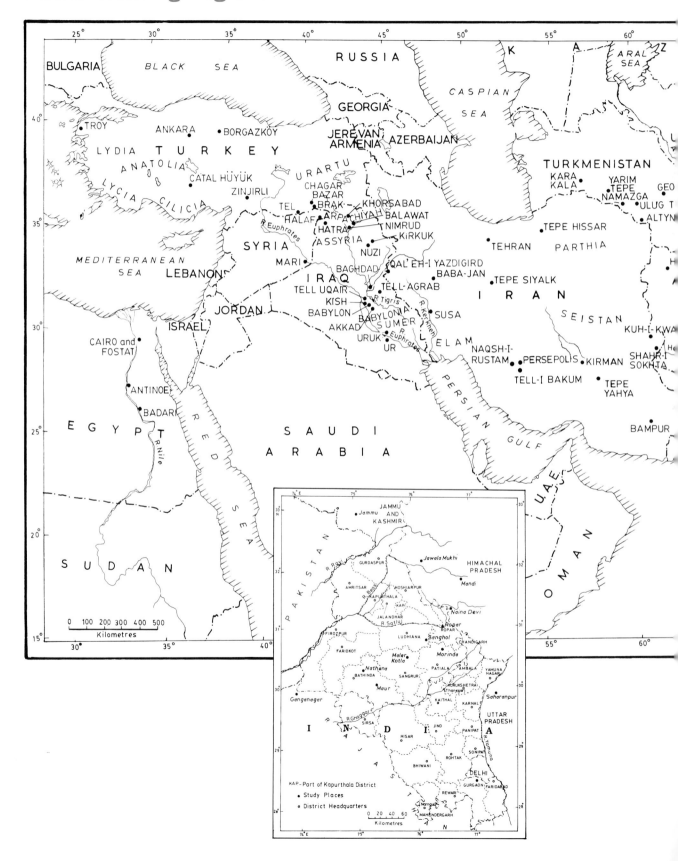

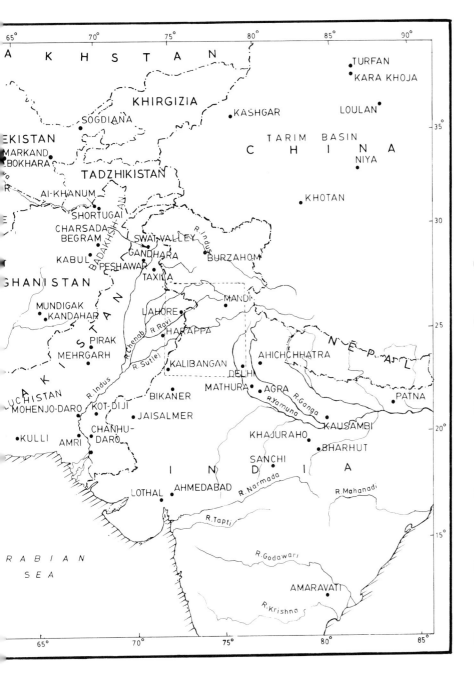

(i) Based upon Survey of India map with the permission of the Surveyor General of India.

(ii) The responsibility for correctness of internal detail rests with the Publisher; for errors and omissions reference may be made to them.

(iii) The territorial waters of India extend into the sea to a distance of twelve nautical miles measured from the appropriate base-line.

(iv) The administrative headquarters of Chandigarh, Haryana and Punjab are at Chandigarh.

(v) The external boundaries and coastlines of India agree with the Record/Master Copy certified by Survey of India.

(vi) © Government of India Copyright 1996.

The World of the Weavers

The Women

Bed durries made for the bridal *bistra,* bedding set, are an essential part of the handmade dowry of most girls in the villages of northwestern India. The great majority of these durries are woven by the girls themselves. In contrast, city girls today rarely weave at home but buy machine-made durries from the bazaar.

Everything about the life of village women points to a long cultural tradition revolving around the land, family, special domestic events, and religious festivals. They lead very active lives, for not only do they run the household and raise a family but they also help with the farm work. Hardworking, efficient, cheerful and affectionate, they invite deep admiration. Nor do they lack courage; no-one who knows them would be surprised that it was a woman who stayed to challenge the legendary dacoit, Jeona Maur. Their approach to life is direct; an observant eye and pithy humour help make light of human vanities and foibles.

These women live largely in a world of their own with its strong attachments and loyalties. Their menfolk are away long hours in the fields or, in many cases, at jobs in nearby towns and cities and even

A weaver, over ninety years old, with her family, Bindrakh village, Ropar district, Punjab.

Right:
Weaver, Mohri village, Ambala district, Haryana.

14

after nightfall, meet separately with their friends. In Haryana they often work in distant cities and return home only for annual holidays.

Usually several women share a household, which is home to three generations of the extended family. This would be composed of grandparents, their sons and their wives, their unmarried daughters and the children of their sons. Since marriages are not arranged between members of the same village or clan, this means a new village for the bride, who will go to live in her husband's family home.

The passing years bring increasing respect and authority for the women. Their position is further enhanced if, as sometimes happens, their husbands choose to leave the household in their hands and retire to live peacefully beside the tubewell in the middle of their fields when they can no longer work on the farm.

Particular affection is given to very old women in their eighties and nineties. They spend winter days lying on a *charpoi,* traditional Indian bed, gently fading away under a benign sun. At the appearance of a camera they would, all seemingly unawares, be wrapped in their best shawl, have a watch strapped on their wrist and be propped up amidst a proud family for a photograph. The only time we were ever asked to make a special visit to a household for photographs was not for a new baby or important anniversary but for a family gathering around a great grandmother over a hundred years old. It was a matter of great urgency and significance for her progeny, who feared they might lose her before she had been recorded on film.

The Setting
The land where the bridal durries are woven is a flat, agricultural plain through which flow the great rivers of northern India: the Ravi, Beas, Sutlej, Yamuna and Ganga. Only the peripheral area of lower Himachal Pradesh lies beyond it in the foothills of the Himalayan mountains. The climate is typical of north India, with cold, usually sunny winters and gruelling summers. The rains of July, August and September bring down the temperature but the humidity is high and relief comes only in the latter part of September, with the first traces of autumn coolness in the evening air.

Modern irrigation schemes which began with the completion of the Bari Doab Canal in 1860-61, have turned vast uncultivated areas into fertile and productive farmland. The introduction of high-yielding crops, particularly long-staple American cotton around 1915, has provided cash income for farmers. Before this the village economy was based on barter. The well-timbered fields of a farmer's land supplied almost all the family needs: vegetables, fruit, pulses, grains and sugarcane, as well as cotton for clothing and bedding. Cows and buffaloes provided milk, from which was made *ghee*, clarified butter, a favourite cooking medium, and also ensured a regular supply of useful cowdung. Wood and mud took care of the material needs of house construction, while chopped straw and cowdung mixed and spread as a floor covering provided a good, hard

surface which could be regularly renewed. Wood was used for household furniture and farm implements, and cowdung, in the form of small sun-dried cakes, and wood provided cooking fuel. Those without land, such as artisans and labourers, exchanged their work chiefly for food. Much of this self-sufficiency remains, and materialism as known today in the city has not yet seriously affected the rural outlook. The major changes resulting from cash income have been in transport, with the use of bicycles, motorcycles and tractors, in building materials, and in the supply of electricity for lighting and television.

The villages are composed of people from a variety of castes and communities, such as Brahmins, Rajputs, goldsmiths, carpenters, tailors, barbers, potters and sweepers, but their major component is frequently the sturdy Jat community of small-holding farmers. In Haryana, they have generally remained Hindu but in Punjab they now mostly follow the Sikh religion. Sikhism is based on the teachings of the Ten Gurus, the foremost among them being the first, Guru Nanak (AD 1469-1539) and the tenth, Guru Gobind Singh (AD 1661-1708). The Jats are also spread over west Punjab in Pakistan. Many of the

Hindu and Sikh Jats came to India at the time of Partition in 1947. Those who remained in Pakistan were mainly Muslim, or have since converted to Islam.

The village itself is a compact maze of narrow lanes and high compound walls, whose residents own the surrounding farm land. Ugly ribbon development may extend from city boundaries but there is none around the villages. They stand, small dun-coloured islands in a sea of well-husbanded fields whose colour changes from brown to green or gold according to crop and season. Many villages now rise five, ten or more feet above the plain. This is a sign of long occupation as one house is built over the ruins of an earlier one.

The dowry or bridal durrie of this part of north India belongs entirely in the joint-family village house where it is woven and used. Traditionally built of dried mud collected from the bottom of the village tank during its annual cleaning, this house construction was cool in summer and warm in winter. It was also, unfortunately, the cause of a great deal of repair work every monsoon and over the past thirty or more years has been steadily replaced by brick and cement. An unfortunate casualty of this change and "progress" is the village tank, now increasingly dirty, weed-infested and neglected.

The village houses vary more in size than in pattern, for they conform to a style that has not altered with the change in building materials. The square or rectangular compound is given privacy and security by a high surrounding wall while the single entrance, which opens into a courtyard, is a gateway on the village street. The living quarters form a rectangle along the opposite rear wall, entered through a pillared verandah. At one end of this is the cooking area which may be either a room or merely a partitioned space. Even though the rest of the construction may be modern brick, often the kitchens still have traditional mud walls with geometric openwork decoration built and maintained by the women of the household. At one side of the house a staircase leads up to the flat roof. An upper storey is only rarely added, though there may be one or two rooms covering a small area of the roof.

Washing is done at a tap or pump in the open courtyard. In another part of the courtyard the family buffaloes are tethered. In large compounds there are farm buildings on all three sides, giving cover for buffaloes as well as tractors and other farm machinery.

No interior has yet evolved to compare favourably with the earlier traditional ones, which were charmingly decorated with wall paintings, openwork and relief patterns on mud shelves, cupboards and storage bins. Factory-made equipment has now replaced

Opposite page:

Top:
Otiya, mud wall for an outdoor kitchen, built by the women of the household, Pandori Bibi village, Hoshiarpur district, Punjab. The *hara,* circular extension at one end, is a hollow basin used for cooking.

Bottom:
Interior of one of the rare surviving mud houses Khuda Ali Sher village, Union Territory of Chandigarh.

17

homemade furnishings; metal drums store grain in place of the mud bins decorated with geometric and animal designs in use since Harappan times (ca. 2800-1750 BC). Cement shelves and metal hooks for clothes are all the decoration now given to most walls. The *sandook,* a carved and painted wooden dowry chest, the most prized possession of the bride, has become a huge metal trunk. Usually plain, it will at most be painted with mass-produced, eclectic, commercial decoration.

Dowry

Robert Briffault in *The Mothers* has made an interesting point about the custom of dowry; in its origin it is the gift of the side with the greater wealth. Thus bride-price developed among pastoral, herding communities whose wealth lay in their flocks, the property of the herders, who were men. Conversely, the traditional Hindu and Sikh dowry, much of it hand-made by the bride, may reflect the predominant role of women in the formative days of agriculture and various domestic crafts, when they were the main creators of wealth.[1] The traditional Indian dowry consists of jewellery, furniture, cooking and eating utensils, clothing and bedding. The custom of sending valuables and bedding with the bride is scarcely new; it is implicit in "The Marriage of Surya," a hymn from the *Rig Veda* which was composed around 1500-1000 BC:

> "Thought was the pillow of her couch, sight was the unguent for her eyes:
> Her treasure was earth and heaven when Surya went unto her Lord." [2]

Above:
A weaver with her *sandook*, bridal chest, Khuda Ali Sher village, Union Territory of Chandigarh.

Below:
Mud storage bin for grain, Bindrakh village, Ropar district, Punjab. Built around 1950.

At the time of the north Indian wedding the dowry will twice be laid out in its entirety on *charpoi* for display to friends and family. These two important occasions are called *dikhawa,* showing. The first is held at the home of the bride at the time of the wedding and the second is held in her husband's village soon after her arrival. The dowry is then lovingly returned to the *sandook,* which remains the preserve of the bride. She usually keeps her chest locked and will take the key with her when she returns to her paternal village to visit her family. Such visits are most frequent soon after the wedding and she delivers her first baby under her parents' roof. When she is well settled with her husband's family she may visit only once a year for about a month, apart from short visits during the marriages and deaths of her close relatives.

The Dowry or Bridal Durrie

The bridal durrie is one of the few household crafts to have survived unscathed in the rapid transformation that the 20th century has brought to the village. It carries with it much ancient tradition in the way it is woven, the purpose it serves and the spirit that motivates the weavers. At the same time, by the switch from labour-intensive vegetable dyes in a limited colour range to cheap, easily prepared synthetic dyes in a variety of colours, and the individual interpretations of old designs, the durrie has maintained both its relevance and popularity.

The tradition of weaving bridal durries is the exclusive preserve of women. A girl is taught to weave by an older woman of the household – her mother, grandmother, paternal aunt or sister – around the age of twelve. The durries for her dowry will be woven over a period of two to five years. Unless she has younger sisters needing her help, she is unlikely to weave again until the time comes to teach her own daughters. The work is done with great pride and affection, for the dowry will be her life-long treasure. In most cases only this type of durrie, which is used on beds and not on the floor, is woven in the villages and any idea that it could be a commercial opportunity is distinctly distasteful, so entirely is it associated with the dearly-held wish to send a daughter handsomely endowed into her new home.

The only bridal durrie ever offered to us for sale had a figure of the Devi, Goddess. It was not traditional, having been copied from a book, and was useless to its owner since no-one could sleep on the image of a deity, something the weaver had realised only after completing her work.

Phulkari and *bagh*, the more widely known and appreciated articles of the Punjab and Haryana dowry, are, by contrast, no longer popular in their traditional role of a *chaddar*, veil, for the bride. These are made of a coarse hand-spun and woven cotton cloth dyed a deep red or brown and are embroidered from the back with silk thread, in darning stitch. The *phulkari*, flower work, has intermittent embroidery whereas in the *bagh*, garden, it covers the entire surface of the cloth. Both illustrate a rich variety of plants and patterns which convey the embroiderers' love of flowers and colour. Now considered old-fashioned, most brides today prefer to wear something brighter, with sequins and machine embroidery in gold yarn purchased from the bazaar. *Phulkari* and *bagh* are also exceedingly time-consuming to prepare, though this would not be a decisive factor for the restless hands of the women. Today knitting occupies much of the time once devoted to embroidery. Unlike the latter, it can be done without constant attention so that the knitter can watch television at the same time, a recreation becoming increasingly popular in the villages.

Durrie weaving is traditionally a seasonal occupation; the horizontal, immovable loom takes up much of the space in the small mud houses, so weaving is restricted to the months when people sleep out of doors and there is no need to leave space for *charpoi* indoors. This season starts from March, when the nights are no longer cold, until the rains begin in late June or early July.

Recently, with the advent of brick houses with cement floors, a variation of the traditional loom has come into use. Instead of wooden corner posts fixed in the mud floor, the frame is composed of free-standing metal piping and can be placed wherever convenient. The loom has become as movable as the *charpoi*. Weaving can now be done at any time of year but summer is still preferred since the women have little work in the fields during that season.

With each durrie woven for her dowry a girl will prepare a complete *bistra*, bedding set, to accompany it. Cotton is used for everything, including the padding in the mattress and quilt. The *bistra* consists of the durrie, placed next to the rough webbing of the *charpoi*, the *chattahee*, a sheet, often hand-embroidered in cross-stitch, and the *khes*, a medium-weight handspun and woven sheet which covers the sleeper. There is also a cotton pillow with a cover which is embroidered in cross-stitch to match the *chattahee*. In winter a *tallai*, a thin padded mattress, is placed between the durrie and the sheet, and the *razai*, a padded quilt, replaces the *khes*.

In the daytime the *bistra* is rolled up and either left at the foot, or rolled to the end of the *charpoi* where it serves as a bolster, or put away until the night.

While the bed durrie continues to be used throughout the area and weaving is found in all communities, it has particularly flourished amongst the small-holding Jat Sikh farmers of the cotton belt which covers much of Punjab and Haryana. These farmers can afford to keep back a proportion of their cotton crop for weaving, so that their only outlay is for the dye and, if they choose, for the millspun warp thread. This is now generally preferred as it is more even, and therefore stronger, than handspun yarn. These days many families can afford anything from five to nine durries and bedding sets for each daughter.

In some peripheral areas (southern Haryana, eastern Rajasthan and western Uttar Pradesh) the case is different since the yarn must often be bought and each durrie is an expense. In these areas fewer durries are made, the quality is inferior and they do not generate the same degree of interest among the weavers as in the cotton-growing areas. In a village in eastern Rajasthan, on being asked if cotton was grown there, a woman surveyed the surrounding dry, sandy land and said sadly, "This is Rajasthan. What do we have here?" In fact some of the villagers did weave durries, made from yarn bought locally, but, whilst the durrie belt crosses into the border districts of north and northeast Rajasthan, it soon peters out in the sandy soil beyond the irrigated areas.

In Haryana durries are not woven in every household; weaving skills depend on the aptitude and interest of individual girls. In the cotton growing districts and the northern parts of the State, however, the art is still prevalent. In other regions many durries are bought for marriage, either from another village woman or girl or from the local bazaar. In southern Haryana where cotton is no longer grown, the stuffing is garnetted from old *razai*, quilts, and *gadde*, mattresses, and then respun and woven. Such yarn however, lacks the lustre and resilience of new cotton. In some areas, such as the villages of Gurgaon district south of Delhi, simple geometrical designs are found, although on seeing photographs of designs woven in other areas the weavers said that these had formerly been part of their repertoire. Clearly, economic factors play a decisive role in determining not only the quantity of durries but the variety and vitality of the designs.

In the hills of the Kangra district of Himachal Pradesh the tradition of weaving durries for dowry still persists, although it may never have been as strong as on the plains. It now faces severe competition from commercially made durries and, in better-off homes, rubber or coir mattresses. The dowry here usually included four durries in two designs and these were kept for visitors, people generally preferring to use *khind*, a quilted mattress made at home of shredded old clothes between two old sheets, which was warmer and softer. Today, durries are found only in some houses and their quality varies from a coarse weave with stripes to a very fine, even weave with the same repertoire of animal, floral and geometrical designs as in Punjab and Haryana.

Durries are also woven for dowry in Jammu, an area which has close links with Kangra. In both areas just a little cotton is grown at home to provide for family needs. Marriages are frequently arranged between families of the two areas, for the Dogri dialect of Jammu is close to the Pahari dialect of Kangra, and many customs are similar.

It is by no means certain to what extent the tradition of bridal durries exists in Pakistan. Apart from two durries seen in Chandigarh, which had been woven at home for dowry around 1930 in the Montgomery district of west Punjab, our information is limited to the reports of those who had once lived there. Jat Sikh women who fled at the time of Partition in 1947 and took up their homes in those abandoned by fleeing Muslims in villages in west Haryana, say that they had no tradition of bridal durrie weaving in the Bahawalpur region of west Punjab but acquired this expertise on arrival in India. Other families from Jajkot village near Lyallpur (now Faislabad) in Pakistan who had settled in Pandori Bibi, near Hoshiarpur, said that durries were woven there by all communities in the same designs as are found in east Punjab. However it was felt that only the better-off, who grew their own cotton, could afford to weave them. This latter picture was several times confirmed by families now settled in or around Chandigarh. Jat Sikh women from landed families who left Pakistan at the time of Partition and are now settled in Delhi, also confirm that durries were included in their dowries. These were durries with simple designs of striped and geometrical motifs which they had not woven themselves but had bought in the local bazaar or from the Lahore jail.

In the Hoshiarpur district of Punjab, where the water table is too high for cotton growing, a small area used to be planted entirely for home use. This is no longer the case and nowadays waste cotton is bought from the mills in Ludhiana, garnetted and respun at home. It is then used for traditional durrie weaving and produces a very thick, velvety texture.

For the time being, the traditional *charpoi* has survived domestic changes and, in our area of study, the durrie seems indispensable to it. Even where wooden bedsteads are beginning to replace *charpoi* in some village households, the durrie is still placed under the mattress. City Punjabis settled in Delhi or Bombay, with no roots in the land, also continue to use bed durries, though their role is slightly altered. Here they have become protectors of the more expensive rubber or coir mattress and may be placed either above or below it.

Other Durries
In some areas where there were until recently large estates, wealthy landlords would employ four or five village women to work together on *farshi*, big floor durries, for their houses. This was occasional work, as need arose. These durries were rather plain, perhaps with simple geometric patterns, and they were used at social gatherings such as weddings. On these occasions, when many guests would be staying, *farshi* would also be spread for them to sleep on at night.

Sometimes, as a service, women will work together on a huge *farshi* for their local *gurudwara*, Sikh temple. We came across an instance of this in the village of Harkhowal near Hoshiarpur, where two durries, each measuring around five metres by one and a half, had been woven in 1989. More often, however, this demand is met by the jail weavers.

According to the older women, in the days before Partition, professional male Muslim weavers would sometimes make durries for the village households. The women invariably spun their own yarn and might weave part of it themselves and have part of it woven professionally. With rare exceptions, such as the small community of Muslim weavers at Mani Majra in the Union Territory of Chandigarh who stayed on after Partition in 1947, this practice has almost entirely died out. Muslim women in west Haryana said that they had no tradition of dowry durrie weaving since they had no tradition of dowry. Indeed these women had never woven durries; like most crafts, this too was done only for sale by Muslim men. However, influenced by the Hindu women in the villages they have, in recent years, also begun to weave durries for household purposes, though not for dowry.

If the bridal durries prove too few for household needs in later years, the women will weave more. These are seldom as fine or lively as the dowry durries and, in Punjab and northern Haryana, may be woven with yarn garnetted from old clothing and bedding. Such materials are sometimes used even for dowry durries in poorer households.

In some districts, efforts are now being made by local officials to have durries woven for sale with the laudable aim of increasing the income of women. This is very helpful for those with low incomes and for widows. Arrangements are made to sell the durries through special exhibitions or the state emporia in towns and cities.

One incident shows what can happen, however, when a craft is separated from its raison d'être; after seeing and recording durries in a village for a couple of hours, we suddenly faltered over one and, at the next, agreed that we had seen enough for the day. This had never happened before but, for no clear reason, we had lost interest. Even when exhausted, every durrie so far had some unique appeal that kept us going to the bottom of the pile, but these two evoked no response. Before leaving, we checked the information sheets prepared and noticed that we had not asked whether the last two had been woven for dowry or household use after marriage. The answer, which was given only on this occasion, was that they were "For sale". These commercial durries had simply lacked the verve and spirit that marked those woven for dowry.

The Web of Tradition: Myth and History

Myth

Around the seventh millennium BC, the generative powers of nature, its feminine fecundity, became personified as the Earth or Mother Goddess. Her cult, with varying names, spread across Europe, West Asia and the Indian subcontinent personifying her either as benign and generative or fiercely destructive. In India, as Devi or Mahadevi, the Mother Goddess has maintained her popularity, with incarnations varying from a benign Lakshmi to a warlike Kali or Durga. Sanjhi Devi is perhaps the most popular form of the Mother Goddess worshipped by the women of rural Punjab. She is particularly worshipped at the Navratri festival in autumn when she is the subject of murals made of small mud discs. Her frontal standing posture, broad hips covered with a *ghaghra*, skirt, and prominent necklaces point to ancient links with pottery Goddess figurines from the Harappan period onwards.[1] The close connexions between the early days of farming with traditions dating back to Harappan times, the tradition of the Devi, Goddess, in rural life, and the role of village women, seem to provide a foundation of particular significance for the durries.

In neolithic times, the universe and all creation were understood as female, the Devi, Goddess, being the embodiment of this feminine principle. The cyclical nature of existence was mirrored in the moon, whose phases combined change and continuity. It represented the circular passage of time, as in night and day, the seasons, birth, growth, death and renewal. The Goddess was all encompassing; life and death in her mythology were not irreconcilable opposites but different phases of the same perpetual cycle of generation.

Women, always seen as those who nurture and assist growth, were the chief worshippers of the Goddess. It is now understood that women, who had been chiefly concerned with gathering berries and seeds while the men concentrated on hunting, were the first to cultivate plants and reap a harvest.[2] This led away from the nomadic life of the hunter to the settled life of the farmer around the seventh millennium BC. With the invention of the plough, men took over this part of the agricultural work from the women who had been using the digging stick. Ploughing the land and planting the seed were done at the same time and the powerful bull, who drew the plough, became symbolic of the fertilizing male principle. The bull came to be identified with the moon, which was seen as male, and thus in its fertilizing role became closely associated with the life of women. The monthly lunar cycle was seen to govern the menstrual cycle in women, and there is plenty of evidence of the belief that women were fertilized by the moon. The moon was thus anthropomorphised as a male god and only much later, when the sun began to usurp its role (for instance the Egyptian sun god, Re, in the mid-third millennium BC), was the moon, the patron of women, sometimes itself seen as female.[3] Aside from agriculture, there is abundant evidence from many parts of the world that women became the first potters and weavers; it was only later, when larger communities allowed for specialised production of crafts beyond the needs of the immediate family, that men also practised these arts.

In the durrie region women no longer make pottery but spinning and weaving remain theirs almost exclusively. Evidence suggests that spinning at least has always been a domestic craft; Harappan sites show scattered spindle whorls and no signs of centralized production.[4] The spindle whorls which survive were the type used in spinning cotton, which is of course, the fibre used in the bridal durries.

The growing and processing of the cotton crop in the north of India today provides a remarkable example of the survival of the influence of the Goddess and the role of women as nurturers and protectors of life, in this case as producers of clothing and bedding. Apart from the ploughing and sowing, which now by tradition belong to the male sphere, the entire work of growing cotton and processing it into cloth is done by women. This is in sharp contrast with the production of other crops, which are basically the responsibility of the men, although the women may help them in tasks other than ploughing and sowing.

The understanding of the forces of the universe that the Goddess represents, remains fundamental to the outlook of rural north Indians. Life is as dependent on the bounty of nature now as it was in early neolithic times, governed by the changing seasons, the water supply, and the fertility of soil, plants and animals. There is no basic change that can render the Goddess, the embodiment of these principles of agricultural life, irrelevant or out of date. The worship of Sanjhi Devi during the Navratri festival recalls ancient customs of trying to ensure a bountiful harvest. On the first of the nine days of the Navratri festival, when the women prepare Sanjhi

Devi figures, they also plant *jau,* barley seeds, either in a small patch of ground directly beneath the Devi mural or in one or five pottery bowls placed nearby. On the final day of the festival they cut the barley shoots and remove the Devi mural, placing both in a handwoven basket of *tut,* White Mulberry, (Morus Alba) twigs which they throw into the village tank or stream. If the shoots have grown well, a good harvest may be expected. On this day the women keep a fast for the health and prosperity of their husbands and families, which they break only on sighting the moon in the evening.

Sanjhi mural,
Kurukshetra district,
Haryana, 1990.

In the planting and cutting of the bowl of barley the women re-enact their role in early agriculture. The barley being planted near the Sanjhi murals clearly shows the close ties of women, agriculture, and the Goddess. It is also fitting that both the murals and cut barley stems should be disposed off in water, a primary symbol of the Goddess. Finally, the fasting and viewing of the moon by the women also reflect the cosmic role of the Goddess and the importance of women as her attendants or agents, for it is in this role that they bear responsibility for the welfare of the family.

Although the powerful gods of the Vedic Aryans, who came to the subcontinent in the second millennium BC, dominated the formal Hindu pantheon, the Goddess never lost her importance among the people already settled there. She became recognized primarily as Shakti, the force that moves the universe and without which no Hindu god can function. Women, who give birth and nurture life, are seen as being of the same nature as the Goddess who, as the earth, produces and supports all living things. They share in the Shakti force, and women either separately or collectively are frequently referred to as Devi. On account of this close identity with the Goddess, domestic ritual is generally carried out by the women of the household. While the Punjabi woman unconsciously performs religious rituals, for the Uttar Pradesh Brahmins the weaving of the bridal durrie is still understood as being a part of the offering to Shakti,the Mother Goddess, and hence the durrie is regarded as a blessed item. For this reason it is never to be placed on the floor and it is imperative that a bride weaves and carries these blessings with her to her new home.

Many of the durrie designs reflect the world of the Goddess, and even when the weavers are no longer consciously aware of her presence, there could surely be no more appropriate medium to represent Shakti in their married lives than these traditional durries woven for their dowry. Foremost amongst these designs is the triangle, one of the most ancient symbols of femininity and the Goddess. As used in the sacred Hindu diagram the Shri Yantra it is a representation of Shakti as the cosmos and its dynamic energy.

Another aspect of the Goddess is her close association with life-giving water. Dr. Gimbutas, working on motifs found on Goddess figurines in southeastern Europe, has identified a group of zigzag and wavy lines on figurines and pottery as symbolic of the watery aspect of the Goddess.[5] In India as the Hindu Goddess Lakshmi, she is born of the waters and, in the *Sri Sukta,* is described as *ardram,* moist, flowing with kindness and compassion. In this connection we find a variety of zigzag and wavy designs on the durries called *lehria,* waves, by the weavers.

Zigzag lines on the durries are also sometimes called snakes, the snake being another symbol closely associated with water. The serpent Sesha symbolizes the cosmic waters on which the God Vishnu sleeps during the intervals between the cycles of creation. Because of the periodic sloughing of its skin, the snake is also associated with immortality and the 'S' figures on durries may be stylized snakes. Dr. Gimbutas has also shown how in old Europe, waterbirds such as the duck and goose, because of their annual migration, are ancient symbols of the cyclical nature of the Goddess.[6] At home on land, sea and in the air, they represent the unity of creation. The same ideas may once have been known in India; for Duck Goddesses such as are found in old Europe are still made for home worship by the women of Bengal.[7]

The *purna kalasa,* flowering vase, is a combination of Goddess symbols; the pot with water, the nurturing womb of both woman and the earth, its overflowing lotus plants the life they bring forth. The lotus is synonymous with the Goddess. In certain villages of South India a clay pot, usually filled with water and decorated with leaves, such as *neem* (Azadirachta Indica), coconut, banana, mango or oleander, is treated as an image of the Goddess and placed in the shrine or carried in procession.[8] Sometimes a lighted lamp serves the same purpose, which suggests a parallel with *jago,* the water pot used as a lamp and carried in procession during the wedding festivities in the Punjab.

Crenellated borders on durries represent the protective function of the Goddess. As the womb protects the foetus, and the house the family, so the crenellated walls protect the fort or town.

Many durrie animals are associated with the Goddess, beginning with her vehicle, the lion. The lion, deer, horse, peacock, parakeet and goose along with the crescent moon and the lotus, all appear on the stone votive Goddess discs of roughly the third to first century BC found at different places in India.[9] The peacock serves as the vehicle of Saraswati, the goddess of learning and the arts, and frequently appears in the Sanjhi murals. Ammavaru, or Ankamma, a goddess of Tamil Nadu whose tale is told by Whitehead, frequently takes the form of a parakeet. Whitehead also mentions Minachi, a fish goddess and patroness of fishermen, whose shrine is at Cuddalore, while in Himachal Pradesh the fish is a symbol of fertility.[10]

The hare found on durries is everywhere connected with the moon in its divine form and the subcontinent is no exception. Several Jataka tales give early evidence of this tradition.

Ears of wheat (stylized on durries) are typical symbols of the fertile earth in wheat-growing areas of the old world, and grains of wheat are part of many religious ceremonies in Hindu households.

Dr. Gimbutas has linked the comb design with the Goddess in Europe, and in north India it is always an attribute of Sanjhi Devi. It may also be significant that the motif of one or two concentric circles with a central dot is found on combs and spindle whorls from Mohenjo-daro and later from Taxila (third to second century BC) as well as on Goddess figurines from the Geoksyur Oasis in southern Turkmenistan.[11] In many ancient mythologies, spinning and weaving are associated with the Goddess, who controls destiny and spins fate.[12] In Gujarat a widespread belief exists that the spot on the moon is the seat of an old woman who sits spinning her wheel with a goat tethered near her.

Other motifs symbolic of the Goddess which appear on the durries are lozenges, diagonal crosses, drums and boats. Unfortunately it is impossible to trace parallels for all of them. However – regardless of when they may first have been woven – the evidence of the dowry durrie weaving tradition as a whole suggests that it is a flourishing contemporary expression of the neolithic agrarian culture of northern India.

Historical Roots
To trace the history of the weavers we have to search for the origins of the Jat community; origins which are both obscure and disputed. However, the Jats bear two outstanding hallmarks of the Indo-

Europeans: language (which includes Punjabi, Haryanvi, Hindi and all the local dialects) and a deep love of horses and horsemanship characteristic of the area before mechanized transport. William Moorcroft, superintendent of the military stud of the East India Company in Bengal, during a visit to the court of Maharaja Ranjit Singh at Lahore in 1820, commented on the latter's attachment to his horses and stud adding, "He is not singular, however, in his passion. Every Sikh in the country keeps a horse and brood mare, and rears colts for his own riding or for sale."[13] This love of horses survives among the Nihangs, a martial group of Sikhs traditionally dedicated to the defence of their faith, who still roam the Punjab on horseback and are famous for their devotion to their mounts.

Although the record is still far from complete, it is today accepted that the Indo-Europeans, from around 4500 BC, were pastoralists, a mixture of physical types and cultural groups living in the Pontic-Caspian region, who intermingled and influenced each other. The Indo-Iranian branch of the Indo-European language family may have evolved in the third millennium BC in the area between the Volga and Kazakhstan.

By about 1800 BC a branch of these Indo-Iranians, probably the southernmost of the Andronovo tribes, had moved south from the steppe into the indigenous, proto-urban settlements of Central Asia such as Namazga and Altyn Tepe. A gradual migration from about 1800 BC led them down into the Indus Valley, with the Gandhara Grave culture of the Swat Valley providing the clearest evidence of the route. These people are generally known as Indo-Aryans.[14]

The material culture of the villages of north India, on the other hand, has maintained a quite extraordinary continuity with that of the Indus civilization. Lasting from ca. 2800 BC to 1750 BC, this first great flowering of civilization in north India is also sometimes identified by the names of two of its major cities, Harappa and Mohenjo-daro, which were among the earliest sites to be excavated. It is still not entirely clear to what extent the civilization declined from internal weaknesses and natural factors, such as a decreased water supply, and to what extent the Indo-Aryan intruders were responsible. It seems to have been a very gradual process, with continued interaction between the two groups. Cultural continuity in this region of north India has in large measure been maintained because, until the coming of radio and television, village society was remarkably self-sufficient and isolated from outside influences. Books were – and remain – rare luxuries, while travel was slow and difficult.

The village house itself remains similar to those of the Indus civilization with a courtyard, windowless outside walls, timber-beam ceilings and flat roofs. Until the middle of this century, walls regularly showed the use of batter, or inward slope, for strength, a feature familiar from Harappan buildings. The drainage system also shows continuity, with plaster wall chutes – from the roof for rain-water and at room-level for household waste – running into drains in the streets which are sometimes covered with stone or brick slabs. Domestic stairways leading to the roof or upper storey of exactly the type known from Mohenjo-daro are still common, as is the Harappan practice of using bricks on their sides as a means of giving extra strength to flooring.[15]

Much of the household pottery has ancient prototypes. The *gharha*, the ubiquitous rough pottery water jar, is still sometimes painted with cross-hatched decoration in black of pipal leaves and palm fronds, typical of Indus culture. The shape of its globular body has been popular since later Harappan times and its concave lid with a central raised knob is identical with a type found at several Harappan sites.[16] Milk is still reduced on a slow cow dung fire in a *karni*, an earthernware pot with a bowl-shaped lid of a post-Harappan shape.

The earthen storage bins for flour can occasionally be found painted with geometric and composite animal designs familiar from a variety of Harappan artefacts. One of the commonest patterns of Indus culture pottery, the intersecting circle, is equally widely used today. Among many other applications, it is frequently seen in the grilles that protect the ventilators in the walls of houses.

Moora, circular mat, made of *bhabar* grass bound with cotton thread. Suketeri village, Ambala district, Haryana, 1988.

Weaving is traditionally thought to have developed from mat-making and the *moorha*, flat round mat, until recently used in every house when sitting on the floor, is made of *bhabar* grass (Eulaliopsis Binata) which grows wild in the area. It is bound with coloured cotton thread in simple geometric patterns, and belongs to what is considered the earliest stage of mat-making, the coiled type. Impressions of evidently similar coiled mats are found on the bases of pottery vessels from Indus sites as early as neolithic times.[17]

Clothing has of course changed considerably since ancient times but the single hair plait, which may be found on Indus seals, remains very popular with girls and young women. The *paranda*, decorative finishing tassel, worn for special occasions, can also be seen on a beautifully sculpted stone figure from the stupa railing at Sanghol, near Chandigarh, belonging to the Kushan period (second century AD).[18]

On the farm, land may quite frequently be found ploughed in the same fashion as an area uncovered at the Harappan site of Kalibangan in northern Rajasthan.[19] In spite of competition from the tractor by those able to afford it, the bullock continues to draw its wooden cart or plough at the same steady place all over the area. Well into this century both cart and plough remained true to their Harappan prototypes. The cart has now changed considerably and the old type is rarely seen in this part of the country, but the traditional wooden plough is still in general use, though a metal version is gradually replacing it, particularly on larger holdings.

With so much evidence for continuity it seems plausible to suggest that, when the same designs which today appear throughout the area are so closely related to those of earlier periods, they must be part of a traditional heritage and by no means random chance. These recurring designs give fresh evidence of the remarkable survival of cultural patterns in an area that has often been trampled under the feet of invading and plundering armies.

The ancient links in designs between India and Iran and Mesopotamia are another theme that has occupied scholars, for they reveal remarkable similarities and parallels. Trading links between India and her western and northern neighbours go back at least to the fourth millennium BC, and people and ideas, as well as goods, continued to pass along these routes through the centuries. Mesopotamia was famed for its textiles and it is likely that they were used in foreign trade from the earliest times. None has survived, but details of clothing in sculpture give some idea of their complexity and variety. A relief from Nimrud shows, on the tunic of King Assurnasirpal II (884-859 BC), many motifs found on the durries, including the Master-of-Animals, the sacred tree and rosettes.[20] Such trade in textiles is one way in which motifs could have been spread from one area to another.

In later times the Punjab often constituted a part of empires or kingdoms spreading to the northwest far beyond the Indus plains. During the reign of Darius (522-486 BC), it became a satrapy of the Iranian Achaemenid empire. By 327 BC Alexander the Great of Macedon had conquered Iran and Afghanistan, and established permanent Greek settlements in both Parthia and Bactria. Less successful in India, he was forced to turn back after reaching the Beas river. His departure enabled Chandragupta Maurya, whose capital was at Pataliputra (Patna) in Bihar, to establish an empire which extended over the Indus plains. After the death of Alexander in 323 BC, Parthia and Bactria first became part of the Hellenistic empire of Alexander's general, Seleucus Nicator, and later, independent Greek kingdoms. These Graeco-Bactrians were able (ca.

155 BC) to conquer Punjab and the Indus valley. During such times the area would have been exposed to outside cultural influences, some of which are probably reflected in the modern durries. Even today, patterns travel from one part of the country to another because of the system whereby girls marry outside their own villages. No doubt local traffic of various kinds has existed in other areas as well, for cultural borders are seldom hard and fast. Forty years after a violent Partition, village links between east and west Punjab also remain strong. Families divided at that time still cross the border to pay long and regular visits to each other's villages.

Durrie Weaving

Certain historical traditions are maintained in durrie weaving. The bridal durries are woven in the tapestry technique and always made of cotton. This pre-eminent textile fibre of the Indian sub-continent is as closely identified with the ancient civilization of India as is silk with China or linen with Egypt. Indigenous, its weaving in different parts of India has produced some of the finest achievements in the history of textile art. There is evidence of its cultivation at Mehrgarh in Pakistani Baluchistan as far back as the fifth millennium BC. A few minute fibres of a cloth dateable to the Indus civilization period (2800-1750 BC), woven in a cotton closely related to Gossypium Arboreum, a cotton still occasionally grown in the area today, and apparently dyed with madder, were excavated at Mohenjo-daro.

No trace of a loom has come to light, but the large numbers of pottery, shell and faience spindle whorls for spinning cotton that were found at Indus civilization sites confirm that spinning and weaving were fully established crafts and very generally practised at the time.[21] Textile imprints are often found on potsherds, as can be seen from a third millennium BC sherd from the mature Indus level at Kalibangan in northern Rajasthan. Such impressions came from the early practice of forming pots by moulding clay around a bag filled with sand. When the clay dried and the pot took its form, the sand bag was removed, but the imprint of the bag that held the sand often remained upon the interior of the pot. The original of the imprint here was apparently a simple plain weave cloth made out of a coarse fibre which was in all probability cotton. Woven mat impressions have also been found at sites in Kashmir, including the neolithic site of about 2300-1800 BC at Burzahom. Roughly contemporary with the Indus period, they are part of a more primitive culture. The impressions here are on the base of the pots which were formed by the coil technique and placed on reed mats during their construction.[22] Several different mat weaving types have been thus recorded and may well have extended to textiles also. Unfortunately no evidence of tapestry weaving in ancient India has emerged, but it seems likely that this was one of the structures used.

Below:
Cloth Impressions on a sherd from Kalibangan, northern Rajasthan, third millennium BC. (Courtesy of the Archaeological Survey of India)

Far below:
Mat impressions on pot bases from Burzahom, Kashmir, third millennium BC. (Courtesy of the Archaeological Survey of India)

Literary sources tell of textiles in the Vedic and late Vedic periods (ca. 1500-500 BC). In Vedic hymns and in a later group of religious texts, the *Brahmanas*, weaving terms – the loom, shuttle, warp, weft and others – are frequently found in beautifully evocative metaphor. The *Rig Veda*, the oldest of the four collections of Vedic hymns, composed between 1500 and 1000 BC, is particularly relevant since it was created in the heart of the modern bridal durrie belt. This area south of Ambala and along the banks of the ancient Saraswati river where it used to flow through Haryana, was the centre of Vedic culture, though it was soon to move eastward into the Gangetic plain.[23]

In the *Rig Veda* 6,9,1, a young poet appeals to Agni, the fire god for enlightenment. Using metaphors from weaving, he seeks insight into the mysteries of the sacrifice. The poet's warp has been seen to represent the metres of the *Vedas* while the woof stands for liturgical prayers and ceremony. These combine into the cloth that represents the sacrifice. The warp and woof can also be seen to represent the subtile and gross elements which unite to form the universe:

> "I know not either warp or woof, I know not the web they
> weave when moving to the contest.
> Whose son shall here speak words that must be spoken
> without assistance from the Father near him.

> For both the warp and woof he understandeth, and in due time
> shall speak what should be spoken

> Who knoweth as the immortal worlds protector,
> descending, no aid from other."[24]

In the *Rig Veda* 10, 130, 1-2, the creation of the sacrifice too is expressed in terms from weaving:

> "The sacrifice drawn out with threads on every side,
> stretched by a hundred sacred ministers and one -
> This do these Fathers weave who hitherward have come:
> they sit beside the warps and cry,
> Weave forth, weave back.

> The man extends it and the man unbinds it, even to this
> vault of heaven hath he outspun it.
> These pegs are fastened to the seat of worship: they made the
> Sama-hymns their weaving shuttles."[25]

In the *Atharva Veda* 10, 7, 42, "two young maids" who stand for day and night, weave the web of time:

> "Singly the two young maids of different colours approach the
> six-pegged warp in turns and weave it. The one draws out the

Carved stone roundel from second century BC. Bharhut showing Queen Maya sleeping on what appears to be a durrie placed on a *charpoi*. (Courtesy of the Indian Museum, Calcutta)

threads, the other lays them: they break them not, they reach no end of labour."[26]

The earliest representation so far recorded of a woven durrie is from the couch of Queen Maya, the mother of the Buddha, in a second century BC roundel from the Buddhist site of Bharhut in Madhya Pradesh. The Queen sleeps on an undecorated textile the same size as a modern bed durrie and of similar weight and stiffness, qualities perfectly captured by the sculptor. Even the couch, with its carved, doubtless wooden, legs has very much the look of present-day *charpoi* from many parts of India.

Buddhist sculpture from Gandhara, a region now shared between Pakistan and Afghanistan, shows patterned textiles covering mattresses laid on couches and cushions placed on square throne seats.[27] A sculpture of the second century AD from the railings of the *stupa* excavated at Sanghol, which lies between Chandigarh and Ludhiana in Punjab, has clear depictions of a heavy fabric with small-scale geometrical designs appearing both as the covering of a cushion with corner tassels and as a larger, folded piece with what well may be fringes, though damage denies a firm identification.[28] On both of these,

Far above:
Tapestry woven fragment with peacock tail design from Kara Khoja ca. second century AD. (Courtesy of the National Musuem, New Delhi)

Above:
Detail of a peacock's tail on a durrie woven in Manakpur village, Ropar district, Punjab, 1980.

figures are standing. Though not a Punjabi custom at present, durries can be folded in this way for extra comfort while sitting and these textiles may well be folded floor or bed coverings, their designs either woven or block-printed.

If no actual examples have survived from these early times in the Indian subcontinent itself, tapestry woven fragments have been preserved from this and an earlier period in not too distant regions. Some were excavated at the site of Pazyryk in the Altai mountains of southern Siberia. This site has been variously dated from the sixth to the fourth centuries BC. Two of these fragments have designs of hooks, and were probably woven in the Altai region. Another is a border depicting a row of lions similar to those encountered in Assyrian bas-reliefs and in sculptures of Achaemenid Persia. This piece was possibly made in Persia and found its way to Pazyryk.[29]

Further to the south, Aurel Stein excavated several tapestry woven fabrics on sites along the Silk Route in the Tarim Basin in what is now Chinese Turkestan, across the Himalayan mountain range from the Indian subcontinent. One was discovered in the ruins of a monastic structure at Kara Khoja in the Turfan oasis, and probably dates from the second century AD. It is coarsely woven with woollen warps and wefts, several strands Z–spun in slit tapestry. The colours are blue, rust, dark brown and ivory. The pattern is apparently that of a peacock's tail. It has some similarity with the tail of the peacock in one of the durries. This is not to suggest that the Kara Khoja fragment was woven in India – though such a possibility need not be ruled out. Certain objects from these Silk Route sites were made elsewhere, including several other woven tapestry fragments that, judging from their designs and the fineness of the weave, must have originated in the east Mediterranean world.[30]

Another fragment, found at the Niya site which flourished in the third century AD, has a pattern of cross-type forms in buff, blue, green and red woollen wefts on buff woollen warps made of yarn more "closely twisted than that used for the weft which generally spreads enough to conceal the warp". Aurel Stein described the motifs as swastika-like and felt they were unmistakably Indian in design. This, taken in combination with the general appearance of the fragment, justified for him the conclusion that not only the sculptural and pictorial arts of Khotan but also the more decorative branches of the textile industry had from an early date received their models from India. He commented on both the brightness of the colours and the condition of the piece, which includes numerous traces of mending and patching. It appears to have been a treasured possession.[31]

The bridal durries are constructed entirely of cotton in the dovetail tapestry technique with only the occasional appearance of slits. In contrast the Central Asian examples are slit tapestry woven in wool but we have included them as evidence of tapestry woven fabrics of an early period found in a region not far from the subcontinent with designs somewhat reminiscent of those of the modern durries of Punjab and Haryana. It is worth remembering, too, that in the early centuries AD when the Silk Route was flourishing, large areas of north India and central Asia were often under one rule such as that of the Kushanas, a people of apparently central Asian origin whose dynasty flourished in the first or second centuries AD. Aurel Stein has further pointed out that the administration of the Niya region seems to have been carried out in a language and script prevalent in north-west India, and that the type of Kharosthi characters used in the script is closely allied to those in the inscriptions of the Kushana period in north west India.[32]

References to flat-woven rugs thought to be durries have been traced by S.J. Cohen from the reign of Ala-ud din Khilji (AD 1296-1316) onwards. These rugs were called by a variety of names: *galim,* clearly associated with the Persian *gelim,* or Turkish *kilim, jambukhana* and *shatrangi.* [33] Today *galim* seems to have disappeared while neither durrie, nor *dari* appear in early texts. *Shatranj* means chess and is an allusion perhaps to the use of certain textiles in board games. In Navalgund in Karnataka, certain durries are woven with the lay-out of another game called *chaupat,* but we have not encountered a north Indian durrie with such a design. The term *shatranj* is often confused with *satrangi* or *satranji,* meaning seven colours which denotes a gaily coloured striped durrie. Both terms are in use in Jaipur, Rajasthan. In Karnataka, south India, they are known as *jamkhane.* However, bridal durries are referred to only as "durries".

A precise etymology for the word durrie has not been traced. It has no apparent connection with the Sanskrit word *dari,* meaning a cave, cavern or valley derived from the root *dri,* meaning to tear, rend, split, or cut asunder.[34] It may come from the Persian word *dari,* for this spelling, rather than durrie, was used in the 19th and early 20th centuries. While this is the most consistent with the usual transliterations of Urdu and Hindi words, "durrie" is in closer keeping with modern Indian usage.

Dari is also the name of the language spoken by the Zoroastrian Irani community of western India. These immigrants from Iran, who settled in India in the first half of this century, are distinct from the Parsis – Zoroastrians who arrived as refugees in India much earlier, around AD 936. The Persian dialect spoken in parts of Afghanistan too is called Dari. It is still to be discovered when and why it came to be applied to the flat-weaves of the Indian subcontinent; certainly it was in current use in 1872 when Baden-Powell wrote about the weaving of Punjab.[35] *Dar* means door in Persian and Urdu; from this we could arrive at *dari,* of the door, because of the use of durries as wall screens, hung over doorways and rolled up or unrolled as needed. In the same way *farshi,* large floor durries, derive their name from *farsh,* floor. It could even be derived from the word *dori* meaning thread or string. This would then refer either to the use of the thickish kind of the thread used in the making of a durrie, or to the string or rope used for the base of the *charpoi,* on which the durrie lies.[36] A truly satisfactory origin for the term "durrie" has yet to be found.

Abul Fazl, who has left detailed accounts about the life and times of the Mughal Emperor Akbar (1556-1605) commented at the end of the 16th century that "his Majesty has caused carpets to be made of wonderful varieties and charming texture; he has appointed experienced workmen, who have produced many masterpieces. The *gilim (kilim)* of Iran and Turan are no more to be thought of ."[37]

Durrie with parakeets
and human figures in
compartments woven in
Lehri village, Bhatinda
district, Punjab, 1909.
(see page 2)

37

Indian weavers were obviously accomplished, for miniature paintings of the Muslim Courts from the 15th century onwards depict a wide variety of floor, dais and throne coverings, some of which may well have been durries. Perhaps the durries in the Calico Museum of Textiles, Ahmedabad, were among these masterpieces.

The famous Widener hunting carpet, made in the late 16th century, has a small durrie covering the base of a bullock cart. A cheetah stands on this durrie waiting for the hunt to begin.[38] Other cheetah carts, complete with striped durries, are also found in paintings of the period. We remain ignorant of what 16th century bedding rolls were composed of, but it seems likely that the durrie played its part in the *bistra* of ordinary people much as it does today.

The earliest extant Indian durrie pieces, generally dated to the 17th century, are in the Calico Museum of Textiles. These are the fragments of a pair of enormous floor durries, which together measure 3.74 x 10.65 m., with typical Mughal ornamentation of the period. With the exception of the lion their motifs and composition appear largely unconnected with the north Indian village bed durries. Both have cotton warps but they differ in other ways; the Ahmedabad durries have woollen

Charpoi with rolled *bistra* during the day shift in Ropar district, Punjab, in front of a *charpoi* with cotton webbing from Kangra district, Himachal Pradesh.

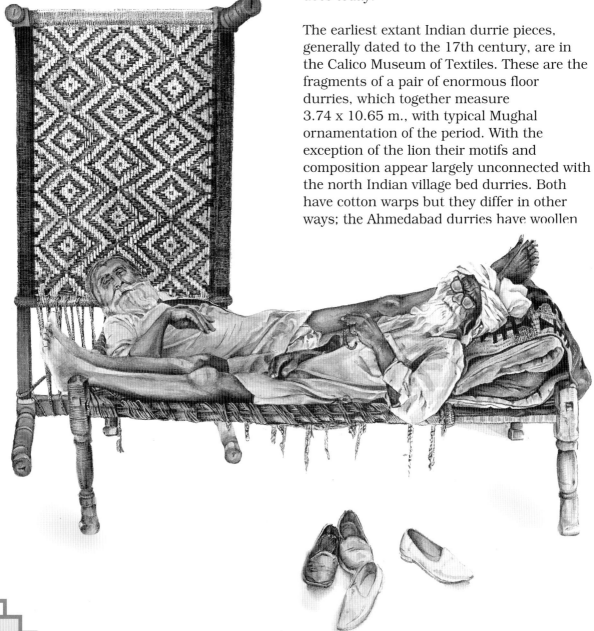

wefts and are woven in the slit tapestry technique with the use also of weft interlocking. Several fragments from three or four different *saf*, multiple prayer rugs from a mosque in Karnataka in the Deccan also appear to be of considerable age, but there is no connection with the bed durries.[39]

Plain striped floor durries are illustrated in many 18th and 19th century miniature paintings and wall paintings from the palaces and temples of the lower hill states of Himachal Pradesh, formerly known as the Punjab Hills. Similar striped floor durries are regularly depicted in 19th century paintings, particularly those of the Company School. Several fine floor durries from the late 19th-20th centuries which have been preserved were the products of jails; the origin of many of the others remains obscure. The identification of centres of production in the 19th and early 20th centuries awaits further research.[40] The designs of such durries come from a variety of sources both Indian and foreign; and they do not seem to be part of the same kind of unbroken tradition as are our north Indian bed durries. Others that do seem to maintain traditions are the prayer durries from the Deccan, with their *mihrab* patterns, and those from Navalgund in Karnataka where Muslim families still make durries with patterns of the traditional game, *chaupat*. The earliest dowry durrie that we recorded in our survey was woven in Punjab in 1909, though obviously the tradition is much older. Sometimes bridal durries are passed on from mother to daughter but it is usual to provide new ones for dowry. Once worn out these durries are thrown away hence the great majority of those examined were woven within the last thirty years. They are not to be found in museum collections and few clues exist as to their antecedents.

Lacking precise archaeological or literary evidence, the conclusion must be that it is still impossible to say where or when the Indian cotton durrie had its origins. The earliest positive indication of what may have been a bed durrie is the example seen of Queen Maya of the second century BC, which appears to be much the same size and texture as those in use today with the structure upon which it lies resembling the modern *charpoi*. This indicates an extremely long ancestry for this craft. As shall be seen in different parts of this study, many of the designs also derive from extremely ancient traditions, not only from the Indian subcontinent, but from far afield in West Asia, and date back to the earliest times.

The Charpoi

A traditional Indian dowry contains at its core the bridal beds, which in rural areas are still a pair of *charpoi*. The *charpoi* is an Indian bed composed of a wooden frame with a webbing base. It is used to sleep on at night and to sit or rest on during the day. When

not in use it is made to stand vertically against a wall, often outside in the compound to provide space indoors. Its small, closely related companion, the *pirhi*, a low square stool with or without a backrest, of identical construction and materials, is the other traditional form of raised seating which is still in vogue today. Its design is ideal for relieving the strain of long hours of squatting for chores such as grinding and cooking.

Most dowries also include one or two *moorhe*, circular grass mats. Still widely used in the kitchens of the Kangra Valley they are less common on the plains, where people now prefer the *charpoi* or *pirhi* and seldom sit on the ground.

Pirhi with *bhabar* grass seat in front of a *pirhi* with home-dyed cotton cord webbing. The owner called the design *phul ballian*, ears of wheat. Union Territory of Chandigarh.

The traditional *bhabar* grass (Eulaliopsis Binata) rope is still used in villages for the *charpoi* and *pirhi*. Although now made on a motorised machine introduced in the mid-1960s, the hand method is still known. For this the ropemaker, who squats at his work, takes a small bunch of stalks, knots them at one end and secures the knot under one foot. The stalks, divided into two equal bunches, are rolled between his palms, first separately but simultaneously and then both together. New stalks are introduced as the rope grows. The work is done at great speed and the product is very strong. The rope, which is not dyed, is always bound to the *charpoi* frame on the diagonal. It is sometimes woven in simple geometrical patterns such as zigzag lines and expanding squares.

Heavy, soft-textured, home-made cotton cord and webbing are also traditionally used for *charpoi* and *pirhi*. Unlike the *bhabar* rope, they are worked on the vertical and horizontal. The webbing is usually white but the cord is often woven in two colours with quite varied patterns. These include half and full stepped lozenges, "S" forms, diagonal and zigzag lines, checkerboards, eight petal rosettes and serrated rhomboids, all of which are also used as durrie designs.

At one end of the *charpoi* the webbing stops short by about 30-40 cms. and is lashed to the frame by a rope. By tightening this rope the webbing is pulled back into shape after it has sagged and slackened with use.

Small votive or toy clay models of *charpoi* found at the Harappan site of Kalibangan confirm its long history though of course no wood has survived from an actual *charpoi* or *pirhi*.[41] Vedic literature too has references to mats, seats, and couches made of grass, reed and wood.

Several votive clay model beds very similar to the Indian *charpoi* have also been excavated at sites in Mesopotamia from levels dated in the late third and second millennia BC. One example from Nuzi near Kirkuk in northern Mesopotamia clearly shows the frame and webbing construction, which is done on the vertical and horizontal in the same way as the cotton webbing in the Punjab. Other votive models of beds from Susa in southwest Iran made around the 16th or 15th century BC, also show similar frames and webbing.[42]

As in the case of the durrie, the earliest sculptural example we have of the *charpoi* too is on the relief of the Dream of Queen Maya from Bharhut of the mid-second century BC. Though only the legs are visible they could belong to a contemporary north Indian village *charpoi*. A similar example is seen on another relief medallion of a railing pillar from Hathin, Gurgaon, in Haryana, of the first century BC, now in the collection of the Department of Archaeology and Museums, Haryana, in Chandigarh.[43] Gandharan sculpture of the third to fifth centuries AD contains many other such examples.

The *charpoi* is light in weight and strong. In its time it has served in many capacities, among them river transport. The rapid waters of rivers in the hills were sometimes crossed by means of inflated bullock skins on which the ferryman would lie, chest down and paddle across. For heavy loads a couple of skins were brought together and a *charpoi,* acting as a raft for the goods, placed across the backs of the two ferrymen.[44] New roles are always being found for this versatile piece of furniture. Villagers bask in the sun, women babysit and knit or dry pickles and *papads* on *charpoi;* it is the focal point for male discussions in the twilight and, on one village roof, a *charpoi* secured to a television aerial served as a mount for a loudspeaker of the nearby Sikh temple.The *charpoi* and the durrie dating back across time travel with each bride to her new home, weaving together the past and the future in a web of tradition.

Warp and Weft

Yarn Preparation

The best bridal durrie is made from cotton grown by the bride's family. Cotton is widely cultivated in northern India as a cash crop, and a portion of it is put away for such traditional domestic purposes. In the villages, once the men have completed the ploughing, sowing and first weeding of the cotton crop, its care is taken over by women. As the seed pods mature, it is picked in a continuous process, from the end of September to the end of February. Traditionally the women also took care of the entire processing of the cotton at home. Until the mid-1970s, a *belna*, a small wooden hand-operated gin with double rollers, was in use in village homes to separate the seeds from the seed hairs or cotton fibres. Before the invention of the cotton gin at the close of the 18th century, the seeds were probably removed by working a single roller on a flat board, in the same way as whole spices are traditionally ground in India on a flat stone.[1]

After ginning, the cotton fibres are batted to loosen them and expel the dirt. This was done with the help of the *tara*, bow, the fibres being vibrated by the string, a method still practised even in major cities to fluff up cotton fibres used to stuff mattresses, pillows and cushions which have become matted together with use. Both these processes have now been commercialized and are carried out by motorized carding machinery introduced around 1965 in small workshops in the village or nearby town.

After carding, the processing continues at home. The women use a *kana*, a light stick about 22 cm. long made of *sarkanda* (Sacharum Spontaneum or S. Munja) to form the cotton into *punia*, loose rolls, convenient for spinning. The *kana* is held in one hand and placed on a small wad of loose cotton spread on a flat surface. The cotton is rolled around the *kana* with the flattened palm of the other hand and removed.

The spinner draws this yarn onto the *takla*, spindle, directly from the *punia*, without using a distaff. The rolls of *nuchla*, spun yarn, are removed from the spindle and plied into *atti*, skeins, on a *teran*, cross-reel, four-ply for durrie, two ply for *khes*. The yarn is generally Z-spun and S-plied.

The *teran* was earlier made from either of the hard woods *sheesham* (Dalbergia Latifolia) or *neem* (Azadiracta Indica), but nowadays softer wood is often used. The *teran* is composed of a central rod about 20 cm. in length. At the lower end another rod crosses it at right angles. At the upper end a heavier crossbar curves upwards from the centre and then broadens and slopes downwards at its outer edges. This curvature holds the yarn in place as the skein grows thicker.[2]

The use of a static reel such as the cross-reel for plying the yarn speaks of the great antiquity of the process, for it is thought to predate the spoked reel. Since the spinning wheel incorporates both spindle and spoked reel, it is considered to be the intermediate stage between the two; both inventions are believed to have taken place in India. It has been suggested that the spinning wheel was invented between AD 500 and 1000. It is unlikely to have been earlier, since there is no evidence of its use in the Roman empire. With so many contacts between India and the Romans, it is improbable that such an advance, had it been known at the time, would have escaped Roman notice. This historical period saw an exceptional flowering of the arts and crafts of India; since the cultural activities in any period tend to keep pace with each other, it is reasonable to suppose that the spinning wheel should have been invented at this time. It probably reached Europe by way of the Islamic civilizations of West Asia, and is first heard of in Europe in the 12th century.[3]

Spinning

The cotton for the weft is still invariably spun at home on the traditional wooden *charkha,* spinning wheel. The women used to sit together and sing to amuse themselves and relieve the monotony, but nowadays few remember the traditional songs that accompanied this work. Two verses however were rendered by a pair of elderly women in Mohri village, near Ambala, in the style of Punjabi folk singing – with verve and a pronounced beat.

> "*Charkha* of iron. I shall put a thread of brass.
> *Charkha* is running. I shall put a thread of brass.
> I would not care to spin if the cloth merchant were alive.
> Since he is dead I have to spin."

> "My husband keeps female camels
> But I do not know how to milk them.
> If I had a golden *gadva* (milk vessel)
> I would milk them very quickly."

> "*Charkha ve khumda piya,*
> *Metho tar kadni na aave*

Charka de ve ki katna,
Mera mar gaya yaar bajaji
Mar gaya yaar bajaji, charkha
De ve katna piya.

Rakhda ve uthenia, metho
Dhar kadni na aave,
Gadva ve sone de, vich
Dhar chhama chhama vajhdi."

There seem to have been no special songs to accompany the weaving, probably because this requires full concentration. The work itself is not rhythmic, so singing would only distract the weavers.

Dyeing

Traditionally the weavers relied on three colours: the natural white of the cotton, indigo blue and a dark brown made from the bark of the *kikar* tree (Acacia Arabica). These remained in use in the villages, together with the new synthetic dyes, until around the time of Partition. The many handsome navy-and-white and brown-and-white, "Coca Cola", durries still being woven in traditional geometric patterns show how effectively a simple palette can be used. Where animals are now increasingly common, small touches of bright red or orange add further contrast.

The modern commercial dyes, which are cheap and easy to use, have given new freedom to the weavers. They are much preferred to the limited, less brilliant vegetable dye colours, so hard to prepare. The women love the wide range and brightness of the colours, very welcome in the dun-coloured world of the farmhouse compound which may have a small tree but seldom a flower.

These women, who dye their own yarn, often arrive intuitively at textbook-perfect harmonies with colours they have never handled before. Most commonly all colours are used in a similar, high density. Red, yellow, pink and parrot green in a very light tone, together with white, are contrasted with very deep tones of blue, purple, brown and green.

Dyeing the yarn is today a simple process because of the use of synthetic, direct dyes. The skeins are immersed in a mixture of dye powder, cooking salt and *patkari*, alum, dissolved in boiling water. Off the fire, the yarn is left to soak for ten to twelve hours and then removed and dried in the sun. More deeply saturated colours are a matter of a stronger dye solution, not longer immersion.

As the natural cotton is slightly off-white, the weavers use Tinopal, a popular brand of commercial bleach, to obtain a better colour. The yarn is soaked for five minutes in a cold solution of the bleach and then removed and dried in the sun. It is then ready to be wound into *guttian*, little bundles, for weaving. This is done by winding it in a figure of eight between the thumb and little finger of one hand.

Since in most cases it is unfortunately the cheapest, non-fast dyes that are used, one wash can make a durrie appear old for it loses all its cheerful freshness and becomes limp and faded. By contrast, an unused durrie that has spent fifty years neatly folded in a *sandook* may appear brand new.

Washing of durries is now done with commercial detergents but older women recall that they used to wash durries with salt deposits that formed on the *kallar*, saline or infertile land, which did not cause fading.

Plain weave. (Tanavoli, the Lion in the Art and Culture of Iran)

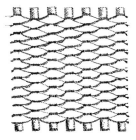

Weft faced plain weave. (Tanavoli, the Lion in the Art and Culture of Iran)

Weaving Techniques

All the durries are woven in weft-faced plain weave with slanting and dovetail tapestry weave joins where two colours meet. The interlocking technique is never used for colour joins. Where there is a vertical line between two colours the dovetail technique is used, in which the colours share the same warp alternately. This gives a slightly fuzzy vertical line but a very strong join structurally.

Where two colours form a diagonal line they do not share the same warp; with each row the weft moves across one more warp so that a very sharp line is formed. The angle of this slanting line is thus determined by the spacing and thickness of the warps. Technically this is the same as the slit-weave tapestry technique but it is used only on the diagonal and never for a vertical line. Applied in this way it has the advantage of producing a clear, sharp line without the structural weakness of a long vertical slit, as occurs in much Persian *gelim* weaving. Diagonal lines of this type are used in many of the oldest geometric motifs and show a perfect harmonizing of design with technique. Occasionally one or two horizontal rows of weft floats are used near the ends of a durrie or between panels of animals or other designs. They are usually floated over three warps at a time.

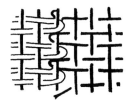

Tapestry weave, dovetail colour joins. (Geijer, A History of Textile Art)

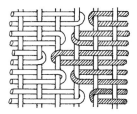

Tapestry weave, slanting colour joins. (Collingwood, The Technique of Rug Weaving)

A popular method of ensuring that the final weft rows do not unravel is a row of *janjeeri*, chains, which is a two-strand countered weft-twining done in two alternating colours while the durrie is still on the loom. This ancient technique is common to weavers in many parts of the world though its usual purpose is to ensure even spacing of the warp threads on vertical looms. Depending on the

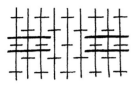

Weft floats.

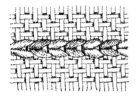

Two-strand countered
weft-twining. (Tanavoli,
the Lion in the Art and
Culture of Iran)

complexity of the design, a durrie may take from one to three weeks in weaving. The decorative warp finishes take a further day to complete.

Warp Finishes

After the weaving is over and the durrie cut from the loom, the warp ends may be given a decorative finish though in about a third of the durries they are left as they are. These finishes are of two types, wrapped and unwrapped. In the former, the warps are divided into groups of four or five and wrapped in two or three bright colours of commercial thread which are looped and bound together to form a variety of patterns usually known as *jali*, lattice. They are sometimes called by the everyday forms which they seem to resemble. The most popular is the *jalebi* pattern, named after a popular sweet, but there are individual cases specially named by imaginative weavers such as *makri ki jali*, spider's web, *jorlu*, simpleton, and *harad*, the dried fruit of Myrobalan (Terminalia Chebula).

The unwrapped warps are sometimes plaited, *mindia*, or twisted into little ropes known as *bumbal*, made by the same method as the *charpoi* webbing, or knotted into a variety of lattices. The finishing touch is given by coloured pompoms called *phunde* or *phulwe*, meaning flowers. In some cases four or five *gungru*, small bells of brass, are attached to the durries as an extra decoration.

All the warp finishes are traditional and could well have as long a history as the durrie. While warp finishes of wrapped and plaited tassels and knotted lattices are common to textiles in many parts of the subcontinent and elsewhere, the looped and interlaced designs made by the durrie weavers with wrapped warps – as well as their names – seem to be unique to this area.

Printing Techniques

Two printing methods are occasionally met with in Punjab. For both, the women weave a plain white durrie at home and take it to the printer's workshop where they choose designs from his collection. The designs, mostly curvilinear floral patterns, are quite distinct from the rectilinear durrie repertoire.

Stencil printing: In this technique the design is cut out of metal plates and dye from a saturated cloth is rubbed through the cut-out areas. The only instance we found of this technique was in Lehri village, Bhatinda district.

Block Printing: Carved wooden blocks are used for this method. The blocks vary in size but are usually about 15 to 30 cm. in their longest dimension and may be square, rectangular or round

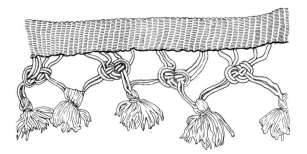

Jalebi, an Indian sweet

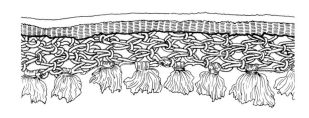

Makri di jali, spider's web

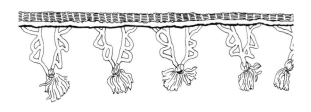

Harad, dried fruit of the myrobalan tree,
(Terminalia Chebula)

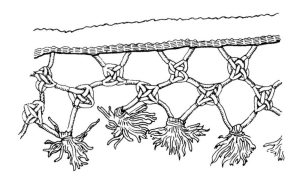

Dubbian, boxes

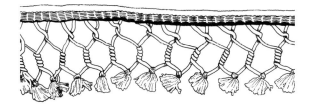

Jali, net or lattice

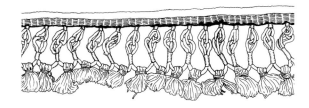

Harad

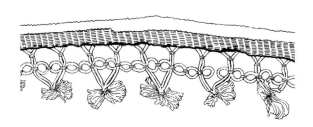

Jurne challe, pairs of finger rings

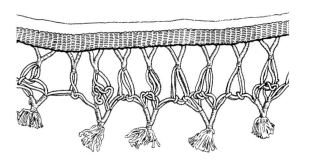

Jali

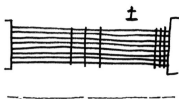

Far above:
Ground loom on pottery
dish from Badari, Egypt,
ca. 5000 BC. (Hall,
Egyptian Textiles)

Above:
Ground loom on seal
impression from Susa,
southwestern Iran, ca.
3100-3000 BC. (Collon,
First Impressions)

Below left:
Traditional, fixed,
wooden Punjab durrie
loom – shed.

Below right:
Traditional, fixed wooden
Punjab durrie loom-
counter – shed.

depending on the design they carry. One block printing workshop was at Hadiya, near Barnala in Sangrur district and a second at Hoshiarpur. A third workshop was in Morinda in Ropar district, where the printer was a Muslim now using a Sikh name. He was not from a traditional printing family but had learned the craft from Muslims in Maler Kotla, for whom it was traditional; they had also supplied him with the wooden blocks he used.

The Loom

No archaeological trace of the north Indian durrie loom – a horizontal ground loom – or its accessories has apparently survived from early times. It is undoubtedly of great antiquity but we cannot yet be sure whether it developed indigenously or was introduced from elsewhere.

The earliest evidence of this type of loom outside India is a drawing on a piece of Egyptian pottery from Badari made around 5000 BC. This was apparently the only loom used in Egypt until the end of the Middle Kingdom in 1782 BC and is still found in the Sudan.[4] The pottery drawing is sketchy and it is not possible to be sure of exact details, but the loom appears very similar to the north Indian durrie loom. The same type of loom also appears on a seal impression from Susa in southwestern Iran of the second half of the fourth millennium BC and is still in use by the nomadic tribes of Iran, the Caucasus and Central Asia for weaving *gelims*[5].

A minor difference between the Punjab loom and the Iranian nomadic loom is that in the former the heddle is fixed while in the latter it is lowered to change the shed. The heddle in Iran is suspended from three wooden rods which form a pyramid over the loom, whereas in Punjab it rests on bricks which have been made there since the time of the Indus Civilization.

The traditional Rajasthani durrie loom is another close relative with a few differences: the weavers sit beside rather than over the weaving, they use a shed bar on their side of the heddle and a shed rod on its far side. The heddle itself is immovable but is suspended from another bar above it and does not rest on bricks on the ground. The weft yarn is wound onto long wooden shuttles instead of into small bundles.

In the north of India the horizontal ground loom on which the women weave their bed durries is extremely simple. It has no

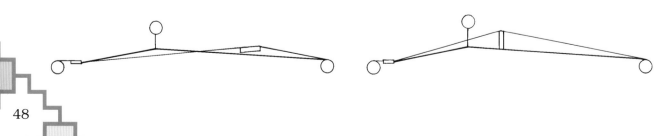

moving parts in its structure and consists of four wooden posts fixed in the ground to make a rectangle. A bar is secured across each of the two short sides at about 15 cm. from the ground and the warp is wound continuously back and forth between these two bars. An immovable heddle is then prepared by setting a rod, which rests on piles of bricks, across the warps about seven to eight cm. above them. Alternate warp threads are individually attached by threads to this heddle rod. These warps are raised above the unattached ones to form the shed or space for weaving between the upper and lower rows of warps.

The counter shed, a row that alternates with the shed, is formed with the help of the rectangular shed board or lease rod which is placed on the far side of the heddle rod. For the shed rows this board is left lying horizontally and pushed away from the weavers so that it plays no role. For the counter shed rows, however, it is pulled up to the heddle and held vertically so that the lower set of warps, not attached to the heddle, is raised above the level of the attached set.

No shuttles are used but the weft yarn is wound into *guttian,* neat little rectangular bundles. The weaver places one hand between the warp rows to give more space and passes the yarn with the other.

The weft is beaten down by a wooden comb with metal teeth which the weavers call a *hatthi,* hand. The more generally known term for this implement, which is used in other parts of India including Rajasthan and Uttar Pradesh, is *panja.* The durries themselves are sometimes referred to by this name outside the area, but never by the bridal durrie weavers. The *hatthi* consists usually of seven curved iron tines about nine cm. in length which are tapered at their outer ends. The broader ends are set into slits in the wooden body of the comb, for which a hard wood such as *neem* or *sheesham* is used. Sometimes iron bands may also be wrapped around the comb to secure the tines. The entire comb, with its long handle, measures about 34 cm. in length.

There is no archaeological evidence for the origin of the iron *hatthi/panja,* weaver's comb. The use of iron is not thought to have occurred before about 1000 BC, but even without it the weaving could certainly have been done with some other kind of beater, such as the flat wooden sword-beater used by the ancient Egyptians during the Dynastic period (ca. 3100-525 BC), which is still used in other parts of India.[6]

Punjabi weavers generally work in pairs, although occasionally either the girl who is preparing her dowry or her mother may weave alone. They squat on a broad plank of wood sometimes supported on small piles of bricks placed either immediately under or over the woven part of the durrie. If it is below the durrie they usually put a cloth under their feet to keep the weaving clean.

To avoid the natural tendency of weaving on the loom to grow narrower, a *panakh*, broad holder or jointed strip of wood of the correct width, is used. At either end it has nails, pointed end out, which are pushed in at the outer cords of the durrie and the joint straightened. It is placed immediately in front of the weaver's squatting plank, at the weaving face.

Jail Weaving

Durrie weaving in jails was first introduced at Jaipur around the 1850s and continues as a popular occupation at many such institutions throughout the country.[7] It has been well documented and many jail durries have survived. The standard of weaving seems very high but, since the design repertoire is eclectic, it adds little to our study of the origins of village designs.

In jails of north India the work is done on a horizontal ground loom, a more complex version of the village loom. This loom has not

Weaving on a movable durrie loom made of water piping. *Hatthi,* weaver's comb, is on the left.

changed since it was described and illustrated by Courtney Latimer in 1905-06. Instead of a rigid heddle raising alternate warp ends and the use of a shed rod to change the shed, all the warp ends are attached alternately to two heddle bars raised and lowered in turn to change the shed. Another difference is that there are two bars at each end. The warps are wound round the inner, lighter bar which is in turn lashed to the stronger, outer bar.

Durrie weaving continues in many jails in the Punjab though the intricate, time-consuming patterns of earlier times are no longer made. Simple geometrical designs are the norm and are made chiefly for the floor rather than the *charpoi*. They vary in size from a small rug to very large floor rugs which are used in tents at large social gatherings, in *gurudwara*, Sikh temples and *mandir*, Hindu temples.

The jail durrie designs may be taken from durries made earlier or be given by the customer. Sometimes the men themselves may discuss and plan a design. In certain cases an imaginative man is given the opportunity to weave what he chooses on his own. There are no scale drawings for the weavers to follow but they draw red lines along and across the warp ends to show the limits of a pattern, though not the actual design.

Men are chosen to train as weavers from among those serving a minimum of seven years, since their training takes time. Older prisoners themselves teach new recruits. The weaving is done in large, bright, airy sheds, the men work an eight-hour day and may weave as much as nine square feet on a plain durrie or as little as half a square foot on a complex one in a day.

The jail weavers have many occupations apart from durrie weaving. In some jails they spin, ply and dye the yarn themselves. In others they now use millspun yarn but dye it themselves, though vegetable dyes have been replaced by chemical ones. They also weave *khadi*, handspun and hand woven cloth, for their own clothing and *khes* for commercial sale. Other commercial products include the hangings for *shamiana*, tents.

Besides durrie weaving, since jails have a substantial acreage within their walls, the inmates, many of whom come from farming backgrounds, grow vegetables and cereals for their own consumption. There is even a special arrangement whereby a man may return home on the basis of a bond for harvest and ploughing twice a year where it is proved that his family cannot manage without his help.

Designs for Dowry

Village women in north India are strong, self-assured and clear-headed; their approach to life is confident and cheerful. These characteristics seem evident in the uncluttered, symmetrical way in which they arrange the designs on their durries. Individual motifs are relatively large, with plenty of space around them. No paper graphs are used; the women copy a design from another durrie in the village, maintaining proportion by counting the weft rows and warp threads.

The weavers, optimistic approach to life makes changes welcome. Anything new attracts instant attention and fresh designs, shared by all communities, "spread like wildfire from loom to loom" as one family put it. The Maruti car has recently become a popular design. Copying from contemporary cross-stitch manuals occurs, but it tends to be adapted into the Punjabi tradition and receives a fresh identity. Designs are common throughout the area, though names may vary from one district to another. Since brides weave in one village and take the durries with them to another when they marry, designs are constantly travelling between districts.

Older women are familiar with most of the figural designs now seen on the durries but before 1960 these were woven only by a few of the most talented weavers, designs on durries being generally limited to stripes and geometric patterns.

During our village trips we were shown many fine wedding veils, both *phulkari* and *bagh,* embroidered by the mothers and grandmothers of the present generation of weavers between approximately 1900 and 1960. These older designs too were almost invariably geometric – many identical with those on the durries – with occasional rows of peacocks. People and animals were also part of the embroiderers' repertoire and among the excellent examples of the late 19th and 20th centuries in the Calico Museum of Textiles, Ahmedabad, are several with motifs still popular on the durries today. These include a girl carrying a water pot, a frontal figure standing between two horses in profile, horses with standing riders, peacocks, camels and eight petal rosettes. While motifs and designs on durries are many and varied, special attention must be drawn to durries which relate a story. Pictorially, or through

Opposite page:
Above:
Design called *gadva*, a milk container; a *gadva* is shown in front of the durrie. Durrie woven in Dandrala Karorh, Patiala district, Punjab, 1979.

Below:
Design called *chhattri,* umbrella. Durrie woven in Parch village, Ropar district, Punjab.

couplets woven into the design, these reflect legends integral to rural culture.

Durrie Names and Symbols

The traditional names of common designs have long been forgotten by the weavers on the plains of Punjab, yet the names they give their durrie designs often provide clues helpful in understanding an earlier symbolism. Durrie names reflect rural concerns and show a deep attachment to the soil and the life it supports.

Crops are constantly named: cotton flowers with their distinctive stalks, maize, wheat, vegetables and fruits. One pattern can have different meanings for different women. The *buti*, small floral ornament, can become an aubergine or tomato, apple or orange, and the leaf form becomes wheat or maize according to local preferences. Irrigation, which has so altered the face of Punjab, is not forgotten; there are designs called after the great Bhakra Dam that harnesses the Sutlej river. Even small water tanks and channels are remembered.

The weavers themselves have no idea of the ancient origins of the designs they weave, yet these remain relevant and personal to each weaver who names them after something of current interest. Designs include everyday objects such as the *chakla* and *belan*, circular dough board and rolling pin, recent additions such as tube lights and electric fans, and reminders of little pleasures such as biscuits and toffees. The most striking example of this process is the traditional *pipal* leaf motif. Frequently represented on seals and pottery from the time of the Harappan culture, amongst younger women it is transformed into a lollipop or an umbrella, while for their elders it is still a *pipal* leaf; clearly it is something quite different to different generations.

One of the oldest geometric designs on durries, the lozenge, may be called *tukri*, pieces, referring to the small, scattered land holdings that dot the villages. To other weavers it represents *burfi*, a favourite sweet of this shape.

53

Another example of this free-wheeling approach can be seen in the motif which is called *gadva*, a metal milk container in one village, yet turned on its head and given a vertical central stripe it becomes an umbrella in another.

A Naturalistic Canvas

The small human figures interpreted by the weavers in a variety of ways, from baby girls and boys to European men, seem to have their origin in the figurines of the ancient Great Mother. Mother Goddess figures appeared first in West Asian sites, on the Russian steppes and in the valley of the Don in Palaeolithic times, when man depended on hunting and gathering for a precarious existence. In a hazardous world, attention centred on the mysterious life-giving processes of generation and birth, as well as their contrary, death. The female figure of the life-producing mother, personification of the generative powers of nature, was a principal expression of these concerns, both in this world and the hereafter.

Detail of durrie with *meman*, memsahibs. Khudda Jassu village, Union Territory of Chandigarh, 1975.

There are striking similarities between the durrie figures and the pottery figurines from the Harappan and later periods in India, particularly in the Sanjhi Devi images worshipped throughout the bridal durrie region. Many terracotta goddess figurines were also

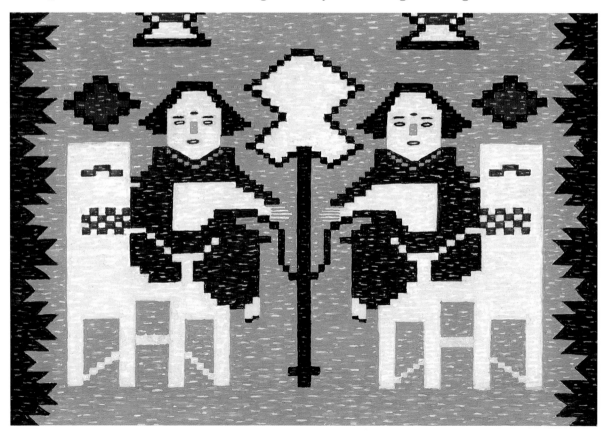

Durrie with *gore*, Englishmen, *phul*, flowers, and a row of *machhi*, abstract fish, at the top. village, Ropar district, Punjab, 1976.

found during excavations at Taxila in Pakistan. Among those of the third or second century BC were some in relief on ex-voto plaques wearing full-flowing drapery, again bringing them close to the durrie figures. Another similarity with figurines of the late first millennium BC at Ropar in Punjab and elsewhere is the way in which the arms are represented: held straight, slightly away from the hips with the hands extended[1]. Tradition and transference combine in the durries when the weavers have used these figures to depict a scene which epitomises the British presence in India and filled it with their usual humour: smug, bored *memsahibs* sit on their straight chairs, sometimes drinking tea or holding flowers. This design and *muchh maror*, twisting mustachios, always had everyone smiling or chuckling when the durries were unfolded.

In some parts these human figures, which are generally known as *kakke*, children, are labelled *gore*, fair, a term applied to Europeans. It is likely they would have entered the durrie design repertoire at a time when the European presence was new to the area and therefore a curiosity to the villagers. One can see reflected in these durrie designs the adventurous, colourful French, Italian and Spanish soldiers who, having fought for Napoleon, were forced to seek their fortune elsewhere after the battle of Waterloo in 1815. A few adventurers found their way to India, where some of them joined the service of Maharaja Ranjit Singh in the 1820s and '30s. The best of them, such as Jean Francois Allard, Jean Baptiste Ventura and Claude Auguste Court, acquitted themselves with great distinction.[2] The durrie figures could equally well, of course, represent any of the far more numerous and less flamboyant British civilians and soldiers stationed in the north of India.

Occasional durries show a crawling infant with its face raised to the viewers. This is also called *kakka*, child, by the weaver. Three durries of this type were seen during the survey, woven between 1958 and 1989, though an old weaver in the Chandigarh area remembered the design from her childhood in the 1920s as a popular motif for embroidered cloth bags. Since the same crawling infant is better known as the god Krishna in childhood in the folk art of Kangra and other areas, and is seen in embroideries from Gujarat, it is probably the same motif but, for the Sikhs, no longer has a religious character.

Guddian: Dolls

Female figures portraying in stylized form the daily life and work of the weavers are frequently seen on durries. A young woman carries a water pot on her head, one arm raised to steady it, the other akimbo for balance. She is a traditional and very popular figure in folk art throughout the durrie area, in Gujarat and Rajasthan and several examples can also be found in 19th and 20th century *phulkari* at the Calico Museum of Textiles. In the western part of Punjab this figure has recently become synonymous with the heroine of a local folk song written in the 1970s, *Pali pani khu ton bara*, about Pali who fetches water from the well. Near Chandigarh, she often represents *Jago*.

Jago, literally "wake up", is a part of the customary earthy ribaldry that accompanies Punjabi marriages. The married women of the groom's family take a procession at night through their village while the men are away for the marriage ceremonies at the bride's village. *Jago* is a *gharha*, earthen water pot, which for this occasion is used as an oil lamp.

Historically, relief sculpture at Amaravati about AD 200, seems to offer the earliest surviving examples of such female figures holding water pots on their heads. These are the *nadi devatas*, river nymphs, in scenes of the Bodhisattva emerging from their bath in the Neranjana.[3]

Goddesses such as Ganga, the river Ganges, and Prithvi, the earth, are often represented in a similar pose, one arm akimbo, the other to the side holding a pot at shoulder height. At Stupa II at Sanchi in

Detail of durrie with *guddian*, dolls, Dhanas village, Union Territory of Chandigarh, 1990.

Durrie with *jago*, female figures carrying the large oil lamp on their heads. Daferha village, Patiala district, Punjab, 1984.

Madhya Pradesh, the goddess Lakshmi appears in this posture but she holds a lotus, *padma-hasta*, rather than a jar. At Kausambi, in a relief of the Ist century BC, she has the left arm akimbo and the right raised in *abhaya mudra*, the hand gesture of reassurance and protection.[4] Among both Sikhs and Hindus of north India, Sanhji Devi figures holding pots are most popular. In the villages she has the extended meaning of a Mother Goddess "common to all" and is worshipped by all religious communities. Her continuing importance is a significant cohesive factor, for she, in her various portrayals, stresses the underlying unity of all creeds.

A fourth century AD terracotta plaque from near Suratgarh, Bikaner, which probably depicts the God Krishna with a *gopi*, female cowherd, also shows a girl holding a water pot on her head with one hand while fingers of the other touch the chin of her smiling face. Despite the religious topic, the effect is distinctly of this world. The pleasing sight of graceful young women carrying water no doubt served as inspiration for Ganga and Prithvi as surely as for this *gopi* or *pali*. Though the figures on the durries now have only secular meaning, they may well have carried religious or talismanic significance in earlier times when modelled in clay or painted in wall murals, and all may equally claim kinship with the neolithic Mother Goddess, whose essential features they incorporate. Punjabi humour touches the Devi murals too: a thief who tried to steal jewellery from the Devi is pictured hung upside down in punishment by the very contemporary looking security guard who had caught him.

The *Pipal* Tree

The *pipal* tree, Ficus Religiosa, is indigenous to the Himalayan foothills and is sacred to both Hindu and Buddhist. Very common on Harappan pottery, it appears in two forms on durries. The simpler form is as individual leaves which are sometimes also called *chhatri*, umbrella, or lollipops.

The second form is a small tree, for which the weavers have no specific name. However, it bears a remarkable resemblance both to certain *pipal* plants on Harappan period pottery[5] and to the *pipal* plants known as *balaur* which decorate house and compound walls in the villages for the Navratri festival beside the figures of the *Devi*. The *pipal* as well as the Goddess, is understood to have been sacred in Harappan times and one seal from Mohenjo-daro also shows a Goddess standing in a *pipal* tree. The lotus, today the primary symbol of the Goddess, is scarcely represented at that date. The earliest known association of Devi with the lotus is Lakshmi, Goddess of wealth in the *Sri Suktam*, a late *Rig Veda* hymn. The association of a village *devi* such as *sanjhi* with the *pipal* rather than

Durrie with *pipal* leaves
Khuda Ali Sher, Union
Territory of Chandigarh,
1988.

Durrie with plants and pairs of parakeets, and bells attached to the sides, Khuda Ali Sher, Union Territory of Chandigarh, 1982.

the lotus therefore supports a pre-*Vedic* date for the Navratri murals. When the *pipal* reappeared in mainstream art of the Sunga period (second-first centuries BC), it had become associated with the Buddha, who searched for enlightenment under a *pipal* tree.[6]

Animals

In the early Punjabi legends, man and nature appear on a remarkably equal footing. Magic plays a leading role and trees and animals are often advisors and guardians to human beings, talking freely with them. It is in the representation of animals that the weavers are perhaps at their best. With simple rectilinear outlines they deftly and affectionately capture characteristic poses and the essential nature of many different species of birds and beasts, filling them with life. The warmth and vivacity of the women of the area are most obvious in these particular durries. Animals sometimes have

Detail of durrie with hares eating cotton flowers, Kajheri village, Union Territory of Chandigarh, 1980.

their favourite food woven beside them; hares with cotton flowers for instance; set in their natural surrounding, squirrels run up *kikar* trees and birds sit in trees or gardens, frequently with a little something to eat in their mouths or within easy reach.

This sympathy with animals has very ancient roots. There are similar scenes painted very naturalistically on Indus civilization pottery from Chanhu-daro where a goat nibbles at a tree, and there are copper tablets from Mohenjo-daro which show hares feeding.[7] This naturalistic animal style continued in Indian sculpture and painting but in textiles such individuality and variety would make the work too slow and difficult. Though the weavers and block printers of Indian textiles succeed wonderfully in capturing the liveliness and nature of animals, repetition is inevitable.

Copper tablet with hare feeding. Mohenjo-daro, Harappan period. (Marshall, Mohenjo-daro and Indus Civilisation)

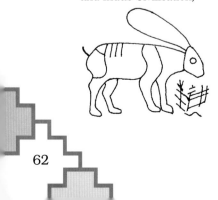

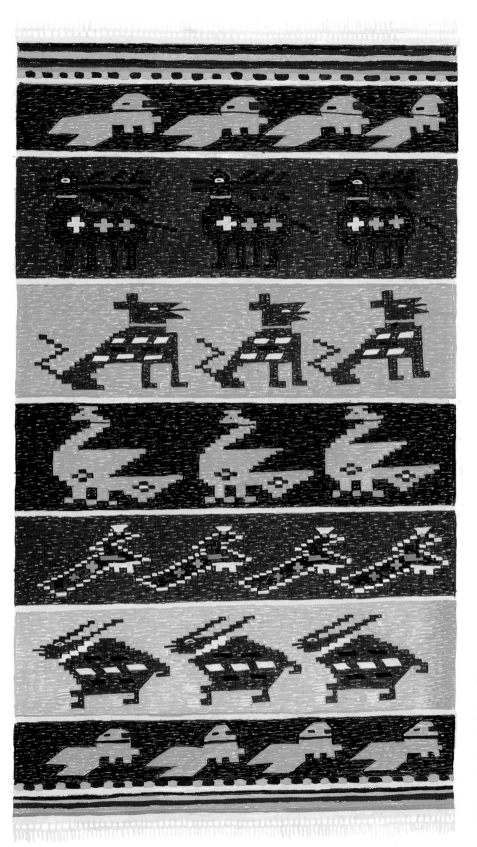

Durrie with rows of animals facing alternately left and right. The weaver identified the animals as (from top) parakeets, deer, dogs, ducks, squirrels, hares and parakeets. On other durries the animals here called ducks and squirrels were usually known as peacocks. Basauli village, Ropar district, Punjab, 1976.

Durrie with pairs of
peacocks confronting a
central plant and a row
of sparrows at either end.
Marakpur village, Ropar
district, Punjab, 1980.

Representations of different animals on the durries have, in most cases, much in common; they stand in profile, their bearing erect and self-assured and their feet square on the ground. Their bodies often have decorative spots, regardless of zoological reality, and they usually wear necklaces. Their mouths tend to be open with their tongues extended – an attribute not denied even to fish. One convention – groups of narrow horizontal lines – serves equally effectively for tails, claws, paws, manes and whiskers. The animals are generally placed in pairs confronting each other, sometimes with a flower or plant between them, or in rows which face alternatively left and right. In both cases there are usually from three to seven pairs or rows on a durrie, sometimes several more where the animals are small.

These conventionalised forms, common to the whole area, imply a long history and tradition. They must have developed gradually, in response to the difficulties of weaving curvilinear forms in a rectilinear medium.

Rows of conventionalised birds and deer shown in identical fashion, in profile and standing erect with feet on the ground, were painted on pottery excavated from sites in Mesopotamia and Iran from the second half of the fourth millennium BC. They are seen again on the pottery of the first half of the third millennium from sites in Baluchistan.[8] At a time of strong links between Iran and the Indus Civilization this is thought to be the trading route by which such designs entered India. During this period the motif of animal processions also occurs at Amri in Sind, at the edge of the Indus plain.[9] The Harappans however made little use of these regimented rows of animals and they differ so markedly from the naturalistic Harappan animal style that, where they do occur, they would appear to be solely of West Asian derivation.[10]

Proto-Elamite seal with ibex facing the sacred tree, from southwestern Iran, ca. 2800 BC. (Frankfort, Cylinder Seals)

Pairs of animals confronting a central plant continue the ancient West Asian tradition of animals flanking the sacred tree of life. This theme from Mesopotamian mythology, later found in the Avestan religion of Iran and the Vedic religion of India, has given to representational art one of its most enduring forms; apart from its symbolic value, it has a pleasing symmetry and offers the artist endless scope for interpretation. It appears on cylinder seals from Mesopotamia of the Uruk period (ca. 3500-3000 BC), and from Susa, capital of the ancient state of Elam in western Iran, made around 3000 BC, and on engraved shell plaques from the Royal Cemetery at Ur in southern Mesopotamia of about 2600-2500 BC.[11]

In Iran its use has continued through the ages and it remains a popular carpet motif today.

As the *ekka asvattha* of the Vedic tradition, the trunk of the tree represents the axis of the universe rising from the navel of the God Varuna as he lies on the cosmic water, while the branches represent differing levels of existence.[12] The *ekka asvattha* appears at Sanchi with pairs of people and animals among the branches. There are also smaller roundels with pairs of animals among lotus plants that grow from the *purna kalasa*, or vase of plenty. At Ajanta a small panel carved in relief on the facade of Cave 19 shows two peacocks confronting a stylized plant and there are similar panels on the Vitthala Temple of the 13th century AD at Hampi.

Details from a silk fragment probably woven in Sogdiana, seventh to eighth century AD. (Courtesy Victoria & Albert Museum)

Around the sixth or seventh century AD, late in the Sasanian period, the motif of the jewelled roundel developed in Iran. At first it contained a single animal or animal head and later a pair of animals which sometimes flank a tree – a continuation of the sacred tree design. Woven in silk, a valuable and easily transported material, it was exported all over the ancient world and fragments have survived in Egypt, West Asia and Europe. Agnes Geijer has shown how its use continued in Swedish folk weaving down to the 18th century. The animals, among them the lion and domestic jungle fowl, are frequently woven in profile and standing stiffly erect. In keeping with the opulence of the Sasanian court, they are sometimes bejewelled and wear necklaces.[13]

Two very similar silk fragments in the provincial Iranian style, thought to have been made in Sogdiana during the seventh or eighth century AD, which reached French ecclesiastic collections at an early date, show several of the weaving conventions used in the dowry durries today. These include the extended horizontal tongue, the diagonal collar and the decorative body markings, here in the shape of crosses, on hounds kept for hunting. This was a period of close ties between India and Iran but, with the lack of surviving Indian evidence to guide us, it is impossible to know whether these shared characteristics are due to direct contact at that time, or later, or where they originated. Similarly the horizontal, extended tongue, body markings and partial collars are also found on the lions of the Patola weaving of Gujarat, which implies a long history over an area much greater than the dowry durrie belt.[14]

There are also resemblances with lions on textiles found in Egypt of the fifth to the ninth century AD. They usually show pairs of identical animals or birds confronting the sacred tree. In common with the dowry durrie lions, these too may have the extended, horizontal tongue, body spots and the tail held up along the back in a horizontal "S" curve. There is, however, no sign of the collar although other animals on these textiles sometimes wear it. It is not always known where such textiles were woven. The dry climate of Egypt has preserved numerous textiles, many of which were doubtless imported from other regions.[15]

In the north of India the diagonal and horizontal neck bands given to many animals are always called *kantha*, necklace. Necklaces or garlands are comparatively rare on animals in Indian art before about the eighth century AD, when they begin to appear regularly on *vahana*, the animal vehicles associated with various Hindu gods. The earliest example we have found in the bridal durrie region is a stone sculpture of this date from Jind in Haryana, now in the possession of the Department of Archaeology and Museums, Haryana, in Chandigarh, which shows two lions and a bull with necklaces. One *vahana*, the dog of Bhaira and Nirriti, wears a collar.[16]

The evidence from the durries is inconclusive. Animals without a particular religious affiliation, such as cats, deer, hares and sparrows may or may not wear necklaces. Certain *vahana* animals such as parakeets always wear a necklace while others such as rats and peacocks are sometimes given one. Possibly the horizontal *kantha* originated in the natural scarlet neck band of the rose-ringed parakeet and it migrated from there to other animals, providing an easily woven touch of interest to the solid body colour. As we shall see, the parakeet is one of the most traditional durrie motifs and was probably established in the weavers' repertoire earlier than many other animals which wear the horizontal band.

The diagonal neck band may originally have been a collar. There is a long history of animal collars in India, beginning with terracotta and bronze models of dogs during the Harappan period. We meet them again at Bharhut (mid–second century BC), where we find an Iranian association in the collar of rosettes worn by a seated stone lion, probably a variant of the rosette collars of bulls and sphinxes from Susa.[17] Animal collars seen on Sasanian and Sogdian silks continue to appear on Iranian lions, as well as cheetahs and hounds, down to the 20th century; several 19th and 20th century

Qashqa'i lion rugs from southern Iran showing stylized versions of this rosette collar. Tanavoli, in his work on these rugs, suggests that the collar implies that the lion has been tamed by its master.[18] Indian miniature paintings from the Mughal period show examples of hunting cheetahs and hounds, as well as pet deer, with scarlet collars.[19] The lion of a 17th century durrie fragment associated with the imperial workshop at Lahore has a curved, three-row, neck band markedly similar to certain diagonal examples on the dowry durries.[20] All the durrie lions in the passant position of the Lahore fragment lion and the Patola lions have the diagonal collar, while its use on other animals is less frequent and shows no consistent pattern. It seems likely, therefore, that this type of collar has an Iranian link and was initially used by the durrie weavers on lions, spreading to other animals with the passage of time.

There are no obvious parallels or precedents for the frequently used groups of narrow horizontal lines, which are most probably a practical weaving solution to the problem of depicting various intricate but important elements of the animals. No doubt they evolved slowly but have gained acceptance because they are successful in showing clearly what they represent, be it hair, claws or whiskers. At the same time these lines are simple to weave and do not weaken the fabric, as would any narrow line other than a horizontal one.

Sher: Lions

The Asiatic lion today survives in the wild only in the Gir Forest of Gujarat but in ancient times its territory extended across much of Europe and West Asia. Originating in Europe, it penetrated as far as India where the tiger, which came down from Siberia into India by way of Assam, was the pre-eminent large cat. Since the lion can live in open country it is well suited to Iran, whereas the tiger, needing jungle cover and water for protection from the heat and for its secretive way of life, adapted best to the Indian terrain.

With this background it is easy to see how the lion was represented as the king of beasts in the ancient art of Mesopotamia and Iran while the tiger did not appear there at all. In India the opposite was the case, with many examples of the tiger during Harappan times but none of the lion.

The leopard, which concerns us to a lesser degree, is very adaptable and can live in almost any environment. It is still found in many areas of West and South Asia and from early times has appeared regularly, if not as frequently, as the lion and tiger in the art of the region.

Durrie with central medallion and pairs of lions. The weaver identified the crenellated border as a *quila*, fort. Timberpur village, Patiala district, Punjab, 1980.

Durrie with a lion, ducks and *aath kallian*, eight petal rosettes. The small red rectangles between the ducks and in front of the lion were specially placed there as food for the animals. Hathoor village, Ludhiana district, Punjab, 1965.

The lion first receives mention in India with the arrival of the Indo-Europeans in the middle of the second millennium BC. It was for them an established symbol of strength, though they did not associate it with any particular deity. The tiger is not spoken of until late in the Vedic period, in the *Atharvaveda*, by which time the newcomers would have become familiar with the local fauna.[21]

Stone lion capital from Sarnath, Mauryan period, third century BC.

From the third millennium BC, the lion is depicted in the art of Mesopotamia and Iran in hunting scenes and contests of strength with man or various animals. Associated with the great Mesopotamian goddess Ishtar, as her special emblem, the lion also became a symbol of royal power and majesty in both Mesopotamia and Iran.[22] Its first appearance in India, on the great pillars of the Mauryan Emperor Ashoka (ca. 269-232 BC), shows the influence of the Iranian model of imperial grandeur.[23]

The lion also became associated with the Buddha, and is shown many times during the second and first centuries BC in the sculpture of Bharhut and Sanchi. In Indian art the animal became quite domesticated and often appears more like a large dog than a ferocious guardian. That this depiction was intentional is borne out by a passage on temple construction in the *Agni Purana*, a sacred Hindu text of the third or fourth century AD, which specifies that the lion should not be fierce-looking.[24] This lack of ferocity is very marked in the durrie lions which, particularly those with a foreleg raised, resemble the solid canine citizens regularly seen trotting purposefully around the fields and villages.

Painted cloth *(kalamkari)* with striking lion from Andhra Pradesh, 20th century. (Private Collection)

The ferocious West Asian lion in his traditional striking pose – standing drawn back on his haunches with a foreleg raised straight ahead, the claws clearly shown, the mouth wide open and the lips withdrawn in a fierce snarl – is not seen on the durries. It appears elsewhere in the country in paintings, particularly of the Deccan[25] and is also well known in Indian folk art and tradition. In Punjab it is distinguished from *sher,* the usual lion, by the prefix "ferocious" *babbar sher.*

Plaque with lion and tiger markings from the wall of the *jharokha* in the Red Fort, Delhi, completed AD 1648.

The extended, horizontal tongue seen on many of the durrie animals probably originated with the lion and entered the subcontinent from Iran, where it can be traced in the fierce West Asian lion from the second millennium BC up to the present. With rare exceptions the tongue is not shown in the animal art of Harappan or earlier times in the subcontinent and when it appears in Mauryan times, it is used quite differently, reinforcing the non-aggressive nature of the lions.[26] Such lions also appear at Stupa II at Sanchi in the late second century BC and are usual on the lion throne, *simhasana,* which also came to India from Iran. The small lion plaques, probably

Durrie with a pair of lions with human faces and tiger stripes and a row of sparrows at either end. Thakora village, Ropar district, Punjab, 1974.

of Indian workmanship, in the back wall of the *jharokha* in the Diwan-i-Am in the Red Fort in Delhi, completed in AD 1648 also show the tongue extended horizontally.[27] The tongue of the durrie lions may follow in this tradition, the angle being adjusted for weaving. It also occurs in the same horizontal form as on the durries in the lions of the Patola weaving of Gujarat, strengthening the possibility that this was originally a lion pose which passed into the common pool of conventionalized durrie weaving forms and was then used for many different animals.

The markings on the bodies of lions and other durrie animals may be simply decorative, to break up the large areas of solid colour, or they may have a different history related to the long-standing artistic confusion of the lion with the tiger and the leopard. Among the durries this is clearly seen in a naturalistic, painted, representation of an animal which a weaver called a *sher*, lion, which had the mane and tail tuft of a lion but the shape and stripes of a tiger. This durrie from Una district in Himachal Pradesh was made by a special painted technique. The weaver traced the lion from a book and transferred it with carbon paper onto a plain-weave durrie she had prepared, and then painted the durrie.

The confusion between the lion and tiger or leopard may be found in Iran as early as the late second or first millennium BC, and also during the Sasanian period, caused probably by the increasing rarity of tigers there. Combinations of lions and tigers or leopards are still to be found in the nomadic Iranian lion rugs of the 19th and 20th centuries.[28]

Lions with tiger markings appear in Indian art in the 17th century. Such beasts can be found on both the durrie fragment associated with the Lahore workshop and the lion plaques of the Red Fort, as well as in paintings of the period.[29] Another variation, in a painted cotton hanging from the St. Thomé-Pulicat region in Madras, made around 1640-1650, has tigers with leopard faces.[30] Two 19th century examples from Varanasi, a sofa and a design for an armchair, show the lion-tiger hybrid,[31] and it also appears frequently in the folk art of Bihar and Gujarat. A fine contemporary embroidery from Saurashtra has a row of well-drawn lions with alternately, tiger stripes and leopard spots. The possibility exists, therefore, that the markings on the durrie lions developed as part of this tradition and, like the tongues, spread to other animals.

The lion body with a human head or face goes back to very ancient times, signifying the greatest physical strength combined with the greatest intelligence. The concept of mixing parts of animals, birds and human beings was common to the Egyptians, Mesopotamians,

Durrie with animals that the weaver called a lion, and pairs of *koel*, Indian cuckoos. Lakhnaur village, Ropar district, Punjab, 1977.

73

Durrie with a pair of
lions with human faces
and rows of deer and
plants. At the top, a row
of abstract fish. Dhanas
village, Union Territory of
Chandigarh, 1974.

Iranians and Harappans, though combinations varied. The use by the Harappans of different hybrids from those of their western neighbours indicates that they were not borrowed directly. The earliest Mesopotamian hybrids, which belong to the Akkadian period (2334-2193 BC), were bulls, lions and birds with human heads, while from Indus civilization sites we find combinations of tiger and elephant parts. There is also a goat with a human face and cases of the hind legs and torso of a tiger attached to a complete female figure.[32]

Stucco parapet with a pair of human-faced lions on a house at Kajheri village, Union Territory of Chandigarh, 1970.

Beginning at Bharhut and Sanchi in the second and first centuries BC the human-faced lion is found in all periods with a wonderful range of expressions from sombre old men to carefree young women.[33]

The two durrie examples of big-cat hybrids were woven in the same village by different women. The tiger hybrid is especially remarkable as it was woven alone by a weaver who lost an arm in a childhood accident. The lion hybrid shows the influence of the Iranian lion-and-sun motif, which is also frequent among the human-headed lions of nomadic rugs of the 19th and 20th centuries.[34]

Among the Sikh weavers of the plains no identity is given to the human-faced lion, but in the Kangra district of Himachal Pradesh it is linked to the story of Indra and Bahula. The God Indra took the form of a lion and threatened to kill a cow named Bahula. He

Detail of durrie showing lion with head seen from above. Dhanas village, Union Territory of Chandigarh, 1974.

granted her plea for one last day in which to suckle her calf before she died. When she returned as promised, Indra was so impressed that he spared her life and revealed his true form. In the contemporary folk painting with which O.C. Handa illustrates this tale, the lion has been given a human face and leopard spots.[35]

Among the durrie lions one is unique in having the head seen from above. We have not been able to trace any precedents for this in Indian art but there are many examples of rampant beasts with their heads held sideways in seals of the third millennium BC from Mesopotamia and Iran.[36] A remarkable resemblance can also be seen with a neolithic leopard painted on pottery from Persepolis.[37] Lions in Iranian art continued to have their faces represented in this way through succeeding periods and are widespread in the nomadic lion rugs of the 19th and 20th centuries.[38] Unfortunately it is impossible to say how or when the motif became known to dowry durrie weaving.

Ghode: Horses

Horses have always been very important in North Indian society. Estimates of their worth for the Punjabi would be hard to exaggerate. The German traveller Baron Charles Hügel was told by Maharaja Ranjit Singh in 1836 that he had fought a war over Laili, a horse belonging to the Barakzai brothers of Peshawar. The war,

Durrie with central figure between confronted horses, woven in Adhuan village, Haryana, 1984.

76

Detail of a horse and rider from a durrie woven in Dilwan village, Bhatinda district, Punjab, 1935.

which lasted several years, cost him 12,000 men and £ 600,000.[39] Even in the 20th century folk tale of Jeona Maur, his horse is extravagantly praised for she galloped so fast it seemed "she was talking with the wind". Though the place of horses, *ghode* or *khode*, in rural life has been greatly diminished by the introduction of mechanised transport, ponycarts are still fairly widely used. Well-maintained ponies are a familiar sight trotting briskly along the shady roads, cockade between their ears and harness bells jingling. Even in the cities today, following a tradition common to much of the subcontinent, the groom still rides to his wedding on a grey horse or pony.

Probably because they are so difficult to weave, horses are comparatively rare on the durries. They are generally seen in pairs facing each other, sometimes with riders and sometimes held by a central figure. The central figures or riders may be soldiers, "military men" in the English of village Punjab, for they wear a pointed head-dress resembling a traditional helmet.

The riders either sit on the horse or are shown frontally, standing above it. The former pose has a precedent in a rare surviving ancient textile, for it is seen in the procession of horsemen on the earliest pile carpet presently known, the Pazyryk carpet, found in a frozen tomb at the site of that name in the Altai mountains of southern Siberia, dated between the sixth and fourth centuries BC. The provenance of this carpet is uncertain but it may have been woven in Achaemenid Iran.[40] In the subcontinent the pose of the standing rider seems to belong primarily to folk art, particularly textiles, for it is found in the *phulkari* embroidery of Punjab of the 19th or early 20th century as well as the folk textiles of other areas, such as the embroidery of Saurashtra and Gujarat, and the *sujani*, embroidered quilts of Bihar. It is also seen in the tribal rugs of Iran and has survived, as apparently did many West Asian motifs, in Scandinavian folk textiles woven as recently as the 18th century.[41] In more enduring materials it is very rare, only one example from the ancient world, on an Iranian bronze belt made between 1000 and 750 BC, being known to us.[42] A standing warrior on his horse, with his dagger, spear and bow and arrow, from a tomb at Hinidan

Durrie with horse and standing rider, woven in Khuda Ali Sher village, Union Territory of Chandigarh, 1975.

in Baluchistan is impossible to date precisely. However, the ancient weaponry and the horse suggest a Hindu Rajput and a date before the area was completely converted to Islam. Other relief carvings of the area, probably made in the 19th century, represent Muslim Brahui warriors with their camels and guns.[43]

One form of standing rider did flourish in the ancient world but it was reserved for deities who are shown on their special mounts, for instance Ishtar on her lion. At first shown frontally and in proportion to their animal vehicles, by the early first millennium BC the deities are shown in profile and towering above their mounts. Realistically portrayed mortal riders seated on equids and, later, on camels also begin to appear in the Akkadian period in Mesopotamia. In contrast with the serene assurance of the standing deities, they cling to their mounts by mane and tail.[44] In a group of paintings from the Kulu Valley in Himachal Pradesh now in the National Museum, New Delhi, there are two of an 18th century AD date, one of which shows a king seated on his horse as he goes hawking while the other shows Siva and Kali standing above their respective mounts the bull and the tiger. Both poses are also found together, embroidered on a 19th century Bengal *kantha*.[45]

The weavers usually represent animals with all their feet on the ground, though horses and lions, and very occasionally other animals, sometimes have one foreleg raised and flexed. In the art of the Indus civilization, as in the rest of the ancient world, the customary walking pose for animals is all four feet on the ground. However, when sculpture re-emerges in India in the second century BC at the Buddhist site of Bharhut, animals – mostly horses and elephants – are sometimes depicted walking with one foreleg raised and flexed.[46] The first appearance of the pose in Mesopotamia seems to be for the horses on the gates of the palace of King Shalmaneser III (859-824 BC) at Balawat.[47]

By the sixth century BC the Greeks had begun to depict horses and other animals with masterly naturalism in the raised foreleg pose, the leg held high and the joints flexed. Thereafter it is found on coins, vases and sculpture all over the Greek world.[48] It may have been these Greeks, settled in cities across the new Asian empire left by Alexander the Great in the late fourth century BC, who introduced the new walking pose into northern India. The archaeological record is still scanty but a silver medallion on which it is found was excavated at Al Khanum, the site of a Greek city in northern Afghanistan.[49] The medallion, thought to have been made in Syria around 300 BC, depicts the Anatolian Mother-Goddess, Cybele, riding in her chariot proudly drawn by a mighty pair of perfectly matched and schooled lions, each with three legs on the ground and one raised foreleg. Lions, elephants and horses in this pose also appear on some coins of the Graeco-Bactrian kings of the second and first centuries BC.[50] From these beginnings it could have passed into the Indian repertoire of animal poses; once established, its use in sculpture, coins, textiles and durries in many parts of the subcontinent can be followed up to the present.

Detail of *barasingha*, swamp deer, from durrie in Basauli village, Ropar district, Punjab, 1976.

Hiran: **Deer**

Deer are a very popular design with the weavers and appear in several forms. The commonest is in pairs confronting each other where both have short, diagonal horns; the fore and hind legs are shown parallel coming straight down and then moving forward diagonally at the same angle as the

Durrie with pairs of
confronted deer, Hulka
village, Patiala distict,
Punjab, 1969.

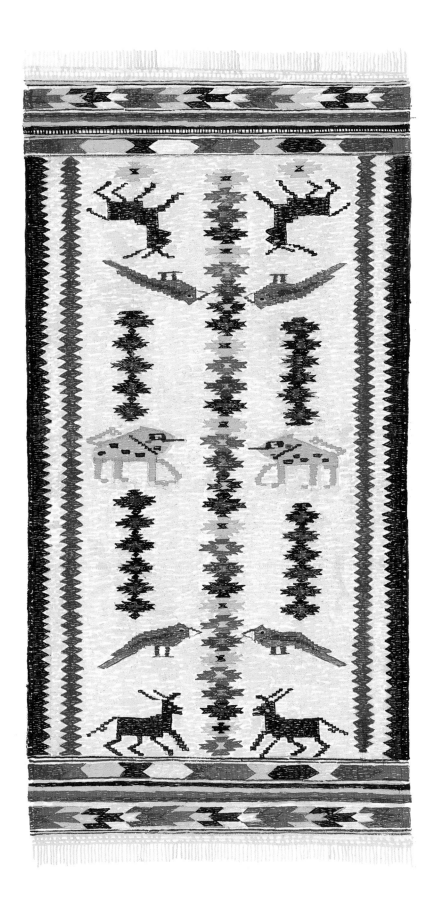

Durrie with pairs of deer, parakeets and lions. The innermost of the end bands represent fish, the outermost *lehria*, waves. Basolan village, Ambala district, Haryana, 1976.

horns. In many cases, the body also has diagonal contours but faces in the opposite direction, thereby balancing the composition. These deer are never given a more specific name by the weavers and are too conventionalised for precise identification; indeed they could as well be wild goats, antelopes or gazelles as deer.

A second kind of deer, which appears in rows of three, has straight legs. The antlers are represented by two horizontal lines behind the head, from which spring either four or six short, diagonal tines. These deer are generally called *barasingha*, literally twelve horns, or the swamp deer (Cervus Duvauceli), which was once common in the area and is still found occasionally in undisturbed places.

In another pose, seen only on two durries, pairs of deer with long diagonal antlers have their legs flexed as if galloping. Again, the weavers only called them deer, and they are too stylized to identify further.

Wild goats, antelopes and gazelles, often hard to distinguish, are commonly seen in the animal processions of Mesopotamian and Iranian art from the late fourth and third millennia BC.[51] They appear, with their legs and horns in an angled pose, on painted pottery of this date from sites in northern Iran. The pose seems to have spread down into Baluchistan, for it is found on pottery there slightly later, in the third millennium.[52]

There is a single case of a pair of deer, rampant and regardant, standing on their hind legs and looking over their shoulders. Although this durrie, woven in 1986, is unique in the survey, the weaver said she had copied the deer from another older durrie. There is no reason to suppose that it is not traditional, and the contorted position of the heads of the animals suggests they were not recently taken from nature. Similar goats and other animals are found in the art of Mesopotamia from the third millennium onwards, the design being particularly popular in the first millennium BC. It could have spread into the subcontinent in the same way as other motifs, for deer in this pose appear at Stupa II (late second century BC) at Sanchi.[53] There is, however, nothing to guide us as to how or when it reached the dowry durrie weavers.

Khargosh: Hare

Hares, *khargosh* or *sahe* (there are no rabbits native to India), are always popular on dowry durries, either sitting upright or crouching to nibble at the plant or flower in front of them. The latter pose is known from copper tablets found at Mohenjo-daro though with only a single hare beside the plant, for symmetrical pairs of animals were not characteristic of Indian art of that period.[54] Since the tablets were amuletic, Marshall thought they might have been sacred. The hare is closely associated with the moon in folklore, as we see from several *Jataka* stories. One of these The *Sasa Jataka* (no.316) uses the hare to give touching evidence of the deep roots of Indian hospitality. In this tale the Buddha had taken an earlier birth as a hare. He was troubled because he had nothing to offer any guests who might visit him, and decided finally that all he could offer was his own flesh. On hearing this Sakka, the God Indra, decided to test his resolve. Disguised as a Brahmin he asked the hare for food. The hare at once offered himself and after shaking his body to free any insects in his fur, and prevent them from perishing with him, he jumped onto a heap of burning coals which Sakka had caused to appear. The hare was puzzled because he did not burn in the fire and turned to the Brahmin for a reason. Sakka revealed his true nature and so moved was he by the virtue of the little animal that in order for this selflessness to be known throughout all time he daubed the hare sign on the orb of the moon. Then placing the hare on a bed of tender grass, Indra returned to heaven and the hare lived happily among his friends in the jungle.[55] In later ages, however, hares have had no particular religious association. Like the ever popular sparrows, the women seem to enjoy weaving hares because they are so familiar and they feel at home with them.

Gilheri: **Squirrels**

The rare appearances of squirrels, *gilheri* or *kato*, in Indian art and on the durries are memorable because of their charming naturalism. They are seen in characteristic poses, either running, climbing or sitting with their tails held up as they concentrate all their attention on the piece of food held between their paws or placed in front of them. Squirrels were fairly popular in Indus Civilization art[56] and are occasionally glimpsed thereafter, such as the delightful examples in the trees on the rear side of Buddhist sculpture from Mathura of the first or second century AD.[57] They are sometimes

Durrie with fish in a
lattice, *machhi jal wich*.
Baraudi village, Ropar
district, 1986.

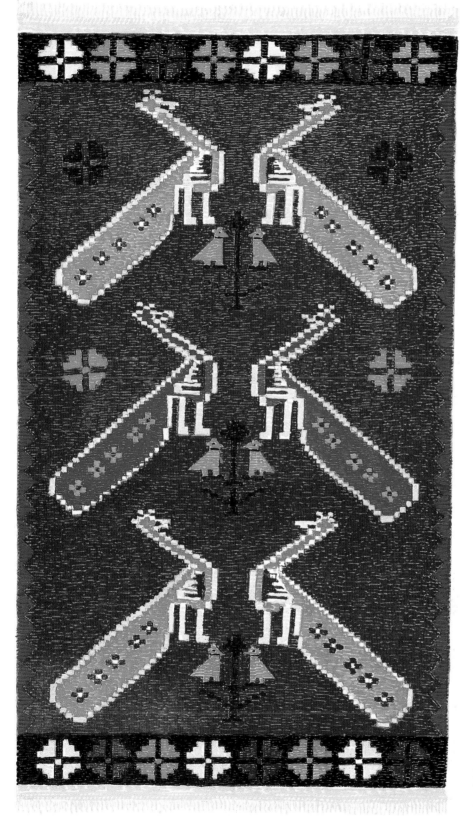

Durrie with pairs of peacocks. Suhagheri village, Patiala district, Punjab, 1987.

85

included in garden scenes of miniature paintings but their finest depiction was certainly the painting devoted entirely to a group of squirrels in a plane tree by Abu'l-Hasan and Mansur of around AD 1610.[58]

Drawing of abstract durrie design called *nagini*, female cobras, by the weaver. Mohem village, Jalandhar district, Punjab, 1978.

It is not clear which member of the squirrel family is intended by the durrie weavers but it is probably the Funambulus Pennanti, or the little Five-striped Palm Squirrel. At home in trees and villages throughout the area, the squirrel's most valuable contribution is the alarm it raises at the approach of a cat, putting every dog and bird on guard.

Nagini, Sanp: Snakes

Snakes are always represented in an abstract form on durries; apart from some of the fish, they are the only animals not shown naturalistically. Called either *nagini*, female cobras or *sanp*, snakes, these durries were seen in three districts. Two snake durries had an all-over pattern of zigzag lines but in one case the weaver had added flowers at the points, making it the same as the design called *bel*, creeper.

In Indian mythology the *naga*, cobra, is a semi-divinity capable of assuming human form. Closely associated with water – probably because it appears mainly during the rainy season – it is linked with fertility of both crops and women. It plays a prominent part in several mythological stories, and shrines to snakes are common in most parts of the subcontinent. The snake cult, like that of the Mother Goddess, is exceedingly ancient.[59] Cobras appear on Harappan seals, in one case partly resting on a dais which is taken as a sign of divinity.[60]

The *nagas* of Punjab are often propitiated through the good offices of Guru Guga – Guga Pir to Muslims – a legendary figure who was supposed to be on very close terms with Basak Nag, the snake king.[61] Festivals are held at the *marhi*, small shrines, of Guru Guga during the monsoon, when it is particularly important to guard against snake bite for at this season snakes are frequently met with in the fields since the saturated soil forces them above ground.

The interior of the late 19th century *marhi* at Dhanas village in the Chandigarh Union Territory is decorated with wall paintings. At the centre Guru Guga rests on the back of his friend Basak Nag, watched by his three mounted companions, Nar Singh, Bhure Singh and Kale Singh. The recumbent figure on a snake traditionally represents Vishnu lying on the coils of the serpent Ananta and has been popular in sculpture and painting since the Gupta period.[62] Thus it is a clear example of the way in which ancient motifs continue in use but are given new meanings according to local preference or legend, their original context quite forgotten – a pattern of transformation frequently repeated in the durrie designs.

The *naga* princesses of legend were very charming, clever and gifted with the power to restore life, so they could have provided the original inspiration for the snakes on the durries identified as *Nagini*. However the weavers could not trace any legends or stories to provide further clues for their presence on dowry durries.

Machhli: Fish

Fish, *machhli* or *machhi*, are woven on durries in a variety of naturalistic as well as abstract forms. Naturalistic fish may be the main subject of the durrie, either in a lattice or among flowers. Their shapes differ but they are clearly recognizable, and all have stylized horizontally extended tongues like the land animals. Fish may also be less prominent, confined to occasional, narrow, horizontal rows among other designs on a durrie. The abstract fish, which appear in two shapes, are found only in narrow, horizontal bands near the ends of the durries.

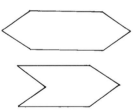

Diagrams of two shapes of abstract fish seen on the durries.

Fish bones and metal fish hooks recovered in excavations show that fish were part of the diet in Harappan times. They are found on the painted pottery of the period, and the fish is a common pictogram in the undeciphered Indus script.[63] This is not surprising since the river Indus, a plentiful source of fish, was crucial to the development of this first urban culture which grew up along its banks. The Indus provided water, transport and, through its annual flooding, fertile and easily worked agricultural land for those who lived beside it.

Since then, and for the same reasons, life continued to be centred along the great rivers of the Punjab plains until the irrigation schemes which began in the 19th century increased the cultivable land far beyond the immediate river tracts. The huge dams built after 1947 brought further changes, for the rivers could no longer be

Durrie with pairs of parakeets, *judwen tote,* crossed, addorsed and regardant and the name of the weaver's brother, Jasvir Singh, at the bottom. Mundi Kharar village, Ropar district, Punjab, 1973.

Durrie with pairs of
confronted cocks.
Dhanas village, Union
Territory of Chandigarh,
1990.

used either for transport or fishing. Although fish are today scarcely known in the villages, their place in traditional Punjabi life is so deep-rooted that they remain popular with the weavers.

Mor: Peacocks

The peacock is among the most popular of the durrie birds and is portrayed in a variety of poses. A native of the subcontinent, it has been a favourite subject for painters and sculptors since the time of the early Indus settlements.[64] The pairs of crossed peacocks at Stupa I (late first century BC) at Sanchi in Madhya Pradesh must rank among the finest of all representations of these proud and elegant birds. Many kinds of symbolism have been associated with the peacock: on pottery from Cemetery H at Harappa (ca. 2000-1500 BC) it has been interpreted as ferrying the souls of the dead.[65] On the stone discs from Murtaziganj, Patna, of about the second century BC it seems to be associated with the fertility goddess.[66] By the Gupta period it appears regularly in sculpture as the *vahana*, mount, of Kartikeya, the god of war, who is the son of Siva and Parvati. Hindu families often place models of peacocks on the roofs of their houses and at the pinnacle of the *vedi*, marriage altar. O.C. Handa has suggested that the reason for these customs is that the bird is felt to offer protection, since it symbolises divine force and virtuous strength through its association with Kartikeya.[67]

In many areas peafowl are protected from man, their most threatening predator, as they are held to be sacred. This belief arose because the cock sheds "tears" during his grand mating display. Legend stated that these were pearls and the peahen, who would be pecking around on the ground nearby, was fertilized by swallowing them.[68] Legend also says that when the peacock is happy he dances for joy at his own beauty but when he looks down he weeps at the sight of his large and ugly feet. It was not always so, according to the story, for once he had small and graceful feet. Opinion is divided over the cause of his misfortune. According to some a black partridge asked to borrow them to wear for a dancing competition, while others maintain it was a pied myna who borrowed them to wear to a wedding. Either way, they have yet to be returned.[69]

The peafowl travelled westwards rather later than the domesticated jungle fowl. Among the *Jataka* tales of the previous lives of the Buddha, often adapted from existing North Indian folklore of the early first millennium BC, is the story of the merchants who travelled by sea to Baveru, Babylon, where they caused a flutter among the residents with a peacock trained to dance at the clapping of hands and scream at the snapping of fingers.[70]

In the *First Book of Kings* (10:22,23), written around 550 BC, the legendary wealth of King Solomon, who lived in the tenth century BC, is given as gold, silver, ivory, apes and peacocks brought to him every third year by his navy.

The peacock does not appear in Iranian art before the Sasanian period (AD 224-642) but thereafter remained very popular. It also lent its magnificient train to the mythical Iranian bird, the *senmurv*.

Tota: **Roseringed Parakeets**

As the mount of Kamdeva, the Hindu God of Love, the parakeet is especially appropriate on dowry durries. The roseringed parakeets, (Psittacula Krameri), one of several subspecies – are among the most numerous and best-known birds of the subcontinent. They live in flocks and, highly destructive of crops by day, return at nightfall with plenty of raucous calling to roost in large trees. They disappear amongst the foliage for their brilliant green colour provides the perfect camouflage. They are small members of the parrot family, though true parrots are particular to Africa. Parakeets have a long history in their more popular role as domestic cage birds, renowned for their gift of mimicking human speech. They figure prominently in folk art and in the earlier legends of India.

The parakeet has held its place in Indian art since Harappan times and reappears at Sanchi.[71] In sculpture of the Kushan (first-second centuries AD) and later periods a favourite scene shows a pet parakeet on the arm or hand of a beautiful goddess, *yakshi*, or young woman.[72]

The parakeet and myna are shown in miniature paintings as domestic pets in cages placed side by side, and appropriately, they sometimes appear together on dowry durries for they are known as the lovebirds of Punjabi folklore. All animals and birds must originally have held a symbolism of some kind but only this pair has retained it for the weavers to the present day. In the Raja Rasalu legend, set by Temple between the eighth and tenth centuries AD, the Raja's young wife Rani Kokilan is watched over in her palace by 80 parakeets, 86 mynas and 80 peacocks. Her favourites are a parakeet and myna, who form a devoted couple. Because Raja Rasalu is constantly away hunting the Rani starts a dalliance with the neighbouring Raja Hodi. When the myna tries to remonstrate with her, in anger the Rani wrings its neck. The parakeet is grief-stricken but manages to escape and flies off to give the sad news to her husband.[73]

Impression of a seal with rampant, addorsed amd regardant lions, their tails and forelegs crossed, Mesopotamia, Uruk period, ca. 3500-3000 BC. (Frankfort, Cyliender Seals)

Durrie with pairs of
confronted ducks in
Mohri village, Ambala
district, Haryana, 1986.

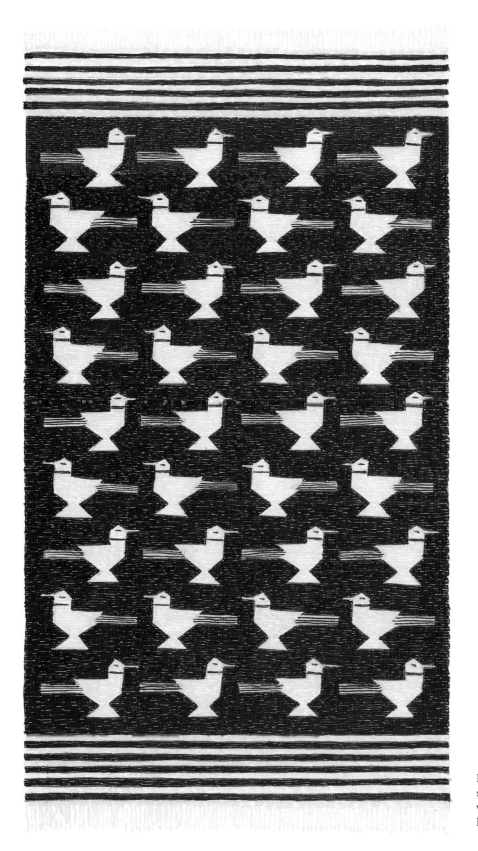

Durrie with rows of
sparrows, Majri Jattan
village, Ambala district,
Haryana, 1983.

On the durries one particular pose, showing a pair of birds crossed, addorsed and regardant, back to back and looking over their shoulders, is characteristic only of parakeets. The stately peacocks from Sanchi of the late first century BC are the sole examples we have found of this pose from an early period in the subcontinent; possibly it was more widely adopted in folk art and has now disappeared. The Sanchi peacocks also seem to be the oldest surviving depiction of birds in this pose, although the composition was widely used in Mesopotamia on seals beginning in the Uruk period (ca 3500-3100 BC), mostly for scenes of bull-men, lions and ibex.[74]

Egypt has provided us with some of the earliest surviving examples of parakeets in this pose, for instance in a mosaic from Bawit[75] and a fragment of a tapestry-woven textile, in which the natural collar of the birds has been converted into a knotted ribbon.[76] Both have been dated to the sixth century AD. The motif is also seen on a Byzantine stone capital from Constantinople of the same period.[77] Nothing comparable appears to have survived in West or South Asia from this time but the motif does seem to be oriental in origin and the influence of Sasanian Iran on textiles found in Egypt has been clearly demonstrated. Parakeets in this pose appear in Iran in the Islamic period, for instance on a silver jug of the 11th or 12th century AD and on brass ewers made in Herat, in modern Afghanistan, between AD 1150-1220.[78] The collection of early textiles at Sens in France also includes an Italian silk chasuble of the 14th century AD with parakeets in this pose.[79] The widespread distribution of these rare surviving examples suggests that the motif may have been well-known in earlier times. Though the similarities are so striking, it is impossible to establish the precise link between the dowry durrie parakeets and the earlier, foreign, examples.

Murgha: Domestic Fowl

It is generally agreed that all domestic fowl are descended from the red jungle fowl (Gallus Gallus), a native of the Himalayan regions, which had been domesticated locally by Harappan times. It appears on seals, pottery and small bronze and terracotta models of the period.[80] It seems to have been a popular item in the early export trade from the Indus civilization to West Asia and was probably known in ancient Babylon by the third millennium BC under the title of "egg-bird".[81] A painting of a cock on a limestone ostracon from Thebes dated between 1425 and 1123 BC proves that it had reached Egypt by that time at the latest.[82]

In Iran and southern Mesopotamia the cock is found on seals and sealings from the Achaemenid period, when it was associated as a sacred bird with the Avestan religion. Later, it became one of the characteristic motifs within the Sasanian roundel.[83]

As a symbol of alertness the cock is among the most traditional figures of Punjabi folk art and was often painted or carved in relief on grain storage bins for protection of their contents. With its proud bearing and elaborate tail, as well as striking colour combinations, it is one of the weavers' most successful creations.

Battakan: Ducks

Birds which resemble either ducks or geese are always known as ducks by the weavers. Both ducks and geese live on many village tanks or ponds, and geese in particular have an important place in Hindu and Buddhist mythology. However, the weavers attach no stories or significance to any of these birds and are content to weave them because of their familiarity from nature as well as from older durries and other traditional household crafts.

Chirian: Sparrows

Sparrows succeed in foraging a good living around the buffaloes and the kitchens of the village compounds, whereas visits from large or more timid birds, found in plenty in the mango groves and trees around the tanks and fields, are rare due to the lack of tree cover. With the men out at work and the children in school, the chirp and bustle of flocks of sparrows are frequently all that intrude upon the quiet of the village morning. Fittingly, they are by far the most popular birds on the durries, either alone, with other birds, or in a row at the end of quite a different design. Wherever it may be, the weavers very often manage to find a little space for them.

The Geometry of Design

Geometrical designs form a large part of the durrie repertoire and have ancient roots. What appears to be a bewildering variety is actually based on a few basic formulas; the variations are in details rather than essence.

Phul

Phul, serrated and stepped lozenges and lattices, are two of the most common types of geometric durrie designs. The basis of one is a lozenge with serrated sides sometimes referred to as a *rhomb*. It may be arranged on its own over the field to form a simple repeating pattern or it may be the centre of a radiating composition sometimes known in the West as a "dazzler". Often it is used as part of a lattice or placed in an arrangement of rows. The motif occasionally appears as but one of several geometrical patterns placed in bands.

The weavers refer to this design by several names but when on its own or specifically referred to, it is most often called a *phul*, flower. At times the motifs are called *tukrian*, pieces, the name also given to the star-shaped motifs that fill the spaces on the dress and surroundings of the *sanjhi* figures worshipped at Navratri. These are also known as *tikki* in Punjab or as *tikria* in Haryana. When it forms part of a lattice, the whole is known as *dibba* or *dubbe*, boxes, *jal*, net, *nimbua da jal*, net with limes, or *lehria*, waves. Whatever meaning or symbolism the motif may once have had is now lost. But its association in the minds of the weavers with a flower is significant.

The second motif is also a lozenge, but here its sides are stepped and not serrated. As with the serrated lozenge, it is used either as a field motif in its own right, or as part of a lattice, forming either small or large compartments. The names accorded to it by the weavers are similar to those of the serrated lozenge. In addition, one lattice is called *shatranj*, chess, and another is referred to as *asman chitare*, stars in the sky. The floral association is, however, once again prominent. In appearance this stepped lozenge is clearly distinct from the serrated lozenge but there is no distinction in use or meaning on the part of the weavers.

Stepped lozenges form the basis of yet another design. This is formed by groups of four stepped lozenges crossed by a stepped

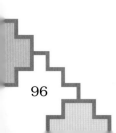

Durrie with design of
radiating serrated
lozenges, Kansal village,
Ropar district, Punjab,
1965.

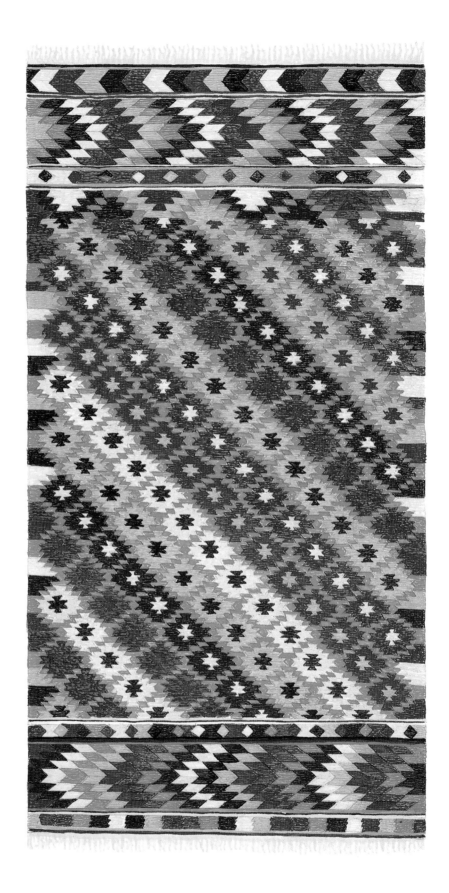

Durrie with lattice
formed by serrated
lozenges, Bhatinda
district, Punjab, 1940s.

Durrie with serrated
lozenges and other forms
in bands. Kansal village,
Ropar district, Punjab,
1969.

99

trellis with which they are linked, in two horizontal rows. In a variation the bands that separate the groups of four little lozenges terminate in hooks. This design is sometimes known as *muchh maror*, upturned mustachios, and causes great merriment, particularly in Sikh families whose menfolk have fine whiskers. In these durries the horizontal rows are divided by serrated bands that are usually known as *sarak*, or road.

Lozenge motifs and lattices are widely used not only in durries but also in rugs and flat weaves of West and Central Asia. Most striking is the resemblance with some of the tapestry woven rugs of the tribes of West Asia, known as *kilim* in Turkey or *gelim* in Iran. Certain Caucasian *kilim* designs are also quite similar.[1] Both serrated and stepped outlines are used. Slit tapestry weave is the most common in these regions, while dovetailing is also found in Iran. North Indian bridal durries are woven in the dovetail structure with some use of slits. The difference therefore lies principally in the fact that the *kilim* or *gelim* are traditionally all wool, though occasionally the warps are cotton, while Indian durries are always made of cotton.[2]

Lozenges, mostly serrated but also stepped, appear too on contemporary Turkmen and Baluch pile rugs, as well as on those from other regions of West Asia.

Lozenge patterns have a long ancestry. They first appear on painted pottery of the Geoksyur culture of the second half of the fourth millennium BC in southern Turkmenistan, but are most associated with the late fourth to third millennium BC at Namazga and related sites also in Turkmenistan and in what is now north-eastern Iran. The parallels between some of these painted pottery fragments and the durrie designs are immediately obvious. Related patterns have also been found on potsherds from other third millennium BC sites in eastern Iran and western Afghanistan notably at Shahr-i-Sokta in Iranian Seistan. There were certainly trade links between some of these sites, as there were also with sites elsewhere in Iran and in the Indus civilization region.[3]

Lozenge patterns are also found at Uruk in southern Mesopotamia around 3200 BC. These are mosaic facings made of clay, or sometimes stone, cones decorating the exterior walls of buildings of uncertain function.[4] This lozenge lattice pattern is close to that of durries and *kilim.*

There is no sign of stepped or serrated lozenges or lattices in the painted pottery of the Indus Civilization in the third millennium BC.[5] On some of the large jars from the site known as Cemetery H. of the early second millennium BC at Harappa are serrated star

Durrie with lattice formed by serrated lozenges, Bahera Sundal Singh village, Uttar Pradesh, 1982.

Durrie with lattice
formed by stepped
lozenges, Nada village,
Ropar district, Punjab,
1982.

Durrie with design of
stepped lozenges and
hooks, Timberpur village,
Patiala district, Punjab,
1980.

Fragment of painted pottery of Namazga III or IV type, Yarim Tepe, Turkmenistan, late fourth to third millenium BC. (Kohl and Heskel, Archaeological Reconnaissances)

Fragment of painted pottery of Namzga III or IV type, Yarim Tepe, Turkmenistan, late fourth to third millennium BC. (Kohl and Heskel, Archaeological Reconnaissances)

Fragment of painted pottery of Namazga III type, Altyn Tepe, Turkmenistan, fourth to third millennium BC. (Kircho, The Origin of Bronze Age)

forms which may be related in some way to the lozenge forms in durries or the Turkmenistan sherds, though these may rather be stellar symbols or even lotuses.

A lozenge lattice emerges on painted pottery of period 11 at Pirak, (ca. 1370-1340 BC) a site to the west of the river Indus. Pirak was a settlement of some importance, with apparent trading links with Turkmenistan and Seistan. Though not identical to the durrie designs, this is close enough to be worth mentioning, and it apparently marks the first appearance of such a design in the pottery of South Asia.[6] How such patterns might have spread after this in South Asia we cannot tell, since painted pottery became increasingly rare in favour of plain or incised wares.

As the potsherds demonstrate, the lozenge has thus had a long ancestry. In the third millennium BC it was concentrated in Turkmenistan and in Seistan and Afghanistan. Appearances elsewhere in the ancient world are rare. But where did the motif come from ? It is quite possible that the potters who made use of its various forms were drawing from textile designs. A pot can be decorated in any way, as easily in curvilinear manner as rectilinear. There are no restrictions except on the part of the skill or will of the painter. On the other hand, quite severe limitations are imposed upon the weaver. Geometrical designs such as these present themselves quite naturally. Their stepped and serrated outlines are part of the very nature of the rather coarse tapestry weaving of the durrie, where a line that is both straight and strong is hard to achieve. This is also true of basket and reed mat making, probably the oldest form of weaving. In many instances in India today, though the potters themselves are usually men, it is often women who undertake the decoration of pots.[7] It is very easy to suggest that all those years ago the prehistoric women, or their men of Turkmenistan decorated their pots with the same designs that were fundamental to their textiles and baskets. In many instances even the serrated and stepped outlines of weaving have been preserved in the decoration of the pots. If these were not strongly a part of the women's weaving tradition then it is hard to understand why such accurate details should have been so faithfully recorded on the painted pottery. These were, after all, domestic pots made for everyday use and the patterns painted on them must have been widely familiar.

Archaeological evidence also suggests an early date in the making of textiles. Actual examples are exceedingly rare, but, as seen, imprints of coarse plain weave fabrics have been found on Indus Civilization pottery fragments. An exciting discovery in Turkmenistan suggests that pile rugs were also woven. Excavations of second millennium

Durrie with lattice formed by stepped lozenges Naya Gaon village, Ropar district, Punjab, 1989.

Fragment of painted pottery of Namazga IV type, Ulug Tepe, Turkenistan, third millennium BC. (Masson and Sarianidi, Central Asia)

Fragment of painted pottery, Shahr-i Sokhta, Iranian Seistan. third millennium BC. (Tosi, Excavations at Sabr-i-Sokhta)

Fragment of painted pottery, Kandahar, Afghanistan, third millennium BC. (Fairservis, Archaeological Studies in Seistan Basin)

BC burial grounds around the Kara-Kala settlement in the Sumbar valley of southern Turkmenistan have revealed curved cutting instruments that closely resemble the curved knives used to trim the pile of carpets made in the region today. Biconic stone spinning wheels, knitting and sewing needles were also found. It thus seems highly probable that pile rugs of the 19th and 20th centuries often bear motifs and patterns that are related to those of the ancient potsherds which further suggests an extremely long tradition.[8]

Likewise in Baluchistan, motifs and patterns of the painted pottery of the third millennium BC from sites such as Bampur sometimes appear on the 19th and 20th century rugs and flat woven textiles of that region.[9] Lozenges, usually halves arranged in bands, of the type under discussion here, mostly serrated rather than stepped, also make an appearance. In the same way as the Turkmen in Turkmenistan, the Baluch tribes are not an indigenous people in what is now called Baluchistan. It is believed that they were forced eastwards as a result of the Turkic invasions of the tenth century onwards from a previous homeland near Kirman in southern Iran to the rather inhospitable lands that they currently occupy which are now shared between Iran and Pakistan. Neither the Baluch nor the Turkmen, however, weave tapestry woven kilims, prefering pile or extra-weft brocaded rugs.

An indication of the early beginnings of *kilim* weaving emerges from the site of Catal Hüyük in central Anatolia, where wall paintings of the seventh and sixth millennia BC are apparently decorated with patterns similar to those on certain 19th and 20th century Anatolian *kilim,* once again suggesting an extremely long tradition. These designs include lozenge lattices. The excavator of this site believes that the paintings represent textiles and it seems likely that *kilim* may have been woven in Anatolia since this time. However uncertainty about the authenticity of the reconstruction of some of the wall paintings in a later publication has kept judgement on this subject reserved.[10]

The mosaic facings at Uruk too may have been copied from textile designs. Perhaps they were intended to reflect on the exterior walls the kind of hangings that may have decorated the interior of the building. At a much later period the patterns of the exterior and interior tile work of mosques and palaces in 16th and 17th century Ottoman Turkey closely resembled those of the contemporary carpets and textiles with which they were adorned, as indeed they did in Safavid Iran or Mughal India at the same period. The practice in antiquity may have been little different. Quite possibly there were also woven floor coverings, reed mats perhaps, or textiles of different types, even durries, brought out as they are today in many parts of

South Asia on special occasions. There may also have been wall hangings in ancient South Asia. The Allchins have commented on the total lack of surviving wall paintings in the Indus Civilization which is surprising, given the varied uses these find in many parts of the subcontinent today, and wonder whether textiles may have filled this role in antiquity.[11]

The development of the lozenge appears to be closely linked to the history of weaving. But is there any further symbolism behind the lozenge? Durrie weavers of Punjab and Haryana often refer to it as a *phul,* flower. In Iran tribal women also refer to it as a flower, *gol* or *gul* in Persian, also translated as rose. Likewise, the characteristic central motif of Turkmen carpets is also referred to as *gol* or *gul,* flower.[12] Thus a floral association with similar motifs that to all outward appearances are completely geometrical and have nothing to do with flowers is shared over a large area. There must surely have been a symbolism that is now lost, and at which we can only guess but which was apparently floral in nature. Perhaps they were associated with the lotus or a symbolic flower.

Glazed brick decoration at the tomb of Akbar at Sikandra, completed 1613.

Whether or not it is related to a flower, the lozenge in its different forms is found as textile decoration in many parts of South Asia today. Perhaps it entered the subcontinent as a textile pattern and has remained part of the textile repertoire. Possibly it developed of its own accord through the limitations of tapestry weave, and the desire to depict a symbolic flower. Whatever the reasons, it is surprisingly little found in other art or craft forms, and since no early textiles have survived, it is almost impossible to trace its development. Stepped lozenges do, however, appear later in friezes on temples in parts of India. In Madhya Pradesh in central India, for example, we have noted its use at a temple of the ninth century AD at Nachna and at several temples of the ninth, tenth and eleventh centuries at Khajuraho. It may well have some religous significance, perhaps as a protective talisman, but this cannot be verified. Stepped lozenges and lattices appear widely in the architectural decoration of Mughal India, such as at the tomb of Akbar at Sikandra near Agra which, begun by Akbar himself before his death, was completed only in AD 1613. They were, indeed, in wide use throughout the Islamic world but their origins are far more ancient than the advent of Islam.

We do not know how the lozenge motifs from the painted pottery of third millennium Turkmenistan and neighbouring regions came to appear in bridal durries – or indeed in the rugs and *kilim* of West Asia. Did the motifs travel as part of the movement of different people in the ancient world? Or was it only in Turkmenistan and the neighbouring regions that textile designs of this kind were painted on pots? It is possible that such patterns were as widespread in basket, mat or textile weaving of the ancient world as they are today. Such designs may have belonged equally to the South Asian repertoire as to that of different parts of West Asia from earliest times. Unfortunately there is no definite answer as yet but the material presented here may provide the basis for further research.[13]

Adhe Phul: Half Lozenges

One of the most common geometrical designs is composed of rows of half lozenges, either stepped or serrated. Predictably, these motifs are referred to by the weavers as *adhe phul,* half flowers; the whole stepped or serrated lozenge being called *phul,* flowers. These half-flowers, however, can also be regarded as whole flowers arranged diagonally but which appear to be half only because of a colour change in the middle of each. *Adhe phul* are used as an all-over pattern and although of great simplicity, distinctive colour combinations can often achieve an extremely sophisticated effect.

Such a composition is once again known from the earliest times right across West Asia and South Asia. A similar example is found in the middle panel on the mosaic cone facing of ca. 3200 BC from Uruk, now in Iraq. The Indus Civilization has numerous examples of the design especially from Mohenjo-daro. Half lozenges are rare in the Turkmenistan finds, but one potsherd shows them with serrated long sides, a feature not noted elsewhere.

Phul Ballian: Serrated Rectangles and Rhomboids

An attractive series of durries have compositions formed by serrated rectangles and rhomboids. These are generally known to the women who weave them as *phul ballian,* ears of wheat. One particularly interesting sample has very much the appearance of a woven basket or mat; not surprisingly, this pattern is shared also in the woven base of many *charpoi.* Its origin must therefore lie in a primitive weaving structure, and is thus of extreme antiquity. In the lower portion the weaver has omitted to put a serrated rectangle and added instead an extra lozenge, which adds to its charm. In some the motifs are more widely spaced, while in yet others they have been arranged to form a zigzag pattern.

Another arrangement, this time of serrated rhomboids, was called by its weaver *bara bihti,* broken bits of pot! Clearly she had no notion of its prehistoric antecedents, for this design has its exact parallel in two fragments of painted pottery from level nine at Altyn Tepe in Turkmenistan dated to the third millennium BC. As has been

Durrie with design of half serrated lozenges, Boor Majra village, Morinda district, Punjab, 1975.

Fragment of painted pottery from Attyn Tepe, third millennium BC. (Masson, Attyn-Tepe)

Storage jar from Mohenjo-daro, third millennium BC. (Khan, The Indus Valley and Early Iran)

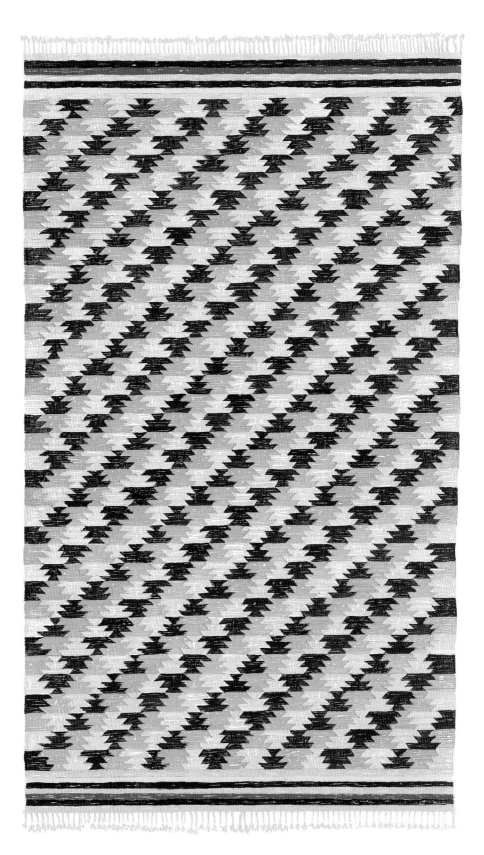

Durrie with design of serrated half lozenges, Badheri village, Union Territory of Chandigarh, 1986.
(see page 6)

Durrie with cut rhomboids in a leafy formation, Karor village, Ropar district, Punjab, 1985.

Durrie with design of
serrated rectangles,
Lamia village, Ludhiana
district, Punjab, 1982.

Durrie with design of serrated rhomboids, Jassaran village, Patiala district, Punjab, 1973-74.

Potsherd from Attyn Tepe, Turkmenistan, third millennium BC. (Masson, Attyn-Tepe)

Durrie with design of serrated rhomboids in a zigzag formation, Badheri village, Union Territory of Chandigarh, 1986.

Durrie with design of
continuous serrated
zigzag bands, Fatehpur
village, Patiala district,
Punjab, 1965.

suggested, such a pattern must surely have had a textile origin, which in its turn was derived from mat or basket weaving. A further identical arrangement of rhomboids, but without serrated sides, is also to be seen on a potsherd of the early second millennium BC far to the west, from the site of Baba Jan in Luristan,western Iran. This is yet another example of how widespread certain designs seem to have been in the ancient world.

The same kind of serrated leaves with their outer short sides cut so that they are no longer proper rhomboids, are sometimes arranged in a more obviously leafy way so that they resemble plants or trees. The weavers call these *sarkan*, roads, the plural form of *sarak*, a reference, doubtless, to the leafy roads of their area. Another example, this time in navy and white, was referred to as ears of wheat. Similar arrangements of more naturalistically drawn leaves were popular also in the Indus Civilization. A later example on the same theme is to be seen on a phyllite plaque from Taxila, near Rawalpindi now in Pakistan, of the second to third century AD and later again on a carved wooden door jamb, perhaps from the last century, in the village of Batta in Haryana.

In other rhomboid forms, the long sides are stepped and not serrated, and the effect is not leafy but severely geometrical. We have found no ancient parallels for this striking design. Again its origins are probably to be found in ancient weaving structures rather than symbols.

Lehria: Serrated Bands

Another extremely common design is composed of continuous zigzag bands with serrated edges. This is known as *lehria*, waves. Sometimes just two colours are employed, white and black for example, or red and blue; there can be a greater variety of colours too, such as blue, rust green and red. Occasionally there are no end panels, or end panels with stripes along with other designs, lozenges for example, in different colours. Such durries are often extremely handsome.

Fragment of painted pottery from Bampur, Iranian Baluchistan, third millennium BC. (de Cardi, Excavations at Bampur)

Fragment of painted pottery from Bampur, Iranian Baluchistan, third millennium BC. (Santoni, Potters and Pottery at Mehrgarh)

Wavy lines must surely be one of the most primordial, natural patterns and are among the first of a child's doodlings. In the hands of someone decorating a pot, the brush does not need to be lifted from the surface as the pot is moved round. In this way it is perhaps more of a potters' pattern than a textile weavers pattern. But so very basic is it that either may have used it independently. It appears on pots all over West and South Asia from the earliest periods but it is interesting, perhaps, to note that once again it is only in prehistoric Turkmenistan, eastern Iran, Afghanistan and Baluchistan that it appears with the serrated edges so characteristic of the textile weavers craft. Examples are from third millennium BC Bampur in

Durrie with design of
diagonal serrated bands,
Shaikhpura village,
Kurukshetra district,
Haryana, 1990.

Durrie with serrated
bands in a "V" formation,
Bakarpur village, Ropar
district, Punjab 1985.

118

Durrie with design of
intersecting circles,
Jahangir village,
Jullunder district,
Punjab, 1982.

Durrie with design of
intersecting circles,
Malloya village, Union
Territory of Chandigarh,
1978.

120

Iranian Baluchistan and another, from Mehgarh in Pakistani Baluchistan, from the same period.

Serrated bands placed diagonally across the field are also a feature of the durries. These too are known as waves. Again, clever use of colour in another extremely basic pattern may render a durrie remarkably attractive and lively. Sometimes such bands may join in points in the centre of the field to form large " V " shapes.

Punkhe: Intersecting Circles

A design that is common in Punjab though less so in Haryana is known to the villagers as *pukhe,* or in Haryana as *punkhe,* fans. The use of such a term is an example of the way in which the weavers express familiar items around them in the designs they use in their durries, even if there is not always a very obvious resemblance.

A durrie with geometrical *punkhe* was seen in the village of Naya Gaon, near Chandigarh. A rare *pukhe* durrie hand block printed was shown at Morinda. In contrast to the woven version this was in the curvilinear style. There are no restrictions on the cutting of a wooden block, and curves are therefore easily achieved in printing. The reverse side has a four-petalled flower design. Hand painting and block printing of textiles was formerly quite common in Punjab, but is now increasingly rare.

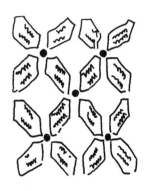

The *punkhe* composition can be regarded in two ways: as formed by intersecting circles which create petal-like forms at their conjunctions, or as a composition of four-petal motifs arranged in rows. Sometimes the four-petal motifs are used to create a lattice.

Whatever the origin of its local name, the design is of great antiquity, for it is surely a descendant of the intersecting circle design which was a feature of the Indus Civilization. Intersecting circles appear on much of the painted pottery from many different sites over the whole of the Indus Civilization region, such as the site of Harappa itself, from Mohenjo-daro, Chanhu-daro and Amri, all now in Pakistan, or Lothal in India and from as far away as Shortughai in north-east Afghanistan. An illustration of this design is from a jar of the middle Indus period of ca. 2500 to about 2000 BC excavated at Harappa. A fragment of pierced stucco from the same period is remarkably similar to the pierced grill of the boundary wall of a house at the village of Dauleh in Haryana, similar to many others made all over the durrie area even today.

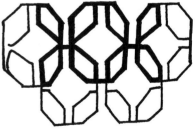

Tracing of a durrie to show the two different readings of the intersecting circle design.

Another Indus Civilization site was Kalibangan, in northern Rajasthan, not far from the area under discussion. Here, from the

Durrie with rosettes known as *aath kallian,* eight petals, Jalaldiwal village, Sangrur district, 1969.

same period as the jar, a splendid tile-flooring was uncovered, decorated with intersecting circles. This looks so very much like a textile that we are left to wonder if woven floor coverings or other textiles were also made at the same time. This may have been so, but unfortunately no textiles, with the exception of a minute fragment of madder dyed cotton found at the well known site of Mohenjo-daro, have survived from this early period.

Painted jar from Harappa, third millennium BC. (Courtesy of the National Museum, New Delhi.)

After the decline of the highly developed Indus Civilization in the early second millennium BC, city life seems to have disappeared for several centuries, although there is plentiful evidence for the existence of agricultural, peasant communities. In many settlements, occupation clearly continued without a break from the mature Indus phase into later times[14]. Jhukar, a site west of the Indus in southern Pakistan which dates to the second millennium BC has pottery which shows a departure from the Indus traditions, with the development of incised wares. One fragment from this site bears an incised, four-petal motif.

No examples of the intersecting circles or four-petal variants on painted pottery were found after about 1500 BC. Yet these patterns were still very common over a millennium later as can be seen from examples decorating the architecture, sculpture and carved stone of the second and first centuries BC and the first and second centuries AD. These adorn mainly Buddhist sites since this became the religion of the rulers after the apparent conversion to Buddhism of the Mauryan emperor Ashok (ca. 272-235 BC).

Unfortunately the invasions of the White Huns between about AD 480-550 caused widespread destruction in north India, as did those of the Muslims from the 11th century onwards, so that there are almost no early Hindu or Buddhist monuments still surviving in the north Indian region. Examples for comparison are thus largely confined to central India. The available material is limited but, where possible, depictions of textiles or textiles themselves are studied.

Intersecting circles decorate the cover of one of the elephants in procession on a splendid carved stone frieze of the second century BC from Bharhut in Satna district, Madhya Pradesh. This cover appears to have a thick, rather coarse texture not unlike a tapestry woven fabric, though it was probably a rich brocade of some sort, more in the tradition of the ceremonial trappings of Indian elephants. Another example of the design decorates the sides of a pedestal upon which is enthroned the Kushana emperor Vima Kadphises, of the first century AD.

Similar decoration was popular in Parthian Iran. It is found at the first century AD palace of Kuh-i Kwadja and that of the second century AD at Qal'-eh-i Yazdigird. At different times during the late centuries BC, parts of Iran, of Central Asia, and of North India had been ruled by Greeks, Scythians, and Kushanas, whose empires extended over vast regions.[15] Motifs and patterns must have passed freely back and forth between the Indian subcontinent and Iran at this time, and intersecting circles were doubtless among them. Since these do not seem to appear on Iranian prehistoric potsherds, it is possible they entered Iran only at this time.

Carved stucco decoration from Qal'-eh-i Yazdigird, Iran, second century AD. (Keall et al., Qal'-eh-i Yazdigird)

Examples in the north of India are rare, but in central India and other areas the pattern can be traced through succeeding periods. The four-petal variant forms a lattice on a cover that adorns an elephant in a frieze at the tenth century Lakshmana temple at Khajuraho in Madhya Pradesh; a fragment of painted silk, probably of the tenth-twelfth century is decorated with intersecting circles. This was discovered by Aurel Stein at Kara Khoto, one of the Silk Road sites in Central Asia and is possibly of Indian origin.[16] Another textile with the same design is a block printed cotton, probably 15th century from Gujarat in western India. This is one of the numerous medieval fragments of uncertain date found at Fostat (old Cairo) in Egypt. As observed earlier, textiles do not long survive the extremes of climate in India; these early export fragments preserved in the dry soil of Egypt are among the earliest Indian textiles known. Today intersecting circles are widely found; carved on wooden architectural brackets in the mountainous Garhwal district of north India, on the backs of the traditional low seats of the valley of Swat in Pakistan, on textiles from Gujarat and Rajasthan and on metal and stucco grills in numerous villages in Punjab and Haryana.It is therefore not surprising to find the design so deeply entrenched in the art of the women of Punjab and Haryana. A line of descent even if it is at times broken, can thus be traced for the design from early times up to the present day.

Block printed cotton textile found at Fostat, Egypt. Gujarat, Western India, probably ca. 15th century. (Nabholtz-Kartaschoff, Golden Sprays and Scarlet Flowers)

Intersecting circles existed much earlier, on painted pottery fragments found thousands of miles to the west, in an area now shared by northern Syria, north-western Iraq and south-eastern Turkey. Here was situated the remarkable Halaf culture which endured from about 5000-4700 BC, its remarkable pottery has been excavated from sites in an area extending from Iran to the Mediterranean coast and as far south as Palestine. Lamberg-Karlovsky has noted the resemblance of the intricate motifs to textile-like patterns and suggested that possibly the later Mesopotamian textile production had already begun during Halaf times.[17] Intersecting circles were clearly so well entrenched in pottery traditions that their use would almost certainly have extended to textiles. Several potsherds with intersecting circles have been excavated from Halaf itself and from the neighbouring sites of Chagar Bazar, Brak and Arpachiyah.[18] The composition is the same as in the Indus sites though in some cases the colouring and decorative detail is different.

Pottery fragment from Halaf, north Syria, sixth-fifth millennium BC. (Courtesy of the British Museum, London.)

In subsequent levels of the Halaf sites, however, there is no trace of this design, nor have we found examples in West Asia over the next five millennia or so. It does not appear in the material culture of the great civilizations of either Mesopotamia or Iran. The intersecting circle pattern apparently quite simply disappears from West Asia and emerges in the Indian subcontinent some two thousand years later.

Although there seems to be no direct influence here, without knowing the symbolism of the design in either culture it is impossible to be certain. The only glimpse of a possible symbolism is its use on the royal Kushan portrait sculpture of Mathura of the second century AD. It decorates the pedestal of the throne of Vima Kadphises, and it also occurs on the belt and hem of the tunic of Castana, and along the side of the footstool and on the scabbard of the emperor Kanishka. It decorates as well the costume of a portrait of the same period believed to represent King Samatruq from Hatra, a commercial city on the western fringe of the Persian Parthian empire.[19] It is quite probable that it had a special meaning which made it appropriate in this context and that its use was due to something more than chance. It is also worth noting that Hatra was near the much earlier site of Halaf.

It is beyond the scope of this book to pursue this design further in West Asia, or indeed in Europe, but such a study would doubtlessly reveal much valuable information and carry forward an understanding of its possible symbolism.

Aath kallian, literally 'eight buds', but here understood as 'eight petals' is a popular variation of the four-petal motif. The name is given to rosettes with pointed leaves, which illustrate the full face of a flower as seen from above. These are composed of two pairs of rhomboids placed at right angles to two other pairs of a different

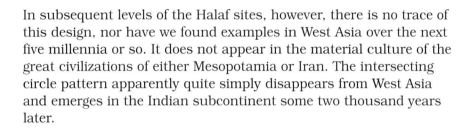

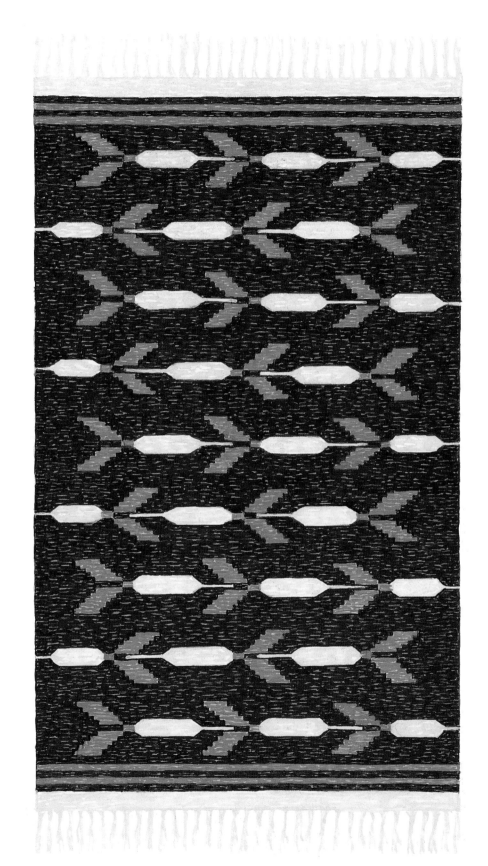

Durrie with *mouli*,
radishes, Dappar village,
Patiala district, Punjab,
1989.

size, usually smaller, which are set within their horizontal axes. The rhomboids are divided vertically and horizontally by straight lines, and on the four diagonals by rows of small squares. The motif is widely used in different parts of the world; we have seen it on hand-knitted sweaters as far apart as Scandinavia and Tibet; as a tiled floor decoration in a 19th century farmhouse in the south of France and as paving in the Municipal Gardens at Bangalore in south India. The same form has been found at many prehistoric sites in Iraq, such as the stone rosettes from Brak, ca. 3000 BC, and in bone and shell from Ur, ca. 2600-2400 BC. Rosettes were frequently associated with the Mother Goddess, particularly the terracotta figurines, both in Iraq and the subcontinent.[20]

In another small group of similar rosettes, the weavers have eliminated the petal points by extending the diagonal rows of squares outwards and including in the petals the triangular spaces between the rhomboids. These may perhaps be woven versions of rounded petals, since they are widely seen in other folk arts. Such properly rounded eight-petal rosettes appear on block-printed durries. In this medium, of course, curved lines are as easy to make as straight ones. In some versions the flowers are further simplified because only the upper half of the motif is used.

The same motifs can be further compressed. These are placed in a lattice composed of the original four-petal forms from which they were derived but from which all superficial resemblance has now been lost.

The name *aath kallian* is also sometimes applied to serrated lozenges if they have eight points. There is also a case of *barah kallian*, twelve petals, and another of *chaubis kallian*, twenty-four petals, where the name is applied to the number of lozenges in each group rather than to the number of points of individual motifs.

From the *aath kallian* rosette a number of other forms are also derived. Stylized flowers in pots are six-petal versions of the parent form placed in a pot or vase. These may represent the *purna kalasa*, vase of plenty. In the border pattern of a durrie the vertical, horizontal and diagonal lines which divide the petals in the rosettes have been joined together to form a continuous pattern. Another six-petal version is placed in a boat and may represent a sail.

Another version is known as *gamle*, flower pots. If further modifications take place then the motif again changes, with purple forms added at the extremities transforming it into a large aubergine plant.

Durrie with a zigzag pattern with simple floral forms extending from the points known as *bel*, Jassaran village, Patiala district, Punjab, 1973-74.

In a further variation of the *aath kallian* rosette the lower four petals have been removed and within the upper pair a stepped lozenge containing a smaller lozenge has been inserted. For obvious reasons this design is called *gobi da phul*, cauliflower. According to Dr. O.P. Parik of the Haryana Agricultural University at Hissar, the cauliflower originated in Syria, and was first introduced into southern Europe in the 15th century. It does not appear to be indigenous to India, and probably made its way here in the British period. The association of the cauliflower with the durrie motif is thus probably based only on superficial appearances, the original meaning of the design having been lost.

The idea of a small plant with leaves is also used in a durrie, known as "tomato" because of the red growth in its centre. The tomato has been cultivated in India only from about 1800.

Using only two of the petals, this time as leaves, and a long hexagonal figure extended at one end by a narrow line, the weavers have produced *mouli*, radishes, of the large white variety grown in the subcontinent. In another striking design the petals, again as individual leaves, are used with rows of small squares to form a zigzag pattern. From the points extend straight lines forming stems, with flowers composed of stepped lozenges.

In this way the weavers have adapted a few basic forms into a variety of motifs known by different names and which, at first sight, appear to have little resemblance to one another. The weavers for the most part copy from other durries designs that have continued to be passed down from mother to daughter. Yet each durrie is different, since all are woven individually, with affection, and imagination and under no compulsions to fulfil a commercial order. The women have no idea that their designs have such ancient antecedents; the copying from mother to daughter must have taken place from the very earliest times for these traditions to have been preserved.

Durrie with design of cauliflowers, *gobi da phul*, Manakpur village, Ropar district, Punjab, 1980.

Durrie with plants the weaver called tomatoes in a lattice, Malikpur village, Ropar district, 1982.

Bel, Aath Kallian, Gamle: Three Plant Forms

Three very popular floral designs, which may represent the same flower, can be examined together. First is the *bel*, creeper, a design of a meandering stem with flowers facing alternately in opposite directions. This is used either as a border or in rows filling the entire

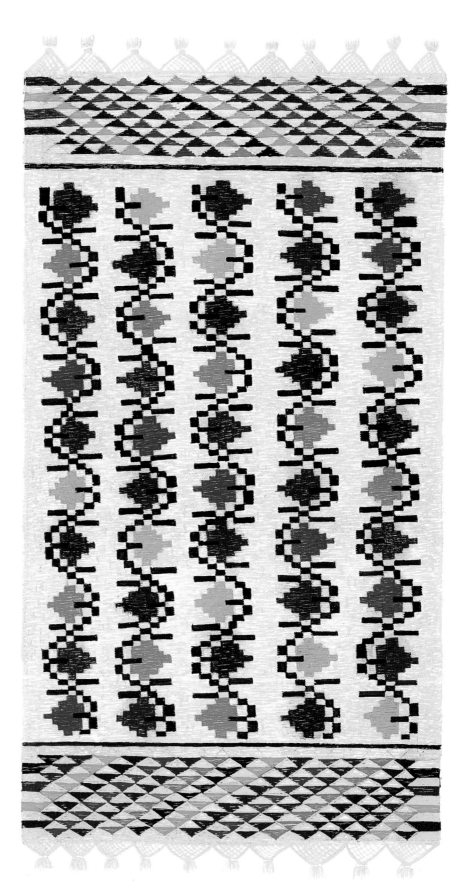

Durrie with creeper, *bel* design and small triangles at the ends called *tukrian*, pieces which some weavers identified as small, scattered land-holdings, Malloya village, Union Territory of Chandigarh, 1978.

Durrie with rows of cross
and triangle motifs,
Makhan Majra village,
Union Territory of
Chandigarh, 1985.

131

field. The second is the rosette, with either pointed or rounded petals, the third form is the *gamla*, flower pot. Though there are variations, this typically shows a plant with a single stem with one occasional variant, which has smaller stems leading from the central one. The pot shapes differ considerably and few show any similarity with the flat-based flower pot in regular use today; these are in any case rare in the villages where people are too busy farming to have much time for gardening.

Very seldom did a weaver satisfactorily identify the flower linked with the *bel, aath kallian* and *gamla.* The occasional name given, such as *laddian,* the tiny coloured electric bulbs used to decorate houses and tents for special events, was clearly an attempt to be up-to-date. In a few cases among the second group of rosettes with rounded petals, there were also random names given such as pumpkin, melon and cauliflower. In a rural society where the names of all local trees, animals and plants are familiar in every household, it is curious that this flower is unspecified. It is probably the result of long usage of one particular plant – to the almost total exclusion of others – so well-known that only the various forms in which it is represented need to be identified. With time, the name of the actual plant has been forgotten in the villages, while the names of these different forms (creeper, rosette, flower pot) survive. Through every phase and school of Hindu, Buddhist and Jain art and architecture, as well as in the Muslim architecture of the subcontinent, up to the present, such a predominent flower has been the lotus. Usually it is the white or pink Indian sacred lotus (Nelumbo nucifera) that is depicted, but the Indian blue water-lily (Nymphaca Stellata) which may be blue, white, purple or pink, is also represented. It appears fully developed in all three forms – the creeper, rosette and flowering vase – in the relief sculpture of the earliest surviving monuments of the post-Vedic age, the Buddhist stone architecture of the second and first centuries BC.[21]

This primacy of the lotus is due to its central role in Hindu thought. In the texts of different periods there are variations but by the time of the *Agni Purana,* a sacred Hindu text of the third to fourth century AD, each cosmic life cycle begins with a lotus growing from the navel of the god Vishnu as he lies on the back of the waters. This lotus is thought of as the tree of life, giving birth to the god Brahma and then to all the forms of existence. The waters themselves are also thought of as the lotus, with the earth its leaf lying spread upon them. In a late addition to the hymns of the *Rig Veda* called the *Shri Sukta,* the goddess Lakshmi is closely compared to and identified with the lotus. In art it is her symbol, for she stands on a lotus pedestal and the plant often surrounds her and she holds its flower. The lotus pedestal also became the support of

Brahma and many other Hindu deities. The lotus is also closely associated with the anthropomorphic form of the Sun God introduced under Iranian influence in the latter part of the first millennium BC as prescribed for his images in texts such as the *Brhat Samhita* and the *Samba Purana* of around the sixth century AD.[22]

Lotus plants fill the *purna kalasa*, the vase of plenty which symbolizes the fullness of life with all its gifts. This vase is referred to in texts as old as the *Rig Veda.* As described by Coomaraswamy:
"Throughout the history of Indian art the full vessel *(purna kalasa, punna ghata,* etc.) is the commonest of all auspicious symbols, employed by all sects .... the form is essentially that of a flower vase, combining a never-failing source of water with an ever-living vegetation or tree of life."[23]

He stresses that the lotus is used by artists to represent all plant life, probably because of its origin in the waters.

The lotus and its symbolism were adopted into Buddhist doctrine and at that time it also became a symbol of purity, since it shows no sign of the mud from which it grows, nor are the flowers or leaves wet by the water on which they rest.[24] Thus we find that the lotus in art may be used as a symbol for, among others, the goddess Lakshmi, the tree of life, the earth, the abundance of nature, all plants and purity.

For comparison of the unspecified plant forms of the durries with lotus forms in early Buddhist sculpture examples are seen from three major sites. These are Bharhut in Madhya Pradesh, which is the earliest, Sanchi, also in Madhya Pradesh, which is the best preserved and most richly carved and Sanghol in Punjab, in the heart of the dowry durrie area, between Chandigarh and Ludhiana. The creeper on the durries can be seen as corresponding with the meandering lotus rhizome, the *padmalata*. This long stem of the plant does not branch but throws out leaves, flowers and roots from nodules appearing at intervals along it. The sculpted and woven forms, therefore, follow the natural growth pattern of the lotus.

The durrie rosettes may correspond with the numerous lotus rosettes of these early Buddhist monuments.[25] Many of these carved rosettes have eight petals; others may have different numbers, usually in multiples of four and sometimes in two or three sculpted levels. In general the petals have a pointed outline as do those of the durrie rosettes, but others have rounded petals and these may have their echo in another group of durrie rosettes. In outline both are strikingly similar to the rosettes found in Indian art of other periods.

Outline drawing of a lotus rosette with 0pointed petals. Relief sculpture in stone from the stupa of Sanghol, Ludhiana district, Punjab, second century AD. (Gupta, Kushana Scultures)

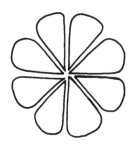

Outline drawing of a lotus rosette with rounded petals. Relief sculpture in stone from the stupa of Sanghol, Ludhiana district, Punjab, second century AD. (Gupta, Kushana Scultures)

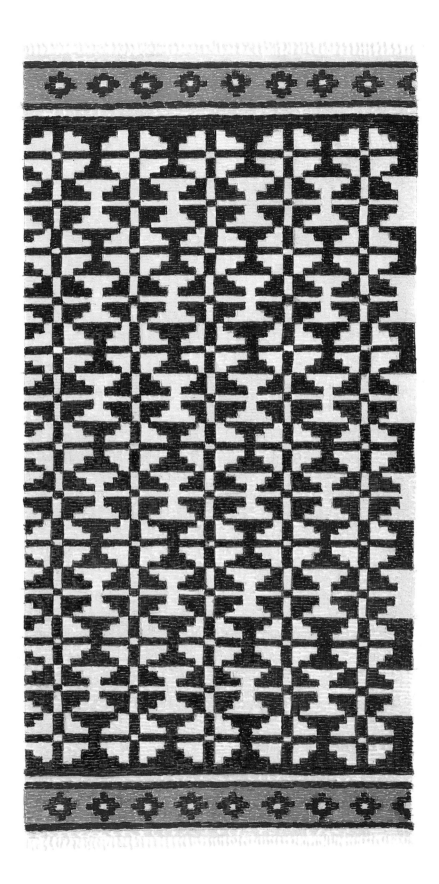

Durrie with design of cross and triangle motifs, Badheri village, Union Territory of Chandigarh, 1986.

134

In the form of the eight petal rosette the lotus has another symbolic meaning; here it represents the ancient concept of the division of space into the four quarters, and then its further sub-division into eight sections.[26] In the carved stone rosettes the outer layers of petals in increasing multiples of four continue the same process.

In Mesopotamia the eight-petal rosette appears with the earliest representations on cylinder seals of the Jamdat Nasr period (end of fourth millennium BC) at the Sumerian site of Uruk in southern Iraq. The Sumerians of this era were seeking to understand and explain the natural world. The forces of nature became their earliest deities and these were given symbols to represent them. Among them was the goddess Inanna, the power in vegetation and fertility, and she was symbolized by the rosette.[27]

The continuity of folk tradition suggests that, in spite of its varied woven shapes, the third floral form, the flower pot, may have its origin in the *purna kalasa,* vase of plenty, for this is the flowering vase which has been popular and familiar at least since the time of its first surviving appearance at the early Buddhist sites. [28] Once among the most usual of village mural motifs, these are now rarely made in the houses of the new brick and cement construction, though they are found painted above or beside the doorways of mud houses in the Una and Kangra districts of Himachal Pradesh, and carved stucco versions still decorate many houses in Haryana. The vase of plenty is also set near the door of the house on festive occasions and kept in the *mandapa,* marriage pavilion. Its use is prescribed for the bases of columns of doorways in Hindu temple architecture[29] and, in the days when a front door meant solid hard-wood double doors and frame, often elaborately carved, the vase of plenty was frequently placed at the centre of the lintel or at the bases of the doorjambs.

Relief sculpture in stone of a medallion with a vase of plenty *purna kalasa* from Stupa I, Sanchi, first century BC.

Phul: Cross and Triangle

A lozenge inscribed with a cross is a common theme in the durries, used either as a field design or as a border. In the border examples, the field pattern is composed of a lattice formed by four-petal, intersecting circle motifs. Inside the compartments are stylized figures, such as aubergine plants. The cross and triangle motif can be viewed in two ways: as four triangles with the points of the two shorter sides meeting at a small central square, or as a cross with triangles at each side. This is sometimes referred to as a Maltese cross, but as we are not here involved with European heraldry we shall refer to it as the cross and triangle motif. In one very splendid durrie, it is placed in rows across the field. These lie one above the other, and are coloured alternately dark green and white. In this way the void pattern is given equal prominence. As we shall see,

Reconstruction of possible origin of the cross and triangle motif from Samarra, sixth to fifth millennium BC. (Parrot, Sumer)

Cross and triangle motifs on potsherds from Mound.R.R. and from Shahr-i Sokhta,Iranian Seistan. third millennium BC. (Fairservis, Archaeological Studies in the Seistan Basin)

positive and void are used to great effect also in other compositions. But here it is the positive with which we are concerned. The outer sides of the triangles are stepped or serrated.

The weavers generally refer to the cross and triangle as *phul,* flower, in the same way as they refer to lozenge as *phul*. Once again, however, there is nothing evidently floral about this group. One girl, however, showed us the base of her buttermilk churner, *madhari,* and claimed that it was from this that she had taken the design. The motifs in this durrie have only three of the usual four triangles and are linked into a trellis created by small squares and larger rectangles, a good example of the way in which a basic motif may be used in a different way.

The cross and triangle motif is of extreme antiquity. Some scholars believe that it is derived from a sixth or fifth millennium BC composition on a pottery fragment from Samarra in Iraq, where four triangular figures with horned heads and curling tails, perhaps intended as deer, are placed on the four corners of a central triangle that may have represented a pond. On other early fragments from the same region the motif is usually simplified, a cross with four

triangles, sometimes with traces of its horns, sometimes not. In this form it decorates a number of sixth to fifth millennium BC potsherds excavated at Halaf, and neighbouring sites in northern Syria.[30] In simplified form, it appears on numerous potsherds from later sites in Mesopotamia and in Iran. On a bowl from Tall-i Bakun, near Persepolis, possibly dating from 4500-3500 BC is an example with stepped edges though without a rectangle in the centre. There is a particularly attractive series of bowls with slightly differing versions of the motif from fourth millennium BC Susa in southern Iran.

Other examples appear in eastern Iran at Shahr-i Sokhta,in the third millennium BC, and at the mound R.R. in the same region. Here the same serrated edges as in the durries have been included. Occasionally squares take the place of triangles. In third millennium BC Turkmenistan are found star forms that may also be read as cross and triangle motifs, but there is no appearance in this region of the motif in its usual durrie form.

It is much less widespread in the Indus Civilization. A rare early example is different from those from West Asia, as it has a diagonal cross inscribed in the middle, It was discovered from the early Indus levels of the early third millennium BC at Kalibangan. In its more usual, West Asian form, without serrated edges, it does not seem to appear until the early second millennium BC, on a jar from Mitathal in west Haryana.[31]

Between the second century BC and the second century AD, the cross and triangle motif makes numerous appearances as a frieze ornament on the carved stone bases on which stand sculptures showing scenes from the life of Buddha from Gandhara. Here it is less severely geometrical, with rounded long sides, and a bud form between each motif. Similar motifs also sometimes appear on Greek vases, and later on Etruscan vases also, beginning with the late geometrical style in the mid-eighth century BC.[32] Many Greek elements are found in the art of Graeco-Buddhist Gandhara and this motif could equally have arrived from that source. Motifs can often be read in different ways and it is hard to know exactly which form the artisan had in mind when he or she created it. In the durries, however, the weaver's name for a given motif remains to give it identity in her eyes at least.

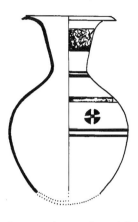

Cross and triangle motif on a jar from Mitathal, Haryana, early second millennium BC. (Allchin, The Rise of Civilization of India and Pakistan)

In later centuries the motif appears on numerous temples in friezes that divide the main exterior decorative registers. Here too it sometimes has a more floral form, but there are enough geometrical versions to show that its origins lie in the cross and triangle motif. One example is from the Lakshmana Temple (ca.930-950) at Khajuraho in Madhya Pradesh. In the same region, a floor inlay of the 19th century Kishoriye Temple at Panna has the same motif in decidedly geometrical form. Today it is also very popular on Indian sweaters. It is such a precise motif that it must once have carried some religious connotation, particularly as it was used as decoration in Buddhist religious sculpture and later as a Hindu temple ornament. It may be that its early use as a terrestrial symbol survived, or at least became a part of a well used repertoire of designs, so that no temple would be complete without it. It was clearly a late arrival in India, and we must presume that it derives from the ancient cultures of West Asia.

As seen, the closest parallels on the durries are with examples on the painted pottery of Shahr-i Sokhta and mound R.R. in Iranian Seistan. These even have the same serrated outlines as those on the durries. Once again it is quite possible that these postsherd motifs were originally copies from textiles, and that it was in the form of textiles that these motifs first made their way into South Asia.

Shamiana: **Eight-Pointed Stars**
Eight-pointed stars are usually known in Punjabi villages as *chananian,* or in Haryana as *shamiana,* meaning tent. Durries with this motif are popular. Such motifs also very often adorn the sides of

Durrie with eight-pointed
stars, Badheri village,
Union Territory of
Chandigarh, 1986.

the huge awnings that are hired out in many parts of the subcontinent for marriages and other ceremonies and festivals. They must thus be auspicious emblems of good luck. Since the tent versions are done in appliqué work they show more variation than on the durries. The solid eight-point outline changes little but the centre may be round, or a square placed horizontally or diagonally. The motif is sometimes divided into eight sections by means of alternating colours. In outline this makes it identical with the *ashtadala*, Sanskrit for 'eight petals', recorded as representing the sun in solar worship in Gujarat in modern times. This is a continuation of the ancient worship of the sun in its natural form, represented by a disc, which may go back to neolithic times, as opposed to the later worship of the sun as an anthropomorphic male god introduced into India in the first millennium BC. The sun was seen in most cultures as a source of benevolent light, warmth and fertility.[33] In the *Satapatha-Brahmana* (ca. 900-500 BC) there is a description of the gold solar disc used in the ceremony of building the fire altar:

> "... for that gold plate is the truth, and ... that truth is the same as yonder sun. It is a gold (plate) for gold is light, and he (the sun) is the light. It (the plate) is round, for he (the sun) is round."[34]

In a single variation of the design, long motifs are placed between the stars. The weavers called these *belan*, rolling pins, and the stars *chakla*, dough boards.

Eight-pointed stars do not appear on Indus Civilization pottery. Indeed they appear nowhere in the ancient world but Turkmenistan, where there are numerous examples on late fourth and third millennium pottery from Geoksyur, Namazga and related sites. The parallel is immediately striking but this pottery motif can also be seen in another way. In the centre is a black square and from its points extend four black triangles, filling the space between pairs of the points of the star. If we take these as forming a motif in themselves, then the cross and triangle motif emerges. The Turkmenistan eight-pointed stars are thus a kind of two-in-one motif, which frequently appears on the nomadic rugs of Iran, the Caucasus, Anatolia and Central Asia. Neither on these rugs, nor on the durries, however, does it appear combined with a cross and triangle.

Elsewhere in ancient West Asia and the Indus Civilization a variety of six and eight-armed stars and rayed discs on pottery and seals have been identified by writers as stars or solar symbols. These symbols frequently appear within the curve of ibex horns or with lions and bulls. On an Elamite seal of the first half of the third

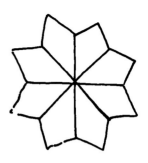

Outline of the *ashtadala*, eight petals, diagram which is recorded as representing the sun in solar worship in Gujarat in modern times. (Enthoven, The Folklore of Gujarat)

Painted pottery design from Namazga, Turkmenistan. Namazga III, late fourth to third millennium BC. (Masson & Sarianidi, Central Asia)

On the left is the eight pointed star motif with central black square and four black triangles. On the right the outline of the eight-pointed star has been removed, leaving the central black square and four black triangles–the cross and triangle motif.

millennium BC there are motifs very similar to the *ashtadala*, but with nine instead of eight points, set in the curve of ibex horns. In his work on the earliest history of West Asian man's understanding of the relationship between the stars and the calendar, Willy Hartner has shown that the lion represents the constellation of Leo, the bull that of Taurus and the Pleiades, and the ibex or mouflon that of the main stars of Capricorn and Aquarius.[35] His study is based on the earliest cuneiform astronomical texts of roughly 1400-700 BC. These use much older Sumerian names for the constellations, implying that they were known in ancient Sumer and may go back to the fourth millennium BC. By reference to these texts and by calculations of the positions of the constellations around 4000 BC, he has been able to show that the ibex with the solar disc or star in the curve of its horns is symbolic of the winter solstice which, at this period, corresponded to the heliacal rising indicated by the solar disc or star of the constellation of the ibex.[36]

The sun symbol over the back of the lion is found in Iran in later periods with various meanings, and seems to have been associated with the Mithraic religion in Parthian times. It was also used to represent the zodiac sign of Leo. Its best-known form, the rayed sun disc with a human face rising behind the lion, was found on coins from the 13th century onwards and later became the state emblem.[37] In addition, certain coins of the Mughal emperior Jahangir show the animals of the zodiac with the same form of the sun disc rising behind them.[38]

On the durries eight-pointed stars or rosettes are not linked with animals in this way. However, this traditional combination, its original meaning lost or altered (since any animal may be so favoured and the rosettes are as often placed between the legs of the animals as on their backs) is to be found in the folk art of other areas of India such as the Madhubani painting of Bihar and the *kantha* embroidery of Bengal. In West Asia six and eight-pointed stars were also frequently used to indicate the divinity of a scene or figure. The pictogram for star in the early Sumerian script stood for 'sky', 'sky-god' and 'god' and throughout the ancient world the gods were thought to belong to the celestial sphere.[39] Dr. Asko Parpola has suggested that the same divine significance may be attached to the stars within the curves of buffalo horns found in Harappan times, for instance on an Early Indus pot from Kot Diji and a seal from Mohenjo-daro.[40] Again, eight-pointed stars and rosettes are not found in this context on the durries but in a 19th century *kantha* embroidery it seems that two pairs of buffalo horns with eight petal rosettes in their curves have been placed back-to-back one above the other and transformed into a flowering tree.[41] On the durries eight-pointed stars are clearly distinguished from the rather similar eight petal rosettes since the stars have a solid form whereas in the rosettes the petals are separated. Although neither form carries any symbolic meaning for the weavers today, they nevertheless hold them to be quite distinct and the rosettes are seen as flowers. On this basis we have associated the eight-pointed stars primarily with the solar disc, representing the natural form of the sun, and the eight petal rosette with the lotus and the goddess Lakshmi.

In other media, however, there is often no such ready distinction between the solar disc and the lotus rosette, with characteristics of one combined with those of the other, so that only the context suggests which is intended. This difficulty is compounded because both the sun god and Lakshmi are associated with the lotus, while in the *Sri Sukta*, Lakshmi is described as having a golden complexion and being resplendent like the sun, so not only the symbol but also its meaning may overlap.[42] For example, a 12th century AD stone sculpture from Andhra Pradesh has a lotus medallion which, since it is surrounded by the twelve signs of the zodiac, represents the sun.[43] On the other hand, a medallion in the pavement of the Devi Temple at Jawala Mukhi in Kangra district of Himachal Pradesh is much closer to the eight pointed solar motif than the lotus rosette which would be appropriate to the temple of a descendant of the Mother Goddess.

The survival and meaning of "art motifs" and their migration from one culture to another has promoted much thought and debate. In the ancient world there seems to have been little time for "art for art's sake." In the 1920s D.A. Mackenzie wrote:

> "It is ... difficult to believe ... that a few "art motifs" were repeated for long centuries, and disseminated over wide areas, simply because early man's aesthetic sense hungered for expression. If the aesthetic sense really made so insistent and inevitable an appeal, why did it ignore many forms of natural beauty, and remain content instead to draw constant refreshment from an exceedingly limited stock of sterile and arbitrary designs?"[44]

If a motif was used it was primarily because of its symbolism, and its use continued for the same reason. A motif such as the eight-pointed star, even with its original meaning forgotten, may still be valued as a good luck emblem. As it moves into new areas a motif may change its meaning and yet retain some of its original significance. The solar symbol, which as already mentioned remained a part of sun worship in India into this century, gives an example of this process. In a slightly different form – a disc with eight projecting rays, alternately straight and wavy – it was the

Inlaid stone rosette in the pavement at the entrance to the Devi Temple at Jawala Mukhi, Kangra district, Himachal Pradesh, 19th century AD.

Durrie with a lattice
design formed by
diagonal crosses,
Kolhapur village,
Kurukshetra district,
Haryana, 1990.

Durrie with design of diagonal crosses, Suketeri village, Ambala district, Haryana, 1989.

143

symbol of the ancient Mesopotamian sun god, Shamash, from late in the third millennium BC.[45] This particular Mesopotamian form, except that it has twenty instead of eight rays, is to be found in the Church of Bom Jesus in Goa, which was completed in 1605. The large, gilded, rayed disc, inscribed with IHS (the first letters of Jesus in Greek) hangs above the main altar. "I am the light of the world", (John 8.12), said Christ and the ancient motif of the disc is thus seen in yet another context. Its symbolism is still fundamentally the emanation of powerful and benevolent rays, but here the source is Jesus rather then the sun.

Another Punkhe: Diagonal Crosses

Another composition of four-armed motifs is also known by the weavers as *pukhe* in Punjab, *punkhe* in Haryana, meaning fans. The same name is also given to the intersecting circle design. The resemblance between the two is however, superficial. The leaf motifs formed by the intersecting circles have pointed ends. Here they are serrated rectangles, identical in shape, in fact, to the "leaves" of the serrated rectangles and rhomboids. They are placed so as to form the arms of a diagonally placed cross. Sometimes a further cross may be inscribed in the empty square formed at the meeting of the arms, sometimes it may have a serrated lozenge or any other appropriate motif. They are arranged so as to form a lattice composition. The word "Welcome" has been placed in the middle of one durrie so that the continuing lattice arrangement is lost, and the seperate motifs are clearly apparent. This is once again an example of how striking and attractive a very simple, basic design can be when used with different details and colour combinations. "S" forms too are inscribed within a lattice of diagonal crosses.

The only example in antiquity that we have found of such an arrangement, without serrated sides however, is on a painted jar of the second millennium BC from Pirak, to the west of the Indus now in southern Pakistan. This is one of the patterns contained in compartments on two friezes that decorate a jar. The similarity with the durrie design is striking.

Examples of such four-armed motifs, used singly and not forming part of a lattice, are more numerous though we have not encountered any with serrated sides. These are found on prehistoric potsherds from different sites in West Asia, in both Mesopotamia and Iran.[46] A potsherd from Tal-i-Regi, or Khusu, in Fars in southern Iran, when regarded from one direction has every appearance of the diagonal cross form. But if the outline is removed, and the ends of the arms left free, it becomes a cross and triangle motif, or *phul.* The sides are rounded because this example is inscribed in a circle but more often such forms have straight sides, as in a series of beautiful

Jar with compartments, one of which is decorated with diagonal crosses, second millennium BC. Pirak, period 11. (Jarrige, Fouilles de Pirak)

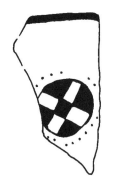

Diagonal cross in a sherd from Tal-i-regi, Fars, Iran. (Starr, Nuzi)

Drawing of above motif, freeing the arms.

144

bowls of the late fourth millennium BC from the cemetery at Susa in southern Iran on display at the Louvre in Paris. Thus this design may be viewed either as a diagonal cross inscribed in a square or as a cross with four triangles. It is the way in which we look at the motif which governs the manner in which we see it.

The cross motif on the durries can be viewed in the same way. When one whole cross form inscribed in a square is taken from the durrie and the borders of the arms are removed, the same thing happens. The cross and triangle motif once again emerges. The durrie weaver, however, gives to this diagonal cross the same name as to the interesecting circle pattern. In her mind it is clear that there is no relationship between her two "fans" and the cross and triangle motif, which she calls a flower. She has simply copied the design and taken the name from another durrie. Any symbolism to her is now quite lost.

But there was once almost certainly a symbolism. Willy Hartner interprets the motif as seen on the Susa bowls as a terrestrial symbol – the "navel of the earth", the "four corners of the earth" or just the Inhabited Earth.[47] One of the cuneiform texts on which his study was based was the first Mulapin tablet, written around 700 BC from observations going back to around 1400 BC. It has the name I-iku for the constellation of the Pegasus rectangle and this name is also given to "the unit of a square measure, the rectangular field, standing metaphorically for the cultivated soil or just for 'earth' ". Its shape on pottery depends on the painter; it may be a square (the cross) to indicate the four directions of the wind or a circle to indicate the circular horizon. A filling of wavy lines represents water while a checkerboard filling represents the cultivated soil. Sometimes, in an obvious allusion to their meaning, the motifs are filled with stylized trees or plants.[48]

Given the many other similarities in the use of motifs and beliefs shared over the ancient world in this huge area from western West Asia eastwards it seems probable that such symbolism extended also to the Indian subcontinent. But like the cross and triangle motif, the diagonal cross version must also have been a latecomer to India, since a jar from Mitathal of the early second millennium BC, remains the earliest prototype for both.

Akkhar: The "S" Form
In some of the diagonal cross, or "fan", durries the compartments formed by the arms of the crosses contain geometrical "S" forms. Such motifs also appear in other durries as a border pattern. On older durries and handwoven hand fans and seats of the low stools known as *pirhi,* they are placed on the diagonal. The weavers usually

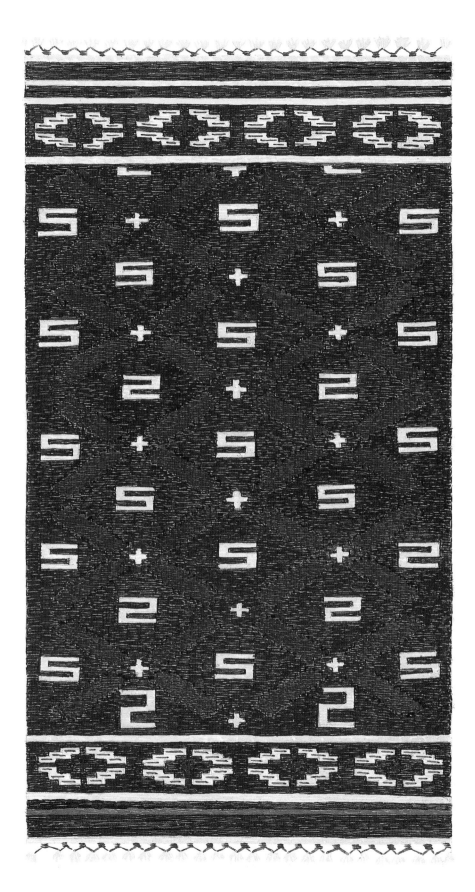

Durrie with "S" forms
inscribed in a lattice
formed by diagonal
crosses, Chilla village,
Ropar district,
Chandigarh, 1986.

146

refer to these as *akkhar*, meaning letter, although there is no such "S" letter or number in Punjabi or Hindi.

Curvilinear S forms are found on sherds at sites of northern Seistan in the third millennium BC, and the same forms occur on punch-marked coins from the Graeco-Buddhist site of Taxila in Pakistan over two millennia later, between the second century BC and the second century AD. It may also be a simplified snake form, as suggested by D.V.S. Agrawala on pottery of the Gupta period, fifth to sixth century AD, from Ahichchhatra in Baraeli district, U.P. [49] It is among the few motifs to have survived among the rare early Indian textiles, for it appears on one of the cotton fragments, resist dyed with indigo, found at Fostat (old Cairo) in Egypt. These were made in Gujarat and maybe as early as the 15th century.

The "S" motif is also found on numerous carpets from West Asia, notably those from Bergama which, though so far to the west in Asia Minor, consistently show many of the same geometrical designs as are found on the durries. This is clearly visible on one of these carpets in the 1533 Holbein paintings "The Ambassadors".[50] In Iran and the Caucasus, both diagonal and rectangular forms are still widely used in the weaving of many different nomadic tribes.

Dumroo: **Combs and Drums**
Several durries have a composition consisting of motifs formed by two triangles joined at the apex. A tiny triangle is placed at the top and bottom in the centre of the two long sides and two or more narrow bands proceed outwards from the middle where the points meet. These motifs are given a variety of names by the weavers, of which *jahaz*, aeroplane, is the most common, along with comb, drum, butterfly wings, or by one lady, policeman's turban. Two triangles so placed is of course a basic concept. The motif appears on prehistoric potsherds from all over the ancient world, such as on a jar found at the port town of Lothal in the mature Indus period in the second half of the third millennium BC. Human figures in prehistoric rock paintings too are often depicted in this manner, with the additions of little heads and stick arms and legs. The *sanjhi* goddesses worked in mud or cowdung that decorate the walls of houses during the festival of Navratri in October, at the time of the worship of the Mother Goddess Durga, are also depicted in the same way.

The waisted appearance, together with the narrow appendages that issue from each side, have led some people – including some of the village women – to suggest that these motifs are the representation of a narrow-waisted drum called *dumroo* which is used in the area. This has strings emerging from the middle which hit the drum

Painted designs on pottery from Ahichchhatra, fifth to sixth century AD. (Agrawala, Pottery Designs)

Durrie with long-armed
motifs, Virdhana village,
Hissar district, Haryana,
1991.

surfaces when the instrument is shaken. In the durries there are sometimes several such appendages. Some of the motifs on durries are much less narrowly waisted than others.

In some durries the motifs are spaced at a little distance one from another. In other examples they are placed close together; they are coloured differently in alternate rows and the void motif is given equal importance. Often there are only two colours, for instance blue and orange, but in one splendid example four colours are used, which achieve a striking diagonal effect. One such durrie was called by its weaver *sarak bazar:* " '*sarak*' because there are so many roads," she explained. In these durries it is impossible to say which is the negative and which the positive. Indeed the differentiation has ceased to exist and at this point has probably lost its importance. The second motif, which we shall call the negative, or the one that is formed in the void, is sometimes referred to as a comb. Sometimes this motif is used singly across the field in its own right, much simplified. A third millennium BC comb from Mohenjo-daro shows the same design as combs of such shape which are still in wide use today. There is undoubtedly a resemblance between the durrie motifs and this type of comb. But whether any of these explanations is correct, or whether these interconnecting motifs are an image of the interaction of opposite forces such as night or day or masculine and feminine it is impossible to know.[51] Interacting designs of a somewhat similar nature appear also on some south Iranian and Anatolian kilims.

Jar from Lothal, third millennium BC. (Rao, Lothal and Indus Civilization)

Another type within the same group has principal motifs which have considerably changed shape, and lost the waisted, triangular effect. These are often spaced much further apart. In some examples there is only one complete motif and two halves in each row. The appendages have become thick bands.

Rock painting at Modi, Rajasthan, about third millennium BC. (Neumayer, Prehistoric Indian Rock Painting)

One durrie has a serrated lozenge lattice pattern in each compartment of which are four forms without any appendages. These motifs are identical to that on a carved brick from Bhamala, near Taxila, a Buddhist site which dates from the third century BC to about AD 600 near Rawalpindi in Pakistan. The same motif is also repeated on column details on Stupa D4 of the fifth century AD in the Jaulian complex at Taxila. Possibly this was some kind of auspicious symbol.[52]

Whatever the origin of these motifs, these durries show a remarkable degree of sophistication both in the different uses of the forms and in the colours employed and are among the most

Durrie with design of
waisted triangular motifs,
Dhanas village, Union
Territory of Chandigarh,
1988.

150

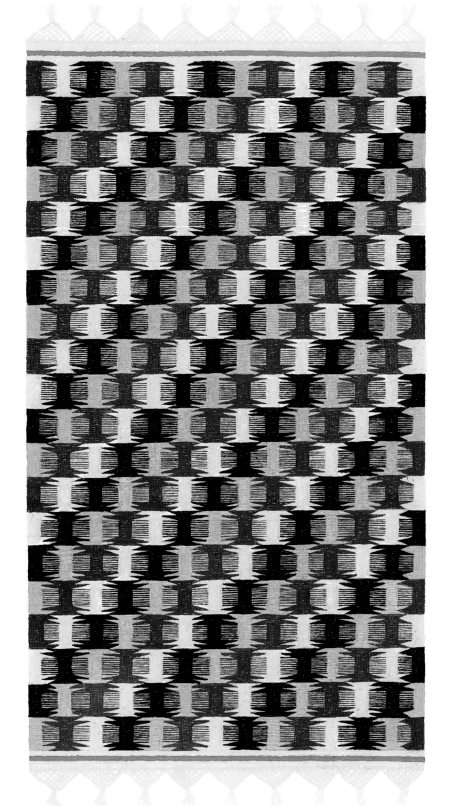

Durrie with positive and negative "comb and drum" motifs, Dhanas village, Union territory of Chandigarh, 1990.

handsome of the whole group. No one durrie is quite the same as another so that many variations are possible.

Sarak: **Rows of Triangles**

Straight rows of adjoining triangles, which tend to degenerate into roughly serrated bands, are a widely used durrie motif. The usual name for them is *sarak*, roads, although in many instances the weavers left them nameless. Occasionally, when more clearly woven, they are known as *diye*, traditional little earthenware lamps of this shape. In a single case the rows had been divided into sections by the use of different colours, and here the weaver saw them as combs. In one instance the geometric patterns between the "roads" were said to represent the shade trees planted beside them. These trees, mostly *kikar* (Acacia Arabica) or *seesham*, (Dalbergia Laltifolia) and sometimes mango, are often so well grown that they close in a canopy high above the road. Such straight, shady roads are found all over the area and are among of the pleasantest features of the landscape.

The most famous of these roads is, of course, the Grand Trunk road, established by Chandragupta Maurya, who came to the throne in 321 BC, to help consolidate his empire. It ran from Afghanistan in the west, across the Punjab to his capital at Pataliputra (Patna) and on to the mouth of the Ganges. It was his grandson, Ashoka, who planted the shade trees.[53]

Around Bhatinda the design is sometimes known as the *thandi sarak*, cold road, which was the name for the Mall, the main road of many British settlements. Wide and tree-lined it used to be regularly sprinkled with water to settle the dust and keep it cool. Designs were probably taken from the well-known *thandi sarak* in the Railway Colony in Bhatinda, an important junction from the late 19th century onwards, which like the old trunk roads is wide and tree-lined. R.C. Temple also praised the Mall in Ferozepur, calling it "certainly one of the greenest and prettiest roads I have seen in any state in India..... It is about three miles long."[54]

Before the water table rose in the Bhatinda area from 60-70' to just 10-12' on account of modern irrigation schemes, there was also a *thandi khui*, cold well, design. We were unable to find an example of this and it seems to have disappeared with the deep, cool well water.

Such rows of triangles, clearly defined, are among the most widespread of designs painted on pottery from Mesopotamia and Iran in the fourth and third millennia BC. The motif is also found on pottery from Baluchistan in Pakistan and from Amri, a site very close to the right bank of the Indus river, in the first half of the third millennium BC.[55] Although we have been unable to trace it through subsequent periods, it is still found on tribal rugs of Iran.[56]

Murrabe Bandi: Lozenges in a Lattice

The Consolidation of Land Act (1957-62) had a great impact on Punjab farmers. They were able to unite their holdings by exchanging small, scattered fields called *tukri,* pieces, between themselves and everyone was assured access to his own land. Lack of such access had previously been the cause of many fights.

Murrabe bandi, in Persian meaning division of squares, was a term introduced in the new Canal Colonies in West Punjab from 1885 onwards. For administrative convenience the newly irrigated land was divided into survey squares *(murrabe)* and rectangles. These squares were based on the traditional measurement of *kadam,* a man's pace which varied between 54 and 66 inches, depending on the height of the local population. As a result, the *murraba* also varied from as much as 27.7 acres in the Chenab Colony to 16 acres in the Bikaner area of Rajasthan.[57] An older name for a similar area – about 25 acres – was a "well", derived from the fact that the land was dependent on artificial irrigation. Desu, the earliest member of the family of Maharaja Ranjit Singh to be mentioned in Sikh annals, was described as owning three ploughs and one well around the turn of the 18th century.[58]

The close links of the women with the land are reflected in all aspects of Punjabi culture. The image of the Jat women taking food to their fathers, husbands or brothers in these fields is a very popular one. A well-known couplet runs:

> *Jati pandaran murrabeanwali*
> *Bhata de ke khet nu chali*

> A Jat girl owning fifteen *murrabe*
> Is going to the fields to give food
> to the men working there.

One of the *guddian* durries too was described by its weaver as girls carrying *lassi* to the fields.

The design usually chosen by the women to represent this popular legislation is a rectangular lattice, the spaces filled with three or four attached lozenges which, in turn, have small, serrated lozenges at their centres. Variations of the design occur throughout Rajasthan and Gujarat. It is to be found, for instance, in the Jain Shri Prashtapadji temple of the 14-15th centuries in Jaisalmer and in the 15th century Muslim complex at Sarkhej, near Ahmedabad.

Durrie with rows of attached lozenges in a rectangular lattice, known as *murrabe bandi*, Consolidation of Land Holdings, after the popular legislation of 1957-1962 when farmers exchanged small, scattered fields in order to unite their holdings. At one end a row of combs replaces the stripes seen at the other, Karanpur village, Ambala district, Haryana, 1968.

Durrie with design known by the weavers as *dubbe,* boxes, which probably has its origin in the sacred Hindu diagram, the *Shri Yantra.* Inside the boxes on this durrie the weaver has placed flower pots, though in others there may be animals, Shahpur village, Ambala district, Haryana, 1985.

Durrie with "earth and sky" design, Suketeri village, Ambala district, Punjab, 1989.

Dharti-Asman: **Earth and Sky**

The *dharti-asman* design is composed of adjoining diamond-shaped compartments with serrated edges, over which pairs of zigzag bands that form small diamonds have been laid. The new compartments thus formed and the resultant triangles left on each side are coloured in two colours, used alternately. It is a simple design yet sophisticated in appearance.

Most of the durrie examples are named earth and sky by the weavers or, in one case, day and night, indicating that the design has a cosmic significance. The nature of this is unknown for the weavers have no idea why they call it by such names. Two women called it *dharti*, meaning a plot of land, another referred to it as houses in a row. One durrie was called quite simply *dubbe*, boxes, relating it to the serrated lozenge and lattice patterns, though the name is the only similarity.

No precise parallel for this design has been found in antiquity, although certain third millennium BC painted postsherd patterns from Namazga and related sites in Turkmenistan seem to have some similarity.

Dubbe: **Boxes**

As a frame for plants or animals, the *dubbe* design is seen in durries throughout the area. So general is its use, with small variations, that we cannot doubt a common origin for all of them. This appears to lie in the sacred Hindu diagram, the *Shri Yantra*, though the design has no religious connotations in the villages today.[59]

The *dubba* is woven either as a square or with two sides extended. This is a form sometimes found in Hindu temple architecture. In one case the outline matches with remarkable precision, the ground plan of the Lakshmana temple at Khajuraho.[60]

Crenellated Borders

Crenellated borders, usually with two steps between the base and top lines, are very common on the durries. In only two cases were they named by the weavers; once called *burji* or *burj*, tower, and once *qila*, fort.

The motif of crenellations has been traced back to about 3000 BC, when it appears on Elamite seals from Susa in southwestern Iran. During the third millennium BC it occurs to the west, in Mesopotamia, and to the east, at Mundigak in Afghanistan, where it is found on the colonnade of a palace dated around 2500 BC.[61] It has been suggested that in Mesopotamia this motif originally symbolized the sacred mountain as did the ziggurats, or temple towers, which had similar outlines. This mountain was symbolic of the whole earth in which "were concentrated the mysterious powers of life" – vegetation and the rains – and where the gods were thought to become manifest.[62] During the Middle Assyrian period (ca. 1350-1000 BC) temples and shrines shown on seals have crenellated walls, suggesting a religious meaning for the motif. By the neo-Assyrian period (883-612 BC) it is a regular part of fortress architecture throughout ancient West Asia, where it served a very practical defensive purpose apart from any symbolism it may have retained. At this period it also seems to have spread, by way of Phoenicia, to the classical world of the West.[63]

Diagram of the typical crenellated border used by the weavers, although it is also woven with either one or three steps between the base and the top.

In Iran the motif has a long history as a crown, often called a mural crown. In an early example of the ninth to seventh century BC it is worn by a neo-Elamite queen in a relief carving at Naqsh-i-rustam. Apart from the prominence of crenellated walls in the architecture of the royal Achaemenid city of Persepolis, the Zoroastrian kings of both the Achaemenid (550-330 BC) and Sasanian (AD 224-642) dynasties are frequently depicted wearing mural crowns. In the relief carving at Bisutun the crown of the emperor Darius has a crenellated border above a band of rosettes. In an interesting survival, this combination of crenellations with rosettes surmounts the walls of several Zoroastrian fire temples built in Bombay in the 19th and early 20th centuries by the Parsi community.[64] The Parsis fled religious persecution in Iran after the Muslim conquest. They settled in India in AD 936 and have continued to follow their Zoroastrian faith. Unfortunately, no significance seems to have survived with the motif, which was described by a temple priest as "just decoration".

The mural crown is also associated with Tyche, the Greek goddess of fortune, who became the patroness and guardian of the welfare of

Durrie with design generally known as *kishtian*, boats, Mundi Kharar, Ropar district, Punjab, 1984.

158

Durrie with rows of
teasets. Here a teapot
with two cups and
saucers on a tray,
Dayerha village, Patiala
district, Punjab, 1984.

cities. In this capacity the crown is a symbol of her protection. She is found, wearing her crown, on first century BC coins of the Graeco-Bactrian kings of northern India, as well as on a carved panel of the same period from the Swat valley in modern Pakistan.[65]

In India, crenellated borders are abundant in the architectural decoration of the Buddhist sites of Bharhut and Sanchi, the crenels, often filled with lotus flowers.[66] The motif continues to be found in temple architecture of later times, for example the tenth century Lakshmana Temple at Khajuraho.

In the bridal durrie area many buildings – forts, sarais, tombs and mosques – dating from the Sultanate period (AD 1206-1526) to the 19th century have crenellated walls. The crenellations vary considerably and we found none exactly matching the durrie pattern. A closer comparison is perhaps the pointed crenellations that often decorate the edges of mud shelves, outdoor ovens and low walls still sometimes made by the village women for their houses. These simple triangular forms could well be abbreviated versions of our motif. It is possible that the zigzag borders of many of the durries were also originally stepped crenellations which have been simplified. The weavers sometimes call these borders *katto*, cuts, but never offer any explanation.

Apart from its religious meaning and architectural use, the decorative nature of the motif has ensured its survival in many media. It is particularly effective as a simple, reciprocal border pattern, providing a balanced meeting for the colours of the main ground and the border. In textiles it is widely used in this way; apart from the durries of our area it appears on the Patola silk weaving of Gujarat and the tribal rug weaving of Iran.[67]

Kishtian: Boats

Detail of a boat with leaf-shaped oars from an album leaf of Jahangir boating in Kashmir, early 18th century. (Childe, New Light on the Most Ancient East)

One design is usually called *kishtian*, boats. The outline is very similar to that of small model boats and depictions of boats on various objects from Harappan sites which have a high prow and stern, central cabin and sail or hole for insertion of a mast.[68] These Harappan boats are sometimes flat-bottomed, like those on the durries, a design which gives a shallow draught suitable for river use. Others have keels and are better suited to ocean sailing. With the modern damming of the great rivers of the Punjab for hydro-electrical power and irrigation schemes, they are no longer a regular means of transport. Until that time, however, traditional, flat-bottomed wooden "Indus boats" were in use on them. These were fitted with a single, large sail which was hoisted when the wind

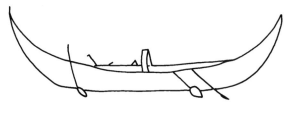

160

was favourable, although they were chiefly hauled by ropes from the banks. They might also have a cabin made of reed mats.[69] In the hands of the weavers in this area, who have no familiarity with river or sea, the central cabin or sail has become a large flower. Smaller flowers complete the prow and stern and the boats overlap at the centre, giving the design more cohesion. It would appear to be one case where the traditional name has endured though the design has been changed to accommodate a little floral decoration.

Similarity between Harappan-period boats and those of ancient Sumer in Iraq, such as appear on seals and tablets from Uruk, has already been noted. The shapes of the silver boat and its leaf-shaped oars found in the royal cemetery at Ur (ca. 2600-2500 BC),and also in Sumer, provide further parallels with ours.[70] Such boats and oars may be seen in Indian drawings and paintings from Mughal and later times and are still in use in many parts of the country today for local transport and fishing on lakes and rivers and along the coast.[71]

Teaset

The brief presence of the British in this area made little impression on the villagers, but the popular teaset design probably finds its origin here. It must have been enjoyed as a novelty, for certainly nobody in the villages would dream of drinking tea from anything but a glass. The habit of drinking tea was made popular by the soldiers returning from the First World War. Brewed with plenty of buffalo milk and sugar, it has become synonymous with hospitality in north India and remains unchallenged by coffee.

Spun Tales: Legends and Couplets

Well into this century entertainment was provided and tradition fostered in north India by wandering bards with their songs and tales of Punjabi saints, heroes and lovers. A particular Muslim caste, the Mirasi, kept the genealogical records of the various Jat clans, which they recited at all weddings and funerals.[1] Retained in wealthier households as family archivists, they would sing daily to their patrons of the noble and generous deeds of their forebears. Most of the Mirasi left for Pakistan during Partition but the folk singers, though reduced in numbers, still remain popular and have enjoyed a revival due to their television performances and cassette tapes.

The folk singers tell of epic deeds of warriors and stories of love and revenge. Nevertheless their frame of reference is always an orthodox, settled world order where the wishes of the individual must be a subordinate consideration. The concept of individual development or action as a matter of personal choice is simply inconceivable in this immutable universal order, a world which Joseph Campbell has called "antithetical to free will".[2] Romantic love is accepted as part of this order but what matters is that it is to be held in check, for the possibilities of chaos that it represents pose an unacceptable threat to the essential rhythm of an ordered existence.[3]

Romances such as Hir-Ranjha, dated no earlier than the 16th century, are still very popular, but the strongest bond between the sexes is generally that between brother and sister as is shown in another popular romance, Mirza-Sahiban. A brother remains the guardian of his sister's honour throughout their lives and the weavers reflect this in their durries. One durrie shows an affectionate reunion between a married girl and her brother who has travelled a long way on his camel to visit her. The couplet woven on the durrie reads:

> Sister: *Killia rangeen gadia; bota banh ye Sarvana vira*
> Brother: *Bota baine pher banh doo, matha tek da ama diye jaiye"*
> Sister: "The coloured stake is here. Tie your camel."
> Brother: "First I greet you, daughter of my mother, then will I tie my camel."

A couplet on another durrie will cause a stab of recognition in every sister, for, which girl has not, at some time, been left behind at home while her brother visits exciting places and people.

Sister: *"Karichakan neem wich de*
Bota vir pajarke legaya"
Sister: "Watching in the *neem* tree
My brother has taken the camel to the fair."

Only four durries with camels were recorded during the survey, three of them from southern Bhatinda District, where the land was mainly desert until modern irrigation schemes reclaimed much of it for farming. Camels are used as pack animals throughout northern India and, in the bridal durrie area, they are particularly common in this southwestern region bordering Rajasthan.

Mirza and Sahiban

There is no more poignant example of the loyalty and affection between brother and sister than in the tale of Mirza and Sahiban, set in West Punjab, now part of Pakistan. On the eve of her marriage to a groom of her parents' choice, Sahiban has had the spirit and courage to elope with her cousin Mirza. After riding some distance he insists on stopping to rest under a tree. The father and brothers of Sahiban are in pursuit and at the terrible moment of choice, when she can save either her lover from her brothers or sacrifice all her romantic dreams, it is Mirza's arrows that she hides in the branches of the tree over their heads. Sahiban betrays her beloved rather than allow him to kill her brothers. She knows too that she is doomed to die at the hands of those same brothers, for a girl who has brought such disgrace upon her family cannot be allowed to survive. There are probably as many versions of this tale as there have been bards to sing it but Mirza is always killed by the brothers of Sahiban and usually she is either strangled by them or commits suicide.[4]

The haunting tale of Mirza and Sahiban has many counterparts in Punjabi legends. In all these stories the theme stressed is not so much the romance itself, for that seems to be taken for granted, as the essential human dilemma: the conflicting demands of stability, represented by family and society with its inevitable compromises and stultification, as opposed to the instability inherent in individual freedom.

These legends maintain a powerful hold on popular imagination for they embody mores still very much accepted. Marriages are arranged between families with scant pandering to personal preferences, so the tales remain potent "symbols of a high romance" for those who "may never live to trace their shadows with the magic hand of chance".

Everyone is drawn to proud and reckless lovers who abandon themselves to a personal destiny, at the same time accepting that such passionate forces are irreconcilable with the patterns of an ordered society. The stories never end with the couple settling down to live happily ever after among their own people. They usually end in death, although in one version of the tale of Hir and Ranjha they are helped away to Mecca "and if, as we believe, they never died, they are living still in one of the islands of Arabia".[5]

The durrie identified with the tale of Mirza and Sahiban was thought by the weaver to illustrate a moment near the end of the story when Bakki, the mare Mirza was riding, returns on her own to the village after the deaths of the lovers. The weaver recited a couplet to accompany the story in which the speaker would have been the dead Mirza's sister:

> Boli: *"Khali ghodi henkadi*
> *Uthe nahin dista vir"*
> "The riderless horse neighs
> My brother is not on her back."

The format of the durrie – a central figure in frontal pose holding two confronted animals in profile – is interesting in the context of the story, since one horse carried the lovers Mirza and Sahiban and it could not, therefore, have been devised traditionally to represent this scene. This durrie illustrates the way in which a traditional format is reinterpreted according to the ideas of the weaver. The motif of a central figure between two animals is an ancient one, found as early as the fourth millennium BC in Mesopotamia and Susa, Iran and it continued to be widely used in the region.[6] In Iran, it occurs on seals as late as the Sasanian period and was adapted to fit the typical Sasanian roundel, for it is found on an Iranian silk fragment of the eighth century AD in the collection of the cathedral at Sens in France. It appears in Egypt during the period of Mesopotamian influence at the close of the fourth millennium BC and during the first millennium BC, also entered Greek art with the Gorgon in the central position.[7] Usually referred to as the "master of animals" it represents the dominance of the central figure over beasts, which were the chief threat to man and his flocks. The central figure may represent either an animal– headed demon or a man with superhuman powers; the animals are usually lions or ibex. The motif has many variations: the central figure may be standing or kneeling and may either grasp the rampant animals by a foreleg, or hold them suspended by a hind leg, or at the neck if they are standing.[8]

In India we find the motif on seals from the Indus Civilization which show the rampant animals as tigers. On pottery from the later

Cemetery "H" at Harappa, the central figure is shown between two stags which stand on all four legs in the same way as the durrie animals. There are also examples of this motif on the *phulkari* of the late 19th or 20th century in the Calico Museum of Textiles, Ahmedabad.[9] It occurs on other durries too, where the figure holds either lions as in the Mesopotamian examples, or two horses or two camels. No doubt a search beyond the scope of this study would find the motif widely used in Indian folk art; we came across it in the work of a contemporary Oriya potter at the Crafts Museum, New Delhi.

Hir and Ranjha

The story of Hir and Ranjha is as popular as that of Mirza and Sahiban and is also found in many versions. The tales are rather similar, for the heroines both belonged to the Rajput Syal tribe and made their own choice of a husband – a difficult situation further complicated since Mirza and Ranjha were Jats, and therefore not acceptable in a caste conscious society, as Syal sons-in-law.

A relatively cheerful version of this story was recorded by Swynnerton in 1889.[10] The young Ranjha having been deprived of his rightful inheritance by his elder brothers, left his home at Takht Hazara in Gujranwala District to seek his fortune. Ranjha, like Orpheus, was a flautist with the power to attract animals and people wherever he played; one escapade with a characteristically earthy touch of Punjabi humour had the cakes in the oven also dancing to his tune. After various adventures, he received divine guidance from the Five Pirs[11] and met the beautiful Hir of Rangpur in Muzzaffargarh district. Hir arranged for him to be engaged by her father as a cowherd and he went to live on an island in the Chenab river. Soon after, Hir dreamt that the Five Pirs gave her in marriage to Ranjha and she went to join him on the island. All went well until they were betrayed to Hir's family, who quickly arranged a marriage for her with a member of the Khera clan. The ceremony had already begun when the Five Pirs again intervened and the lovers were carried away in the sky to Mecca.

In other versions the story is less happy and ends in the murder of Hir at Rangpur. Temple, writing in 1884, mentions her tomb near Jhang and the fact that in his time it was still an insult to mention either Hir or Sahiban in front of a Syal, nor would one remain present if either tale were recited.[12]

For this unusual durrie the weaver first made a small picture in cross-stitch – a far easier medium – which was used as a guide. It is not clear where she found her inspiration, for she said the idea was her own. It was her first attempt at this difficult design, which explains the irregular proportions of the durrie. The cross-stitch

Durrie illustrating the tale of Hir Ranjha, Kajheri village, Union Territory of Chandigarh, 1980.

version was far better balanced. Even so, and it is unique among the durries, she has succeeded in imbuing the figures with zest and movement. Hir dances while Ranjha plays a drum, rather than his flute. The couplet, of which only the first line is woven, runs:

> *"Mahi sang Nachdi mein*
> *Kade na thakha mein"*
> "I shall dance for my husband
> I shall never grow weary."

Jeona Maur

Amongst the floral patterns used in stencil printing by Gurbachan Singh in Lehri village was one of a different kind: the horseman Jeona Maur, who was a local hero in the 1920s. Folk singers have taken his story into their repertoire and it remains very popular, touching the quick of Punjabi social values at several points.

Jeona and Kishna were brothers from Maur village in Bhatinda District. Jeona was a soldier while Kishna was a dacoit. Kishna kept his loot with Dogar, his *pagwat-yaar,* very close friend, the friendship sealed by the exchange of *pug,* turbans. However, this arrangement turned sour when Dogar decided to betray Kishna to the police and keep a large haul of loot for himself. He invited Kishna to dinner and gave him, to quote a village translation, "liquor so much, that gone out of sense, and fell down", whereupon Dogar called the police. Kishna was captured and sentenced to deportation to the dreaded jail in Kalapani, the Andaman-Nicobar islands.

Stencil printing of the tale of the dacoit, Jeona Maur, at Lehri village, Bhatinda district, Punjab, 1988

To avenge his brother, Jeona ran away from the army and became a dacoit. He did a great deal of looting but suddenly, after robbing all the young married women of Longowal village of their jewellery and new clothes when they were celebrating their special festival of *tian,* he underwent a change of heart. He became withdrawn and sad and finally decided to return the jewels. On seeing him all the villagers ran away but one brave girl stood her ground and shouted at him, asking him what he wanted from them now since he had already taken all they possessed. Jeona explained that he had come to return the jewels and henceforth would become her brother and protector.

Sometime later he received a letter from Kishna telling him of the treachery of Dogar and challenging Jeona, if he be indeed his brother, to kill Dogar, for otherwise the neighbours would taunt them and they would have no right to live after losing their family honour.

Jeona immediately galloped to the village where Dogar lived and called him out of his house. He offered his rifle to Dogar and gave him the chance to shoot first. Dogar tried but missed his target so Jeona shot him dead.

Jeona then went to the Naina Devi temple and made an offering of a gold *chhattar,* canopy, which the legend said weighed *sawa man pacca,* 60 kilos. However, the police followed him there and, when Jeona saw there was no escape, he jumped to his death from the mountain top, preferring death to dishonour.

Postscript

This study of bridal durrie weaving has confirmed the survival and growth of a living culture. The weavers, earthy and hardworking women, have unconsciously preserved traditions from the earliest history of human civilization. They weave together in their durries a legacy from their land; its legends, animals, plants, designs, and their dreams for the future. In a changing landscape where villages are being rapidly absorbed by urbanisation and television beams day and night into most homes, a young girl still sits at the loom with her mother, aunt or elder sister and absorbs, perhaps unwittingly, her heritage along with the durrie designs. These traditions do not form a rigid straitjacket, for each girl sees and weaves according to her own imaginative concepts: the ancient *pipal* design continues as cheerful lollipops; prehistoric intersecting circles are transformed into modern ceiling fans. The blessings of the Earth Mother, Sanjhi Devi, are required as much today as in the past, and thus creativity fuses with traditional roots as each young devotee weaves the bridal durrie for her new home and her future.

Appendix of Natural Dyes

During the course of the fieldwork, the only traces of the process of natural dyeing were the three following accounts.

The procedure used is more or less the same for all colours but no one remembered precise timings or proportions. The recipes have not been tested before writing:

Kartar Kaur, Gehri Bara Singha village, Bhatinda District, remembered the dyeing from her childhood, in the late 1920s and 1930s, in her village of Muraj, near Nathana in Bhatinda District. Her procedure is as follows:

1. The yarn is thoroughly soaked in water.

2. The dye is boiled separately for about an hour, with salt added as it boils, to give fastness. For darker colours, a stronger solution is boiled longer.

3. The dye pot is removed from the fire and the yarn soaked in it for up to two or three days, depending on the colours and the depth required. Pounded alum, *patkari,* is sometimes added as a mordant to ensure that the dye blends with the yarn.

4. To make the colours fast, dried, powdered *harad,* Myrobalan fruit (Terminalia Chebula) is used. The powder is boiled

separately for half an hour and the dyed yarn is soaked in this solution for at least two hours, or overnight.

5.   Finally, the yarn is rolled in cowdung, left for an hour or two and then washed out. This also enhances the fastness of the colours.

Brown: The bark of *kikar*, Gum Arabic (Acacia Arabica). To make it darker, the bark of *malaberi*, wild jujube (Ziziphus Nummularia) is added. For the very dark brown, now known as Coca Cola, the Gum Arabic bark is mixed with powdered *harad*, Myrobalan fruits.

Green: *Mehndi*, henna leaves (Lawsonia Inermis). A different shade is obtained by adding wild jujube leaves.

Parrot
Green: *Mehndi*, henna leaves and *gachni*, a yellow clay brought from Shrikolait, Bikaner district in Rajasthan, which is also used to plaster house walls.

Yellow: *Gachni*, yellow clay.

Pink: *Phalsa*, Flame-of-the-Forest flowers (Butea Monosperma) and *gachni*, yellow clay. Not a fast colour.

Red: *Phalsa*, Flame-of-the-Forest flowers. Not a fast colour.

Purple: *Nila tota*, indigo and *gachni*, yellow clay.

Blue: Nila tota, indigo.

Muslim dyer Lalari, who went to Pakistan at the time of Partition, used to visit the villages and make the dye for the weavers as it is a laborious process.

From Chanan Kaur, Dhansingh Khanna village, Bhatinda district:

Brown: Added tea leaves with the bark for a darker shade.

Yellow: Added *haldi*, turmeric, for a stronger yellow.

Black: The bark of *pipal* (Ficus Religiosa) and Gum Arabic, ink ground from a block, ashes and tea leaves.

From weavers at Daun Kalan village, Patiala District:

Brown: The bark of *pipal* and Gum Arabic.

Violet: The bark of *pipal* and *jamun*, Java Plum (Syzgium Cumini). The *pipal* is only used to make the colours fast, having no colour of its own, and the process is the same for both colours.

1. The two barks are first boiled together.

2. The yarn is added, the pot removed from the fire and the yarn left to soak overnight.

3. In the morning the yarn is removed, ash is rubbed into it and it is left for the day.

4. In the evening the yarn is washed in cold water to remove the ash and the whole process is repeated. Depending on the shade required, the yarn is treated upto five times, each time becoming darker.

Professor M.L. Gulrajani of the Textile Technology Department of the Indian Institute of Technology, Delhi, has very kindly offered the following clarification of these dyeing methods. The salt (sodium chloride) is added to improve the absorption of dye into the yarn. It ionizes in water, forming sodium ions and chloride ions, and the sodium ions neutralize the negative charge on the fibre, thereby promoting the dye uptake.

Usually Myrobalan, with its high tannic acid content, is used as a mordant at the beginning of the dyeing process. (A mordant is a chemical that forms a link between certain dyes and fibres which have no natural affinity for one another, since it can both combine with the dye and be fixed on the fibre. Alum is the only mordant noted in this appendix.) In the dyeing methods given here, however, the Myrobalan is used after the dyeing, in a process known as back tanning. The tannins form a lake (precipitate) with the dye, and the inorganic salts of the cowdung, in which the yarn is afterwards rolled, react with the tannin, making it insoluble in water. Whilst this treatment improves the washing fastness of the dyed yarn, the brownish colour of the Myrobalan gives it a dull shade.

Much further information on the chemical structure of the natural dyes of India and methods of dyeing with them may be found in M.L. Gulrajani & Deepti Gupta, eds., *Natural Dyes and Their Application to Textiles* (Delhi: Indian Institute of Technology, 1992); Mohanty, BC, Chandramouli, K.V., Naik, H.D., *Natural Dyeing Processes of India*, Studies in contemporary textile crafts of India (Ahmedabad: Calico Museum of Textiles, 1983); Mohanty BC, and Mohanty J.P., *Block Printing and Dyeing of Bagru, Rajasthan*, Studies in contemporary textile crafts of India (Ahmedabad: Calico Museum of Textiles, 1983).

Endnotes

The World of Weavers

1. Briffault, R. *The Mothers. A Study of the Origins of Sentiments and Institutions,* 3 vols, *London: Allen & Urwin,* 1927, Vol.2, 337-338.

2. Griffith, R.T.H. *The Hymns of the Rig Veda.* 2 Vols 1889; reprint, New Delhi. Munshiram Manoharlal, 1987, Vol.II. 10, 85, 7. The Sanskrit word *kosah* literally means 'treasure' but by extension 'treasure chest'.

The Web of Tradition: Myth and History

1. Allchin, B. & R. *The Rise of Civilization in India and Pakistan.* Cambridge, C.U.P., 1982; reprint, 1988, 134, 207 & pl. 8-14 & Marshall Sir John ed. *Mohenjo-daro and The Indus Civilization. 3 vols.,* London, Probsthain, 1931, 49.42, pls. XCIV XCV.

2. See Marshack, A. *The Roots of Civilization: The Cognitive Beginnings of Man's First Art, Symbol and Notation.* New York, McGraw Hill, 1972, 43-55

    Briffault, R. *The Mothers* Vol.3, 2.

3. Briffault, R. *The Mothers.* Vol 3, 191-195, 1-2, 46-47 & Campell, J. *The Masks of God: Oriental Mythology.* New York, Viking Press, 1962; Penguin Books, 1976 93-94, 255, Campell, J. *The Masks of God: Occidental Mythology. New York,* Viking, Penguin, 1964, Penguin Books, 1976 3-92. See also Marriott, McKim. *Village India Studies.* 209-212. This describes the "Pitcher Fourth" festival in Kishan Garhi village, Aligarh, Uttar Pradesh, in which women fast and worship the moon for the welfare of their husbands.

4. Ratnagar, S. *Enquiries into the Political Organization of Harappan Society.* Pune Ravish, 1991, 27-28.

5. Gimbutas, M. *The Goddesses and Gods of Old Europe.* second ed. London, Thames & Hudson, 1982, Gimbutas, M. *The Language of the Goddess.* London Thames & Hudson, 1989.

6. Gimbutas, M. *The Language of the Goddess*, 29.

7. Ray, S. K. "Folk Art of Bengal: The Theriomorphs". *Roopa-Lekha XXVIII,* (1958) 72-79.

8. Whitehead, Henry. *The Village Gods of South India.* Calcutta, Association Press, 1921, 37-39.

9. Agrawala, P.K. "The Early Indian Mother-Goddess Votive Discs". *EW* 29, (1979) 75-111.

10. See Robins, B.D. & Bussabarger, R.F. "Folk Images of Sanjhi Devi". *AA, XXXVI* , (1974) 296-7.

    Whitehead, H. *The Village Gods.* 126-138, 24-25 and Handa, O.C. *Pahari Folk* Art. pl.32 & fig. 39.

11. Gimbutas, M. *The Language of the Goddess.* 298-301, Marshall, J. *Taxila.* 3 vols., Cambridge, C.U.P., 1951, 655 nos. 19, 20, 23; pl.199.

    Gupta, S.P. *Archaeology of Soviet Central Asia and the Indian Borderlands.* Delhi, 1979, figs. 2, 15, no.17 & 2.17.

12. Dayton, J.E. "The Faience of the Indus Civilization" in K. Frifelt & P. Sorensen ed., *South Asian Archaeology,* (1985) Scandinavian Institute of Asian Studies Occasional Papers No.4, ed. K.R. Haellquist London, Curzon, 1989, fig.2.

Gimbutas, M. *The Language of the Goddess,* xxii, 109, 189, 209, 318-9.

13. Moorcroft, W. & Trebeck, G. *Travels in the Himalayan Provinces of Hindustan and the Panjab; in Ladakh and Kashmir; in Peshwar, Kabul, Kundur and Bokhara.* ed. Wilson, H.H. Calcutta; Asiatic Society, 1837; reprint Patiala Dept. of Languages, 1970, 60.

14. Mallory, J.P. *In Search of the Indo-Europeans.* London Thames and Hudson, 1989; reprint 1991, 230-31, 263.

    Allchin, B. & R. *The Rise of Civilization in India and Pakistan.* 237-241, 303-6.

    Burrows, T. "The Proto-Indoaryans". *JRAS,* (1973) 123-140.

15. Mackay, E.J.H. *Further Excavations at Mohenjo-daro,* Manager of Publications, Delhi, 1938, 89-90, pl. XXXVIII b.d., 164.

    Marshall, J. ed. *Mohenjo-daro.* 16, 17, 251, 272, pl. LXXV, pl. XLIII b.

    Bisht, R.S. "Further Excavations at Banawali: 1983-84". In *Archaeology and History; Essays in Memory of Shri A. Ghosh* eds. Pande, B.M. & Chattopadhyaya, B.D. Delhi, (1987) pl. 17.

16. Mackay, E.J.H. *Further Excavations at Mohenjo-daro, 204 & pl.* LXII; Mackay, E.J.H., *Chanhu-daro Excavations,* 1935-36, New Haven, American Oriental Society, 1943, pl. XXVI; Marshall J. ed. *Mohenjo-daro,* 308 &   pl. LXXXII, 36-43.

17. Crowfoot, G.M. "Textiles, Basketry and Mats" in *A History of Technology,* eds. Singer, C., Holmyard, E.J. & Hall, A.R. Oxford, Clarendon,

1964-5, Vol. II, 415-6;

    Allchin, B. & R. *The Rise of Civilization in India and Pakistan,* 109-111.

18. Gupta, S.P. ed. *Kushana Sculpture from Sanghol,* National Museum, New Delhi 1985, 66-67.

19. Allchin, B. & R. *The Rise of Civilization in India and Pakistan,* 162, 192.

20. Lamberg, C.C. Karlovsky and M. Tosi, "Shahr-i Sokhta and Tepe Yahya: Tracks on the Earliest History of the Iranian Plateau", *EW 23,* (1973) 52; Kohl, Philip L. "A Note on Chlorite Artefacts from Shahr-i-Sokta", *EW 27,* (1977) 111-127 & Frankfort, H. *Cylinder Seals,* London, 1939, 308-9.

21. Allchin, B. & R. *The Rise of Civilization in India and Pakistan.* 109, 191 & J. Marshall,ed. *Mohenjo-Daro,* 32, 468-69, & pls. CXXXI, 62-71; CLVI, 8-10; CLVII, 36, 40-1, & 47.

22. We are indebted to Dr. M.B. Pande of the Archaeological Survey of India for explaining how cloth and mat impressions were formed and for pointing out the references: Pande, B.M. "The Neolithic in Kashmir: New Discoveries", *The Anthropologist.* Vol. XVII, no. 1 & 2, 1970, Saar S.S., *Ancestors of Kashmir,* New Delhi Lalit Art Publishers, 1992, 30, il.32, 33, il.35.

23. Basham, A.L. *The Wonder that was India.* London, Sidgewick & Jackson, 1954; reprint Calcutta, Rupa, 1981, 32.

24. Interpretations of ancient texts give rise to endless debate; we have chosen those most apt to our context. See Griffith, R.T.H. *The Hymns of the Rig Veda,* Vol.I, 603-4.

25. Griffith, R.T.H. *The Hymns of the Rig Veda,* Vol. II, 623-24.

26. Griffith, R.T.H. *The Hymns of the Atharva Veda.* 1895-96, reprint, New Delhi, Munshiram Manoharlal, 1985, II, 24-25.

27. Ingholt, H. *Gandharan Art in Pakistan.* New York, Pantheon, 1957, figs. 137, 138 & 189; Marshall, J. *The Buddhist Art of Gandhara.* Cambridge, C.U.P. 1960, figs. 54, 56, 68, 128 & 129. *Exhibition of Gandhara Art of Pakistan,* Tokyo, 1984.

28. Gupta, S.P. ed. *Kushana Sculptures from Sanghol,* National Museum, New Delhi 1985, 75, no.14.

29. Rudenko, S. *Frozen Tombs of Siberia, the Pazyryk Burials of Iron Age Horsemen.* London, 1970, 298-99, Also *Frozen Tombs: The Culture and Art of the Ancient Tribes of Siberia.* London, British Museum, 1978. See illustration No.41.

30. Several such fragments are in the National Museum, New Delhi. See Stein, M.A. *Innermost Asia.* Reprint, New Delhi, 1981. Vol.I 231, Vol.V pls. XXX - XXXII, Vol.IV, p. XLIV. Stein notes their "distinctly Hellenistic nature", but believes them to be of local origin.

31. Stein, M.A. *Ancient Khotan.* Reprint, New Delhi, 1981. Vol. 2, 333-334. See also his *Archaeological Explorations in Chinese Turkestan.* London, 1901, (Preliminary Report) 42-54 and *Serindia,* Oxford, 1921, 1.241.

32. Stein, M.A. *Serindia,* I. 242-3, The Kushanas flourished for about 150 years in the first and second centuries AD.

33. Cohen, S.J. "The Development of Indian Floor Coverings and

Their Appearance in Miniature Paintings". Ph.D. Thesis, SOAS, London, 1986, 112, 135-6.

34. We are indebted to Prof. Devendra Handa for this information.

35. Baden-Powell, B.H. *Handbook of the Manufacturers and Arts of the Punjab.* Vol.II of *Handbook of the Economic Products of the Punjab, Lahore, 1872.*

36. We are indebted to Dr. Chhahya Haesner and Dr. Lotika Varadarajan for pointing out this latter meaning out to us.

37. Brand, M. & Lowry, G.D. *Akbar's India: Art from the Mughal City of Victory.* New York, The Asia Society Galleries, 1986, 109; Abul Fazl. *Ain-i-Akbari I*, 96.

38. Brand, M. & Lowry, G.D. *Akbar's India,* 109.

39. Franses, M. and Pinner, R. "Dhurries, The Traditional Tapestries of India". *Hali* 4, No.3, (1982,) 239-251. Also see Nos. 6,7,8,9.

40. Cohen, S. *The Unappreciated Dhurrie.* London, David Black, 1982; Franses & Pinner *Dhurries.* Cohen, "The Development of Indian Floor Coverings."

41. Bala, M. *Bhartiya Purattvam-Navintama Uplabdhya.* New Delhi, Swati, 1989, pl.21. Dr. Haesner informs us that she remembers excavating at Kalibangan in the 1970's pieces that formed an almost complete model *charpoi* with slip patterning that indicated the webbing of the base. See also Sarkar, S.C. *Some Aspects of the Earliest Social History of India.* London, O.U.P., 1928, 47-56.

42. Starr, R.F.S. *Nuzi.* Cambridge, Harvard University Press, 1937-39, 377 & pl. 57, il.

Amiet, P. *Suse: 6000 Ans d'Histoire.* Paris, Musée du Louvre, 1988, 84 no.4. Mundkur, B. "Notes on Two Ancient Fertility Symbols". *EW 28,* (1978) 270 & fig.23.

43. Cunningham, A. *The Stupa of Bharhut,* London, W.H. Allen, 1879, 125, pl.XXVIII; Ray, N. *Maurya and Post-Maurya Art.* Delhi, I.C.H.R., 1945, pl.30. Punia, D.S. "New Evidence of Pre-Kushan Sculpture from Gurgaon District Haryana". *EW 31* (1981) 133-4 & fig.2.

44. Moorcroft W. & Trebeck, G. *Travels in the Himalayan Provinces.*

Warp and Weft

1. Schlinghoff, D. "Cotton Manufacture in Ancient India". *Journal of the Economic and Social History of the Orient,* 17 part 1, (1974) 81-90, pl.IV.

2. Gupte B.A. in "Notes on Female Tattoo Designs in India". *TIA, XXXI,* (1902) 293-8, wrote that, in Punjab, the *teran* was used as a caste mark tattoo for women of the spinning castes, originally nomads and still unsettled in their habits, who were now mat and rope-makers.

3. Born, W. "The Indian Hand Spinning Wheel and its Migration to East and West". *Ciba Review,* (1939) 2130-2136, see also Forbes, R.J. *Studies in Ancient Technology.* 4 Vols. Leiden, 1964, Vol. IV 151-174.

4. Hall, R. *Egyptian Textiles.* Princes Risborough, Shire 1986, 14-15.

5. Amiet, P. *Glyptique Susienne, Memoirs de la Delegation Archeologique en Iran* 43, Paris, 1972, no. 673, quoted in Collon, D. *First Impressions Cylinder Seals in the Ancient Near East.* London, British Museum Publications, 1987, 145-6, 148, no. 629 and Wuff, H.E. *The Traditional Crafts of Persia.* M.I.T. Press, 1966, 199-201.

6. Baden Powell, B.H. *Handbook of the Manufacturers and Arts of the Punjab.* Vol. II of the *Handbook of the Economic Products of Punjab.* Cohen, S. *The Unappreciated Dhurrie,* Banerjei, N.N. "The Cotton Fabrics of Bengal". JIAI, VIII, (1900) 65-72, Hall, R. *Egyptian Textiles* lb. Sudhir Kumar, A. "Naga Shawl". *Swagat,* (November, 1992) 34-45.

7. Latimer, C. *Monograph on Carpet Making in the Punjab.* 1905-06, Lahore, 1907.

Designs for Dowry

1. Marshall, J. *Taxila.* Cambridge, C.U.P., 1951, pl.132.9 and 10-16.

Chandra, P. *Stone Sculpture in the Allahabad Museum.* Poona, American Institute of Indian Studies, 1970, pl. V no.13 & 14.

Sharma, Y.D. "Past Patterns in Living as Unfolded by Excavations at Rupar". *L.K.* nos. 1-2 (April, 1955 - March, 1956) pl.125 & pl. XLVI, fig.13.

Shere, S.A. "Stone Discs Found at Murtaziganj". *JBRS* XXXVII, (1951) pl.V.

Zimmer, H. *The Art of Indian Asia.* 2 Vols. Princeton,

Princeton University Press; paperback edition 1983 Text Plate B3a, and Dikshit, K.N. "India The Work of the Archaeological Survey of India During the Year 1935-38". *Annual Bibliography of Indian Archaeology*, XI, (1936) 4.

2. Grey, C. *European Adventurers of Northern Indian 1785-1849*. 1929. Reprint. Patiala; Language Dept., 1970.

3. Fergusson, J. *Tree and Serpent Worship*. London, 1873, pl. LXVII. Coomaraswamy, A.K. *Yakshas II*. Washington, 1931; reprint, New Delhi, Munshiram Manoharlal, 1980, 66-71.

    A similar figure appears on the eastern gateway at Bharhut with one arm akimbo and the other raised above her head. There is no clear identification of what she is holding or doing. See Cunningham. *The Stupa of Bharhut*. pl. XII.

4. Coomaraswamy, A.K. "Early Iconography II, Sri-Laksmi". *Eastern Art I* No.3, (Jan.1929) 75-189. See also Ray, N. *Maurya and Post-Maurya Art*. Delhi, I.C.H.R., 1975, no.56 and Chandra, P. *Stone Sculpture in the Allahabad Museum*. 58 & pl. XXX 77a-b.

5. Mackay, E.J.H. *Chanhu-daro Excavations*. pl. XXXII 1a.

6. Marshall, J., ed. *Mohenjo-daro*. 63-66, pl.XII, 18 & pl. CXII, 387.

    Zimmer, H. *The Art of Indian Asia*. 158-168.

    Marshal, J. l & Foucher A. *The Monuments of Sanchi*. Calcutta; 1940, 142-3.

7. Mackay, E.J.H.*Chanhu-daro Excavations*. 102,pl.XXXVI, 25.

    Marshall, J., ed. *Mohenjo-daro*. pl. CXVII, 5-6.

8. Porada, E. "The Relative Chronology of Mesopotamia, Part-I". *Chronologies in Old World Archaeology*. ed. Ehrich, R.W. Chicago, University of Chicago Press, 1965, 147 & fig. VI, II.

9. Casal, J.M. *Fouilles d'Amri*. Paris, Klincksieck, 1964, fig. 63, No.208.

10. Starr, R.F.S. *Indus Valley Painted Pottery*. Princeton, Princeton University Press, 1941, 71-73 & fig. 145-50.

11. Frankfurt, H. *Cylinder Seals*. London 1939 pl. IV j. Porada, E. *Ancient Iran: The Art of Pre-Islamic Times*. London, Methuen, 1965, 31 pl.5, and Woolley, L. *Ur Excavations. Vol. II The Royal Cemetery*. London, British Museum, 1934, pl.105.

12. Coomaraswamy, A.K. *Elements of Buddhist Iconography*. Cambridge, Harvard University Press, 1935, 7-18.

13. Bier, C. "Textiles" in P.O. Harper, ed, *The Royal Hunter: Art of the Sasanian Empire*. New York, Asia Society, 1978, 119-140. Geijer, A. A *History of Textile Art*. London, Philip Wilson, 1979; reprint, 1982, 117-124 pls. 14-26 & 88-89a, Ghirshman, R. *Iran: Parthians and Sassanians*. tr. Gilbert, S. & Emmons, J. London, Thames & Hudson, 1962, 226-237.

14. *Tresor de Sens* 57 & pl.24, Victoria and Albert Museum Acc. No.763, 1893.Buhler, A. & Fischer, E. *The Patola of Gujarat*. New York & Basle, Krebs, 1979, 199-200, fig. 187a-c and Trilling, J. "The Roman Heritage Textiles from Egypt and the Eastern Mediterranean 300-600 AD". *TMJ* 21, (1982).

15. Van Rosevelt, A. "Coptic Textiles: An Introduction". *The Art of the Ancient Weaver, Kelsey Museum of Archaeology*. Ann Arbor. The University of Michigan 1980, 15-21, 30-31, and Kozloff, A.P.ed. *Animals in Ancient Art from the Leo Mildenberg Collection*. Cleveland Museum of Art, 1981, 194 no. 181 & colour pl. V.

16. Handa, D. *Asian History, Archaeology, Art and Architecture*. Delhi, Sundeep Prakashan, 1984, pl. 67.

17. Mackay, E.J.H. *Further Excavations at Mohenjo-daro*. pl. LXXIX, 6, 11-12 & p.307; Vats, M.S. et al, *Excavations at Harappa 1920-21 and 1933-34*. Delhi, Manager of Publications, 1940, 306 & pl. LXXVII, 49-50, 52-54,

    Cunningham, A. *The Stupa of Bharhut*. pl. XXXIX,

    Ghirshman, R. *Persia: From the Origins to Alexander the Great*. tr. Gilbert, S. & Emmons, J. London, Thames & Hudson, 1964, 137, fig. 186.

    Ghirshman, R.G. *Persia: From the Origins to Alexander*. no. 260-216, no. 264, 217, no.226.

    Mention may be made of a distinctive necklace or collar with a pattern of alternating circles and lozenges which appears on a relief carving of an eagle, dated AD 187 from Hatra, an important commercial city on the western edge of the Parthian Empire in Northern Iraq, Colledge, M.A.R. *Parthian Art*. London, Elek, 1977, pl. 34.

18. Pope, A.U. ed. *A Survey of Persian Art*. London. O.U.P., 1938-39 & 1958, Vol.VI, 723, Tile from Kashan with

Cheetah, AD 1267, & Vol. IX 130 lc, bronze mirror with hounds 13th century AD; Tanavoli, P. *Lion Rugs: The Lion in the Art and Culture of Iran.* Basel, Wepf, 1985, fig.8, 14,30,37,39-47. Also 17-18,28-30 & 49.

19. Victoria and Albert Museum, *Indian Animals Daybook*, n.p. The range of the cheetah; or hunting leopard, used to extend from Africa across West Asia into India. It is now deemed to be virtually extinct in the subcontinent where it was trained and used for hunting since the 11th century AD. Basham, A.L. *The Wonder that was India.* Prater, S.H. *The Book of Indian Animals.* Bombay, Bombay National History Society, 1948, rpt. 1980, 80-81.

20. "Warp and Woof Historical Textiles, Calico Museum, Ahmedabad." *Marg* XXXIII No.1, 1979, 60.

21. Macdonell, A.A. *The Vedic Mythology.* Varanasi, Chowkhamba Vidyabhavan, 1961, 58, 79, 83 & 90., *Rig Veda* 4, 16; 1,64,8; 5,83, 3 & 3,6; 3,2,11, also Hopkins, *E.W. The Religions of India,* Boston, Ginn, 1895, 35.

22. Gray, J. *Near Eastern Mythology.* London, Hamlyn 1969, reprint. 1988, 44, 56, 76 & 91 and Rosenfield, J. *The Dynastic Arts of the Kushans.* Berkeley & Los Angeles, University. of California, 1967, 184. The lion later became associated with the goddesses Durga and Parvati and appears as their *vahana*, mount.

23. Irwin, J. "The True Chronology of Ashokan Pillars". *AA* XLIV, (1983) 263-4. Rosenfield, J. *Art of the Kushans.* 184.

24. Shastri, J.L. ed, *Ancient Indian Tradition and Mythology.* Delhi, Motilal Banarsidass, 1984, Vol. 27. *The Agni Purana.* trans. Gangadharan, N. 42.18.

25. Talwar, K. and Krishna, K. *Indian Pigment Paintings on Cloth. Vol. III; Historic Textiles of India at the Calico Museum Ahmedabad.* Ahmedabad, Calico Museum of Textiles, 1979, pl. 113A & col. pl XII, no. 138 (Painted cotton *patachitra*, late 18th century - tiger; Welch, S.C. *India Art and Culture 1300-1900.* New York, Metropolitan Museum of Art, 1985, 51-52 no. 19, Andhra Pradesh, ca. 1625.

The same lion, with wings and coronet, appears in his European heraldic role on an early 17th century cotton quilt made in Bengal for the Lima family of Villa Novada Cerveira but, since this pose does not appear on the durries, its story cannot be followed here; Victoria & Albert Museum, Indian Embroidery, London, H.M.S.O. 1951, no. 11, Acc NO.T438-1882.

26. Casal, J.M. *Fouilles de Mundigak.* Paris, Klincksieck, 1961, fig.62, no. 154; Mackay, E.J.H. *Further Excavations at Mohenjo-daro.* pl. LXXXVII, 259; Lloyd, S. & Safar, F. "Tell Uqair: Excavations by the Iraq Govt. Directorate of Antiquities in 1940 & 1941". *J.N.E.S.,* 11, (1943) pls. X-XI.

Tanavoli, P. *Lion Rugs.* fig. 5, 7, 8, 22, 24, Rug nos. 50, 52, 54, 55, 56. Porada, E. *Ancient Iran: The Art of Pre-Islamic Times.* London, Methuen, 1965, 136, pl. 39 and Welch, S.C. *Royal Persian Manuscripts.* London, Thames & Hudson, 1976, pl. 4-5 & 30.

27. Goswamy, B.N. *Essence of Indian Art.* 188, no. 146; Koch, E. *Shah Jehan and Orpheus.* Graz 1988, pls. 18, 28, 39.

28. Pope, A.U. ed. *A Survey of Persian Art.* vol. IV, pl. 52c, pls. 204, 205, 208 and Tanavoli, P. *Lion Rugs.* nos. 21-23.

29. "Warp and Woof Historical Textiles Calico Museum Ahmedabad". *Marg* XXXIII, 60 no. 1.

Koch, E. *Shah Jehan and Orpheus.* pl. 18 & 41, note 42. 18th century copy of *Badshah Nama,* B.M. Add 20735 fols. 366v &608v.

30. Irwin, J. & Hall, M. *Indian Embroideries.* Colour pl. 1.

31. *The Indian Heritage.* London: Victoria and Albert Museum, 1982, nos. 188, 572.

32. Collon, D. *First Impressions. 183-186;* Mackay E.J.H. *Further Excavations at Mohenjo-daro,* 332-4, Seals. 411, 450, 521, 636, 338-9; pl. LXXXIX, 347, 337-8, pl. XCIX A no. 430; Marshall, J. ed. *Mohenjo-daro.* pl. CXII, 378, 380; Thaper, B.K. "Kalibangan, a Harappan Metropolis Beyond the Indus Valley". *Expedition* 17, (1975), 28, no. 4; Vats M.S., *Excavations at Harappa.* 324, no. 249. Also Parpola, A. "New Correspondences Between Harappan and Near Eastern Glyptic Art". *South Asian Archaeology (1981)* ed. Allchin, B. Cambridge, Cambridge University Press, 1984, 176-195.

33. Cunningham, A. *The Monuments of Sanchi.* Vol. III pl. LXXV, 8a.

Burgen, J. *The Buddhist Stupas of Amaravati and Jaggeyyapeta.* London, Trubner, 1987 pls. XXXIII-XXXIX & LXV, 7.

Gorakshkar, G. ed. *Animals in Indian Art.* no. 137,

Irwin, J. & Hall, M. *Indian Embroideries.* pls. 89 & 91. In Calico Museum other examples of Bengal Kanthas include acc. 1058 & 1062.

Leoshko, J. "The Case of the Two Witnesses to the Buddha's Enlightenment". *Marg* XXXIX 47, no. 4.

34. Tanavoli, P. *Lion Rugs.* nos. 12-13, 19,33,35-36,39, 40-43,45,51,54,56-57 & 60.

35. Handa, O.C. *Pahari Folk Art.* Bombay, D.B. Taraporewala, 1975, 10-12 & fig. 1.

36. Collon, D. *First Impressions.* 24, 27, nos. 75,81-3, 127-30,158,161,163; Legrain, L. *Ur Excavations. Vol. X: Seal Cylinders*, London, British Museum, 1951, pl. 11.

Wiseman, D.J. *Cylinder Seals of Western Asia.* London, Batchworth Press, N.D., 28.

37. Herzfeld, E.E. *Iran in the Ancient East.* London, O.U.P. 1941, pl. XI.

38. Ghirshman, R. *Iran: Parthians and Sassanians.* 306, no.404; Pope, A.U. *Masterpieces of Persian Art.* New York, Dryden, 1945, pl.61; Tanavoli *Lion Rugs.* nos. 7,18,28-29, 31,37,54-55.

39. Hugel, G. *Travels in Kashmir and the Punjab.* tr. Jervis, T.B. London, 1845, 333-4.

40. Rudenko, S.I. *Frozen Tombs of Siberia.* 304 & pl. 174-6. Also see N. Diyarbekivli, "New Light on the Pazyryk Carpet". *Hali* 1, no.3, (1978), 217, N.Otkay, Aslanapa. *One Thousand Years of Turkish Carpets.* Istanbul, 1988, 10.

41. Housego, J. *Tribal Rugs.* London, Scorpion, 1978, pl.20. Geijer, A. *A History of Textile Art.* 260, pl. 95b.

42. Moorey, P.R.S. *Catalogue of the Ancient Persian Bronzes in the Ashmolean Museum.* Oxford, Clarendon, 1971, pl. 71, no. 463.

43. Gupte, B.C. "Some Rock and Tomb Inscribed Drawings from Baluchistan". *T.I.A.* XXXIX, (1910) 180-1, pl. II fig.5.

44. Collon, D. *First Impressions.* nos. 344, 351, 432, 447, 560, 573, 725-6, 685, 772-3, 737, 779-80, 786; also Zimmer, H. *The Art of Indian Asia.* 42-48.

45. Bhattacharya, A.K. "A Set of Kulu Folk-Paintings in the National Museum of India". *AA* XX (1957) fig. 3 & 7.

Kramrisch, S. "Kantha". *JISOA*, VII, (1939) pl. XIII.

46. Cunningham, A, *The Stupa of Bharhut.* pls. VIII, XII, XIII, XXIII, XXVI, 5, XXVII, 9, XXXII, 5-6.

47. Frankfort, H. *The Art and Architecture of the Ancient Orient.* 165, ill. 191. Collon, D. *First Impressions.* no. 918, illustrates a Babylonian seal impression with a goat in this pose which might be as early as the 11th century BC though a first millennium BC date is more probable letter from Dr. Collon.

48. Cook, J.M. *The Greeks in Ionia and the East.* London, Thames & Hudson, 1962, 32.

Gardner, P. *A History of Ancient Coinage 700-300 BC.* Oxford, Clarendon, 1918, pls. IV, 8, 9, 11, VII 12-13, XI, 1,7; Woodford, S. *An Introduction to Greek Art.* London. Duckworth, 1986, reprint. 1989, nos. 74, 80, 127, 192.

49. Allchin, F.R. & Hammond, N. ed. *The Archaeology of Afghanistan.* London. Academic Press, 1978, 229, fig.4-33.

50. Gardner, P. *Coins of the Greek and Scythic Kings of Bactria and India in the British Museum.* London, Languages, 1886, pl. IV, 6,8. VIII, 8, IX, 8. XVI, 5; Guillaume, O. *Graeco-Bactrian and Indian Coins from Afghanistan.* Osmund, N. Bopearachchi, Delhi. O.U.P. 1991, pl. V, C & V, D.

51. Collon, D. *First Impressions* nos. 55, 58, 879; Eisen G.A. *Ancient Oriental Cylinder and Other Seals with Description of the Collection of Mrs. William H. Moore.* University of Chicago Oriental Institute Publication, XLVII, Chicago, Universiy of Chicago, 1940, nos. 4 & 15; Munn Rankin, J.M. "Ancient Near Eastern Seals in the Fitzwilliam Museum". *Iraq* XXI, (1959) no.2.

52. Fairservis, W.A. *The Roots of Indian Civilization.* figs. 38 & 44; see also Starr, R.F.S. *Indus Valley Painted Pottery.* 71-73.

53. Frankfort, H. *The Art and Architecture of the Ancient Orient.* ills. 79 & 81; Collon D. *First Impressions.* nos. 421, 773; Eisen, G.A. *Ancient Oriental Cylinders.* nos. 79, 98, 99; Munn Rankin, J.M. *Seals in the Fitzwilliam Museum.* no. 30; Parker, B. "Excavations at Nimrud 1949-1953, Seals and Seal Impressions". *Iraq* XVII, (1955) pls. XII, 1 & XIII, 1 ND.3582 & ND. 3226. Marshall, J. & Foucher, A. *The Monuments of Sanchi.* pl. LXXXIII 44c.

54. Marshall, J. ed. *Mohenjo-daro.* 398-9, pl. CXVII 5 & 6. Other Indus Valley hares include, Mackay, E.J.H. *Further Excavations at Mohenjo-daro.* 291 & pl. LXXIV, 20; Mackay, *Chanhu-daro Excavations.* 89-91; Rao, S.R. *Lothal.*

535-551 & pl. CCXLIII B fig. 117; Vats, M.S. *Excavations at Harappa.* 324, no. 568.

55. Cowell, E.B. ed. *The Jataka* or *Stories of the Buddha's Former Births.* Cambridge, C.U.P. 1895, 3 vol. nos. 20 (Nalapana Jataka,) 316 (Sasa Jataka,) & 454 (Ghata Jataka).

56. Mackay, E.J.H. *Chanhu-daro Excavations.* 88 & pl. XXXIII, 6 & pl. XXXVI, 23. also Mackay. *Further Excavations at Mohenjo-daro.* 285, 303 & pl. LXXVII, 20; Marshall, J. ed. *Mohenjo-daro.* 43, 205, 221, 351, pl. XCVI, 7; Rao, S.R. *Lothal.* pl. CCVI A & p. 494, Vats, M.S. *Excavations at Harappa.* 304 & pl. LXXVIII 28-30.

57. Pal, P. "A Pre-Kushan Buddha Image from Mathura". *Marg* XXXIX no. 4, fig. 8; Snead, S. *Animals in Four Worlds.* Chicago, University of Chicago Press, 1989, pl. 63,; Vogel, J.Ph. *La Sculpture de Mathura.* pl. XLb. Cunningham mentions but does not illustrate two squirrels at Bharhut, on the sides of a pillar below the central medallion, eating fruit while holding on to a small branch of a tree. *The Stupa of Bharhut,* 44.

58. Welch, S.C. *India Art and Culture 1300-1900.* New York, Metropolitan Museum of Art, 1985, 214-216, 326.

59. Sen, A. *Animal Motifs in Ancient Indian Art.* Calcutta, Mukhopadhyay, 1972, 41-53; Vogel, J.P. *Indian Serpent Lore or the Nagas in Hindu Legend and Art.* London, Probsthain, 1926; Zimmer, H. *Myths and Symbols in Indian Art and Civilization.* New York, Pantheon, 1962, 59-68.

60. Mackay, E.J.H. *Further Excavations at Mohenjo-daro.* 360.

61. Temple, R.C. *The Legends of the Punjab.* 1884, reprint. Patiala, Language Dept., 1962, Vol.I 121-209, 414-528, Vol. III 261-300.

62. Aijazuddin, F.S. *Pahari Paintings and Sikh Portraits in the Lahore Museum.* Karachi, O.U.P., 1977, 75 no. 2(V); Desai, K. *Iconography of Vishnu.* New Delhi, Abhinav 1973, fig.21-25.

63. Mackay, E.J.H. *Chanhu-daro Excavations.* 15, 45, 184, pl. LXXIII, 5-8, 17-18 & LXXVI 15. Also 91-149,pls. XXXIII, 4, XXXVI, 17, 21 & LII, 33.

Mackay, E.J.H. *Further Excavations at Mohenjo-daro.* 219, pl. LXX, 10.

Marshall, J., ed. *Mohenjo-daro.* 501, 664, 670, 673, pl. CXLIII 24-25. Also 557 pls. CXXXII, 19-20, 32, 40 & p. 392.

64. Casal, J.M. *Fouilles d'Amri.* fig. 77; Mackay. *Chanhu-daro Excavations.* 1935-36, 88-9, 91-2 & 102, pls. XXXIII 2, 3 & 12, pl. XXXVI, 14 & 16; Mackay, E.J.H. *Further Excavations at Mohenjo-daro.* pl. LXX, 32; Marshall, J. ed. *Mohenjo-daro.* 349 & pl. XCVI, 4; Vats, M.S., et al, *Excavations at Harappa.* 302 & pl. LXIV 6-8.

65. Vats, M.S., et al, *Excavations at Harappa.* 207 & pl. LXII, 2.

66. Shere, A.S. "Stone Discs Found at Murtaziganj". *JBRS* XXXVII, (1951) pls. V & VI.

67. Handa, O.C. *Pahari Folk* Art. 34-35.

68. We are grateful to Mr. J.S. Sarrao of the Bombay Natural History Society for the information. Also see Thaker, J.P. "Peacock: The National Bird of India". *Pavo,* 1, no. 1, (March 1963) 1-18.

69. Local Tradition – see also Crooke, W. *The Popular Religion and Folklore of Northern India.* 2 vols., second ed, 1896, reprint. N. Delhi, Munshiram Manoharlal, 1978, vol. 2, 251.

70. Cowell, E.B. ed. *The Jataka.* vol. III 83-4, Jataka No. 339, Baveru Jataka.

71. Marshall, J. ed., *Mohenjo-daro.* pl. XCVI, 2 & p. 349, Vats M.S. *Excavations at Harappa.* pl. LXXVIII, 2; Marshall, J. & Foucher, A. *The Monuments of Sanchi.* pls. XIX a-b & LXIX d.

72. Hackin, J. *Begram.* nos. 7, 83, 139, 143, 233. *Sanghol.* (unpublished).

Sivaramamurti, C. *Birds and Animals in Indian Art.* New Delhi, National Museum, 1974, fig. 63.

Tartakov, G.M. & Dehejia, V. "Sharing, Intrusion and Influence: The Mahisasuramardini Imagery of the Chalukyas and the Pallavas". *AA* XLV, (1984), fig. 11 & 41.

Vogel, J. Ph. *La Sculpture de Mathura.* pls. XIXa, LIXa.

73. Temple, R.C. *The Legends of Punjab.* 1884; reprint Patiala, Language Department, 1962, vol. I, pl. 65.

74. Marshall, J. & Foucher, A. *The Monuments of Sanchi.* pls. XXX, XXXII, XLII & XLIV; Collon, D. *First Impressions.* 12-15 no. 8; Frankfort, *Cylinder Seals* pl. IVe; Legrain L. *Ur Excavations. Vol. X, Seal Cylinders.* pls. 11, no. 138-140, 142 & 144 & 14 no. 176.

75. Kitzinger, E. "The Horse and Lion Tapestry. at Dumbarton

Oaks". *Dumbarton Oaks Papers* 3, (1946) figs. 24 & 25.

76. Trilling, J. "The Roman Heritage". no. 15.

77. Kitzinger, E. "The Horse and Lion Tapestry". fig. 23.

78. For instance Geijer, A. "A Silk from Antinoe and the Sasannian Textile Art". *Orientalia Suecana* 12, (1963) 3-34, & Kitzinger, E. "The Horse and Lion Tapestry". 3-59. Pope, A.U. ed. *A Survey of Persian Art*. Vol. IX, pl. 1353A, 1322-3 & 1325.

79. *Tresor de Sens*. 12 & pl. 2-3.

80. Allchin, B. & R., *The Rise of Civilization in India and Pakistan*. 191.

Mackay, E.J.H. *Further Excavations at Mohenjo-daro*. 218-9, 296 & pls. LXXIV, 1 & 5; LXXVII, 10 & 12; LXXVIII, 24; LXXX 20 & 27.

Marshall, J. ed. *Mohenjo-daro*. 395, 398, 424-5, pl. CXI 338, CXVI, 14 & CXVIII, 10.

Rao, S.R. *Lothal*. 535 & pl. CCXLV, B.

Vats, M.S. *Excavations at Harappa*. pl. LXXVIII, 12.

81. Carter, H. "An Ostracon Depicting a Red Jungle-Fowl". *JEA* IX, (1923) 2.

82. Carter, H. "An Ostracon". pl. XX fig.1.

83. Legrain, L. *Ur Excavations*. Vol. X: *Seal Cylinders*, 52 & pl. 42, nos. 821-826; Ward, W.H. *The Seal Cylinders of Western Asia*. Washington, Carnegie, 1910, 421 & figs. 554, 556 & 1126.

Zettler, R.L. "On the Chronological Range of Neo-Babylonian and Achaemid Seals". *JNES* 38, no. 4, (Oct. 1979) 262, fig. 5a.

Ghirshman, R. *Iran: Parthians and Sassanians*. 230, no. 280.

The Geometry of Design

1. See for example Petsopoulos, Y. *Kilims The Art of Tapestry Weaving in Anatolia, the Caucasus and Persia*. London, 1979, 82, fig. no. 102 and p.102, fig. No.121.

2. Similar patterns and structures are also found in the tapestry weaves of central and South America.

3. For a discussion of such trade see Ratnagar, S. *Encounters. The Westerly Trade of the Harappa Civilization*. Delhi, 1981. See also different sections of Allchin, B. & R. *The Rise of Civilization in India and Pakistan*.

4. See Nissen, H.J. *The Early History of the Ancient Near East* 9000-2000 BC. Chicago, 1988, 98, 99, fig.39.

5. We have consulted numerous works on these sites, as listed in the bibliography. See in particular Allchin, B. & R. *The Rise of Civilization in India and Pakistan*.

6. See Jarrige, J. *Fouilles de Pirak*. 2 vols. Paris: 1979. Also Allchin B.& R. *The Rise of Civilization in India and Pakistan*. 233, fig. 9.6.

7. We are indebted to Dr. S. Bhan of Kurukshetra University for this information and also for his thoughts in a private discussion on the importance of textile designs on potsherds.

8. See Khlopin, I.N. "The Manufacture of Pile Carpets in Bronze Age Central Asia". *Hali*, 5, no.2, (1982), 116.

See Pinner, R. "Decorative Designs on Prehistoric Turkmenian Ceramics". *Hali*, Vol.5, no.2 (1982), 118. See also Dalley, "Ancient Assyrian Textiles", 119.

9. de Cardi, B. "Excavations at Bampur, a Third Millennium Settlement in Persian Baluchistan, 1966". Vol.51, Part 3. *Anthropological Papers of the American Museum of Natural History*, New York, 1970.

See also Allchin, B. & R. *The Rise of Civilization in India and Pakistan*. 140.

10. Mellaart, J. *Catal Hüyük, A Neolithic Town in Anatolia*. London, 1967, 152.

See Eiland, M. "The Goddess From Anatolia". *Oriental Rug Review*, 10, no.6, (1980) 19-26, for his review on Melloart, J., Hirsch, U. and Balpinar, B. *The Goddess from Anatolia*. Adenau, 1989.

11. Allchin, B. & R. *The Rise of Civilization in India and Pakistan*. 212.

12. This was ascertained by Jenny Housego during field work in Iran in the 1970's.

13. We are extremely grateful to Dr. Oliver Guillaume for reading a draft of this chapter and for his comments, and also to Simon Digby for his help.

14. Allchin, B. & R. *The Rise of Civilization in India and Pakistan*. P.241

15. See Basham, A.L. *The Wonder That Was India*, and various parts of Thapar, R. *A History of India*. Vol.I, for a discussion of this little documented period of foreign invasions.

16. The dating of this silk was suggested by Dr. Chhayha Haesner. Dr. Lotika Varadarajan believes however,

that it is probably of Central Asian origin.

17. Lamberg-Karlovsky C. and Sabloff, J.A. *Ancient Civilizations. The Near East and Mesoamerica.* California, 1979, 102.

18. Mallowan, M.E.L. "Excavations at Tall Arpachiyah, 1933". *Iraq* II, (1935); Mallowan, M.E.L. "The Excavations at Tall Chagar Bazar". *Iraq* III, (1936); Mallowan, M.E.L. "Excavations at Brak and Chagar Bazar". *Iraq* IX, (1947).

19. Rosenfield, J. *The Dynastic Arts of the Kushans.* 170-171, 186; figs. 3 a,c,d & 138.

20. For details of the design see: Mallowan, M.E.L. "Excavations at Brak and Chagar Bazar". *Iraq* IX, (1947) pl.V.

    Woolley, C.L. *Ur Excavations,* Vol. II *The Royal Cemetery,* London, British Museum, 1934, pls. 95-6, 98 & 103.

    Frankfort, H. "Ishtar at Troy". *JNES,* VIII, (1949) 196, fig. 1, no.4, seal from Tell Agrab, (ca. 3400-2900 BC).

    Parrot, A. *Le Temple D'Ishtar, tome I, Mission Archaeologique de Mari.* Paris, Geuthner, 1956, 154 & pl.LVIII, ivory and shell inlaid roundels, (ca. 3000-2340 BC).

    Van Buren, E.D. *Clay Figurines of Babylon and Assyria, Yale Oriental Series - Researches.* Vol.XVI, New Haven, Yale, 1930, pl.XXII, fig. 110, Tello, (ca. 2300 BC) and fig. 111, Babylon, (ca. 2300 BC).

    Vats, M.S. *Excavations at Harappa.* pl.LXXVII, 34-40.

    Coomaraswamy, A.K. "Archaic Indian Terracottas". *Marg* VI, (1952-53), fig. 18, said to be from Mathura, (ca. 1000-300 BC).

21. *The Wealth of India.* (Delhi, Council of Scientific and Industrial Research, 1948.) Vol.VII, 7-9, 72-73. The representations of plant forms may have developed earlier but in perishable materials like wood, of which no trac has been found.

22. Coomaraswamy, A.K. *Yaksas, II.* Washington, 1931, reprint N. Delhi, Munshiram Manoharlal, 1971, 23-24, 56-58; *Sri Suktam.* trans. B.B. Konnur, Bombay, Bharatiya Vidya Bhavan, 1987; Coomaraswamy, A.K. "Early Indian Iconography II Sri Laksmi". *Eastern Art I,* no. 3, (1929) 175-189. Also Kramrisch, S. "An Image of Aditi-Uttanapad". *AA* XIX, (1956) 259-270 and Bhat, M.K. *Varahamihir's Brhat Samhita II,* Delhi, Motilal Banarsidas, 1982, 559-560.

23. Coomaraswamy, A.K. *Yakas II.* 61; Agrawala, P.K. *Purna Kalasa or the Vase of Plenty.* Varanasi, Prithvi Prakashan, 1965; Rosu, A. "Purna ghata et le Symbolisme du Lotus dans L'Inde". *Arts Asiatiques* VIII, (1961) 163-194.

24. Coomaraswamy, A.K. *Yaksas II.* 57; also, *Elements of Buddhist Iconography* 21.

25. Cunningham, A. *The Stupa of Bharhut.* pls. VII-XIII, XVII, XXI-XXIV, XXXIV-XXXVIII,XL; Marshall, J. & Foucher, A. *The Monuments of Sanchi.* pls. VIII, XXIII, XXIV, XXVI, XXVIII, XLIII, XLIV, L, p, LVIII, LXXIV, LXXVIII, 23b,c,XCI,a, XCIII, CIII, CIV, I and Gupta, S.P. ed. *Kushana Sculpture from Sanghol.* l92-97, 105-113.

26. Coomaraswamy, A.K. *Yaksas II.* 18; See also Adalbert, G. "Planets and Pseudoplanets in India Literature and Art with Special Reference to Nepal". *EW,* XXX, (1980), 140, who refers to *Vishnudharmottarapurana* III 86, 52b, in which a temple called *Kamala,* Lotus, is included in a list of 101 temple types. It should be built on an octagonal base with eight sanctuaries with eight doors facing the eight cardinal directions, one for each of the *Dikpalas,* guardians of the eight directions.

27. Jacobsen, T. "Formative Tendencies in Sumerian Religion". *The Bible and the Ancient Near East* ed. Col. Wright. Cambridge, Mass; 1961 267-8 & Maxwell - Hyslop, K.R. *Western Asiatic Jewellery.* (ca.3000-612 BC) London, Methuen, 1974 151-2.

28. Cunningham, A. *The Stupa of Bharhut.* pls. XXXVI, I, XXXVIII, 1&3; Marshall, J. & Foucher, A. *The Monuments of Sanchi.* pls. XVIs, XVIII, XXVIII, XXX, XXXII, XXXIV-XXXVI, XLI-XLVIII, LXXVII-LXXXIII, LXXXV, LXXXVI, LXXXVIII-XC.

29. Bhat, M.K. *Varahamihir's Brhat Samhita.* Part I. 539, Shastri, A.M. *India as seen in the Brhat Samhita of Varahamihira.* Delhi, Motilal Banarsidas, 1969 398-400.

30. Parrot, A. *Sumer.* London, 1961, figs. 60-61. Many finds from Halaf and associated sites are preserved at the British Museum.

31. Bala, M. "Maltese Cross on Proto-Historic Pottery". *Puratattava.* no. 11, (1979-80).

32. Boardman, J. *Greek Art.* London, Thames & Hudson,

1985, p.27, Cambridge, C.U.P., 1991, fig.17.

Rasmussen, T. & Spivery, N. ed. *Looking at Greek Vases*, Cambridge, C.U.P., 1991 fig.17.

Dunbabin, T.J. *The Greeks and Their Eastern Neighbours.* London, S.P.H.S. 1957.

Payne, H. *Necrorinthia: A Study of Corinthian Art in the Archaic Period.* Oxford, Clarendon, 1931, p.53-55.

33. Enthoven, R.E. "The Folklore of Gujarat," supplement to *TIA* XLVI, (1917), 8 and Srivastava, V.C. *Sun-Worship in Ancient India.* Allahabad, Indological Publications, 1972. 19-28.

34. *The Satapatha-Brahmana.* tr. J. Eggeling, *The Sacred Books of the East.* ed. Muller, F.M. Vol. 41, Oxford, Clarendon, 1894; reprint, New Delhi, Motilal Banarsidass, 1989. 265, VI, 7,1,1-2.

35. Hartner, W. "The Earliest History of the Constellations in the Near East and the Motif of the Lion-Bull combat". *JNES, XXIV,* (1965) pls. XII,XIII,XV; and 3.9. Also Starr, R.F.S. *Indus Valley Painted Pottery.* 52-53, 70-75; Collon, D. *First Impressions.* 24-25, no.55.

36. Hartner, W. "The Earliest History". 9.

37. Tanavoli, P. *Lion Rugs.* 36-39.

38. Wright, H.N. *Catalogue of the Coins in the Indian Museum.* Calcutta. Vol.III. *Mughal Emperors of India.* Oxford, Clarendon, 1908 nos. 570-582, 603-605, 627-636 & pls. VI & VII.

39. Parpola, A. "New Correspondences Between Harappan and Near Eastern Glyptic Arts". *South Asian Archaeology* (1981), ed. B.

Allchin, Cambridge, C.U.P., (1984); Porada, E. "Remarks on Seals Found in the Gulf States". *AA* 33, (1971), 336. The planets are still known by the names of Roman gods and stars above or beside divine figures are found on Roman coins.

40. Parpola, A. "New Correspondences". 187, figs. 23.16, 23.33.

41. "Warp and Woof ". Historic Textiles, Calico Museum, Ahmedabad". *Marg.* XXXIII, no.1, December, (1979).

42. *Sri Suktam.* 19, (verse 14).

43. Gorakshkar, S. ed. *Animals in Indian Art.* no.34.

44. Mackenzie, D.A. *The Migration of Symbols and Their Relations to Beliefs and Customs.* New York, Alfred Knopf, 1926, X.

45. Pope, A.U., ed. *A Survey of Persian Art.* pl 18C.

46. Starr, R.F.S. *Early Indus Painted Pottery.* Princeton, Princeton University Press, 1941, 56.

47. Hartner, W. "The Earliest History". 12-14; also Van der Waerden, B.L. "Babylonian Astronomy. ii. The Thirty-six Stars". *JNES,* VIII, (1949), 6-26.

48. Pope, A.U., ed. *A Survey of Persian Art.* pl.33,(fig. 6a); pl. 2B, 3A, fig. 6B); pl.2A, (fig. 6c); pl. 1C; *Memoires de la Delegation en Perse XIII.* Paris: Leroux, 1912. pl. IV, 1, fig. 6d.

49. Agrawala, D.V.S. "Pottery Designs from Achichchhatra". *LK*, 3-4, (1956-57), 78, 80-81, nos. 71-73.

50. Harris, N. *Rugs and Carpets of the Orient.* London, Hamlyn, 1977, 6, 31.

51. We are indebted to Henri Daumas for this suggestion.

52. We are indebted to Dr. Chhahya Haesner for this suggestion. Dr. R.C. Sharma pointed out other examples of this motif on stone carvings from sites in Gandhara at a lecture delivered at the National Museum, New Delhi.

53. Forbes, R.J. *Archaeologisch Historische Bijdragen III.* "Notes on the History of Ancient Roads". 1934, 85-94.

Hultzsch, E., ed. *Corpus Inscriptionum Indicarum, I, Inscriptions of Ashoka.* Oxford, Clarendon, 1925 2-4, 130-137.

54. Steel, F.A. "Folklore of the Punjab". *TIA,* XI, (1882) 167.

55. Fairservis, W.A. *The Roots of Indian Civilization.* London, George Allen & Unwin, 1971. figs. 25, 45, 49; Perkins, A.L. *The Comparative Archaeology of Early Mesopotamia.* Chicago, U.C.P., 1957 fig. 5, 10, 11 & 19.

Starr. R.F.S. *Indus Valley Painted Pottery.* 49-52.

The motif of stacked triangles combined with snakes from Mesopotamia and the eastern Mediterranean has been interpreted as a fertility symbol. See Mungkar, B. "Notes on Two Ancient Fertility Symbols". *EW* 28, (1978), 263-282.

56. Housego, J. *Tribal Rugs.* London, Scorpion, 1978 pl. 61.

57. Douie, J.M. *Punjab Settlement Manual.* Lahore, Punjab Govt., 1930, 117-119, & Appendix XIV, LXII-LXVI; Mr. Gurbachan Singh, Chief Conservator of Forests, Punjab, (Retd.)

58. Lawrence, H.M.L. *Adventures of an Officer in the Punjaub.* 2 vols. 1883; reprint, Patiala, Languages Department, Punjab, 1970 241.

59. Zimmer, H. *Myths and Symbols in Indian Art and Civilization*, 140-148; Kramrisch, S. *The Hindu Temple*. Calcutta, University of Calcutta, 1946 21-39, 67-68, 244-253.

60. Kramrisch, S. *The Hindu Temple*. 255. We thank Mr. Kulbushan Rishi, Dept. of Cultural Affairs, Archaeology and Museums, Punjab for suggesting the *Shri Yantra* link and Professor Devendra Handa of the Dept. of Ancient Indian History, Punjab for pointing out the similarity with the Lakshmana Temple.

61. Garbini, G. "The Stepped Pinnacle in Ancient Near East". *EW* 9, (1958) 89; Casal, J. *Fouilles de Mundigak*, fig.22.

62. Garbini, G. "The Stepped Pinnacle". 86-90; Frankfort, H. *The Art and Architecture of the Ancient Orient*. 22.

63. Frankfort, H. 132, ill. 150, a-b;GunterA. "Representations of Urartian and Western Iranian Fortress Architecture in the Assyrian Reliefs". *Iran*, XX, (1982) 103-112; Oppenheim, A.L. in "The Golden Garments of the Gods". *JNES*, 8, (1949), 172-193, suggested that the designs on some of the gold ornaments stitched to the garments of kings and images of deities in Mesopotamia from the 12th century BC until the Achaemenid period would have special and protective meaning. The most usual motifs on these brackets are stars and rosettes, but fortress walls with towers are also shown. Real walls of this kind would generally be crenellated. See also Garbini, G. "The Stepped Pinnacle". 90.

64. Porada, E. *Ancient Iran*. 67, 159, 201, fig. 42, 85, 110.

    Ghirshman, R. *Iran*: 157-8, 160-5.

    Hill, G.E. *Catalogue of the Greek Coins of Arabia Mesopotamia and Persia*. London, British Museum, 1922 pls. XXXIII & XXXIV.

    Oppenheim in "Golden Garments" 190-91, draws attention to an Assyrian relief of the period of Ashurnasirpal, 885-860 BC, in which circular disk-like ornaments are carved just below the battlements of a city wall.

    The Wadia Atash Behram, Princess Street, (1830), Thoothi Agiary, Walkeshwar, (1861), and Sodawater Agiary, M. Karve Rd, (1920), all preserve these motifs.

65. Gardner, P. *The Coins of the Greek and Scythic Kings of Bactria and India in the British Museum*. London, 1886 pl. XVI, 3, (Maues); Gnoli, G. "The Tyche and the Dioscuri in Ancient Sculptures from the Valley of Swat". *EW* 14, (1963), 29-37 & fig 6; also Rowland, B. "The Tyche of Hadda". *Oriental Art*, XII, (1966), 183-189.

66. Cunningham, A. *The Stupa of Bharhut*. pl. XLVII.

67. Buhler, A. & Fischer, E. *The Patola of Gujarat*. fig. 170, & Tanavoli, P. *Lion Rugs*. nos. 20, 21, 25, 29, 37, 44, 55, 59.

68. Mackay, E.J.H. *Further Excavations at Mohenjo-daro*. 340 and pls. LXIX, 4 & LXXXIX(A); Rao, S.R. *Lothal*. 505, 511-513, pls. CLXXV, CCXX and CCXXIII.

69. Lawrence, H.M.L. *Adventures of an Officer in the Punjaub*. 403-4.

70. Childe, V.G. *New Light on the Most Ancient East*, London, Routledge & Kegan Paul, 1952, 128,176, pl. XXIV.

71. Cf. "Jahangir boating in Kashmir". Album Leaf, early 18th century. B.M. Oriental Antiquities No. 1920.9.17.01.

Spun Tales: Legends and Couplets

1. Hershman, P. *Punjabi Kinship and Marriage*. Delhi, Hindustan Publishing Corp., 1981, 92.

2. Campbell, J. *The Masks of God, Oriental Mythology*. New York, Viking, Penguin, 1962, Penguin, 1976, 128-9, 179, 286.

3. Zimmer, H. *The King and the Corpse*. Bollingen Series XI, Princeton, Princeton University Press, 1956, 239-316.

4. Temple, R.C. *The Legends of Punjab*. Vol.III, 1-23.

    Swynnerton, C. *Romantic Tales From the Punjab*. 1903; reprint, Patiala, Language Department, 1963, 301-336.

5. Swynnerton, C. *Romantic Tales*. 37, "as told by the bard, Sher, at Abbottabad, October, 1889".

6. Hansen, D.P. "New Votive Plaques From Nippur". *JNES*, XXII, (1963), 158.

    Kantor, H.J. "A Bronze Plaque with Relief Decoration From Tell Tainat". Oriental Institute Museum Notes, No.13. *JNES*, XXI, (1962), figs. 7-12.

7. Pope, A.U., ed. *A Survey of Persian Art*, pls. 28-29, 32, 34, 38, 56, 123 C, M; 256 S,T,W; Tresor de Sens, 51 & pl.23.

Kantor, H.J. "A Bronze Plaque". 101 & fig.16.

8. Kantor, H.J. "A Bronze Plaque", figs.101-108.

    Wiseman, D.J. *Cylinder Seals of Western Asia.* London, Batchworth Press.n.d., 15, 19, 49, 50, 70, 73, 74 & 106.

9. Collon, D. *First Impressions.* 14 2-144, no. 614; Mackay, E.J.H. *Further Excavations at Mohenjo-daro.* 337 & pl.LXXXIV, 76 & 86.

    Vats M.S., et al. *Excavations at Harappa.* 207 & pl. LXII, 1a-b.

    See Calico Museum of Textiles, Ahmedabad. Acc. no.2962.

10. Swynnerton, Charles. *Romantic Tales from the Punjab.* 1-37.

11. The Five Pirs, *Panj Pir,* are the five original saints of Islam – Mohammed, Ali, Fatima, Hasan and Husain – but the term may also be used for any five saints. Five leading north Indian saints are known in the area as the Five Pirs and it is likely that these are intended here. They are Baha-ud-din Zikariya of Multan, Shah Ruqa-i-Alam Hazrat of Lucknow, Shah Shams Tabriz of Multan, Shaikh Jalal Makhdum Jahaniyan Jahangasht of Uchcha in Multan, and Baba Shaikh Farid-ud-din Shakkarganj of Pak Patan, now in Pakistani Punjab. See Crooke, W. vol.1, 202-203.

12. Temple, R.C. *The Legends of Punjab.* vol.II, 177; see also Rose, H.A. "A Version of Hir and Ranjha". *TIA* LIV, (1925), 176-9 & 210-19, in which Hir is poisoned by her parents and Ranjha dies of grief.

For further reading on this legend see also Shah, W. "The Story of Hir and Ranjha," *TIA* L. (1921), supplement 1-31 and LI. (1922), supplement 33-64; Singh, A. "A Version of Hir and Ranjha". *TIA* LIV, (1925), 176-219; Singhal, C.R. "Some Corrections to "A Version of Hir and Ranjha". *TIA* LVIII, (1929), 181-6; Told by a peasant proprietor of Jhang to H.A. Rose, in 1884-85, "The Sequel to Hir and Ranjha," *TIA* LV, (1926) 14-19, 36-39.

Bibliography

Abbreviations

AA	Artibus Asiae
AP	Ancient Pakistan
BMMA	Bulletin of the Metropolitan Museum of Art
EW	East and West
JASB	Journal of the Asiatic Society of Bengal
JBRS	Journal of the Bihar Research Society
JEA	Journal of Egyptian Archaeology
JIA	Journal of Indian Art
JIAI	Journal of Indian Art & Industry
JISOA	Journal of the Indian Society of Oriental Art
JITH	Journal of Indian Textile History
JNSI	Journal of the Numismatic Society of India
JNES	Journal of Near Eastern Studies
JRAS	Journal of the Royal Asiatic Society
LK	Lalit Kala
LMB	Lahore Museum Bulletin
ME	Man and Environment
PA	Pakistan Archaeology
RSA	Royal Society of Art
TIA	The Indian Antiquary
TMJ	Textile Museum Journal

Abbott, J. "On the Ballads and Legends of the Punjab. Rifacimento of the Legend of Russaloo". *JASB*, XXIII, 1854.

Adalbert, G. "Planets and Pseudoplanets in Indian Literature and Art with Special Reference to Nepal. *EW* XXX (1980).

Agrawala, P.K. *Purna Kalasa, or the Vase of Plenty*, Varanasi: Prithvi Prakashan, 1965.
——"The Early Indian Mother Goddess Votive Discs". *EW* 29, 1979.

Agrawala, V.S. "Pottery Designs from Ahichchatra", *LK* 3-4, (1956-57).

Ahmed, Z. ed. *Selections from Journal of the Punjab Historical Society*. 3 vols. Lahore, 1982.

Aijazuddin, F.S. *Pahari Paintings and Sikh Portraits in the Lahore Museum*, Karachi: O.U.P., 1977.

Akbar, M. *The Punjab Under the Mughals*. Delhi, 1974.

Ali, S. and Ripley, S.D. *Compact Handbook of the Birds of India and Pakistan*, Delhi: O.U.P., 1987.

Allan, J.W. "Mamluk Sultanic Heraldry and the Numismatic Evidence: A Reinterpretation", *JRAS* (1970).

Allana, G.A. *Art of Sind*, Islamabad, Lok Virsa Publishing House. n.d.

Allchin B. & R. *The Rise of Civilization in India and Pakistan*. Cambridge, C.U.P. 1982; reprint 1988.

Allchin, F.R. and Hammond, N. eds. *The Archaeology of Afghanistan*. London, Academic Press, 1978.

Amiet, P. et. al. *Art in the Ancient World. A Handbook of Styles and Forms*. London, 1981.
——"Glyptique Susienne, Memoirs de la Delegation Archeologique", *Iran* XLIII, Paris. (1972),
——"*Suse: 6000 Ans d'Histoire*", Paris, Musee du Louvre, 1988.

Anand, M.R. *Madhubani Paintings.* Delhi, Ministry of Information and Broadcasting, 1984.

Aryan, K.C. *100 Years Survey of Punjab Painting, 1841-1941.* New Delhi, Rekha Prakashan, 1975.
—— *Punjab Murals.* New Delhi, Rekha Prakashan, 1977.
—— *The Cultural Heritage of Punjab, 3000 BC to AD 1947.* New Delhi, Rekha Prakashan, 1983.

Aryan, K.C. and S. *Rural Art of the Western Himalayas.* New Delhi, 1985.

Askarov, A. *Sites of the Andronovo Culture of the Lower Basin of the Zeravaban,* Tashkent, 1962.

Auboyer, J. *Daily Life in Ancient India From Approximately 200 BC to AD 700.* New York, Macmillan, 1965.
—— *Le Trone et son Symbolism dans L'Inde Ancienne.* Paris, 1949.

Baden Powell, B.H. *Handbook of the Manufactures and Arts of the Punjab. Vol.II of the Handbook of the Economic Products of Punjab.* Lahore, 1862, 1876.

Bala, M. "Maltese Cross on Protohistoric Pottery". *Puratattva* 11 (1979-80.)
—— "Recently Explored Sites in Punjab", *ME* V (1981)
—— *Bhartiya Puratattvam Navintama Upalabdhyah* New Delhi, 1989.

Banerjee, N.N. "The Cotton Fabrics of Bengal", *JIAI* VIII (1900).

Basham, A.L. *The Wonder that was India.* London, Sidgwick & Jackson, 1954; reprint, Calcutta, Rupa, 1981.

Beer, A.B. *Trade Goods. A Study of Indian Chintz in the Cooper Hewitt Museum.* Washington, 1970.

Belenitsky, A. tr. Hogarth, J. *Central Asia.* London, Nagel 1968.

Bhatia G. "A Home in the Desert". *Swagat* (January, 1990).

Bhatia R.K. *Handicraft Survey Report, Panja Dari.* (Census of India 1981 Series 17, Part XD).

Bhatt, M.R. *Varahamihir's Brhat Samhita.* Part II. Delhi, Motilal Banarsidas, 1982.

Bier, C. "Textiles" in P.O. Harper, ed., *The Royal Hunter: Art of the Sasanian Empire,* New York, Asia Society, 1978.

Birdwood, G.C.M. *The Industrial Arts of India,* London, 1880; third U.K. reprint 1986.

Biscione, R. "Baluchistan Presence in the Ceramic Assemblage of Period I at Shahr-i Sokhta". *South Asian Archaeology* (1981).

Bisht, R.S. "Transformation of the Harappan Culture in Punjab with Special Reference to the Excavation at Sanghol and Chandigarh" in *Archaeological Congress Seminar, Kurukshetra,* ed. U.V. Singh, (1972).
—— "Harappan Culture in Punjab: A Study in Perspective". *Indus Civilization, Problems and Issues.* eds.B.B. Lal and S.C. Mallik.
—— "Further Excavation at Banawali: 1983-84", in *Archaeology and History: Essays in Memory of Shri A. Ghosh.* eds. B.M. Pande & B.D. Chattopadhyaya, Delhi, 1987.

Biswas, T.K. "A Special Treasure", *The India Magazine* (October, 1990).

Black, D. and Loveless, C. ed. *Rugs of the Wandering Baluchi.* London, David Black Oriental Carpets, 1976.

Boardman, J. *Greek Art.* London: Thames & Hudson, 1964; reprint, 1989.

Born W. "The Indian Hand Spinning Wheel and its Migration to East and West". *Ciba Review* (1939).

Brand, M. and Lowry, G.D. *Akbar's India: Art from the Mughal City of Victory.* New York, The Asia Society Galleries, 1986.

Briffault, R. *The Mothers: A Study of the Origins of Sentiments and Institutions,* 3 Volumes. London, Allen & Unwin, 1927.

Buddha, P. *Political and Social Movements in Ancient Panjab.* Delhi, 1964.

Buhler, A. and Fischer, E. *The Patola of Gujarat.* New York and Basle, Krebs, 1979.

Burgess, J. *The Buddhist Stupas of Amaravati and Jaggeyyapeta.* London, Trubner, 1887.

Burney, C. " Excavations at Haftavan Tepe. Third Preliminary Report", *Iran,* 11 (1971).
—— "Excavations at Haftavan Tepe. Fourth Preliminary Report", *Iran* 13 (1975).

Burnham, D.K. *Warp and Weft. A Textile Terminology* Toronto, Royal Ontario Museum, 1980.

Burrows, T. "The Proto-Indoaryans". *JRAS* (1973).

Burton, R. and Arbuthnot, F.F. tr. *The Kama Sutra of Vatsayana* London, Unwin Paperbacks, 1988.

Bussabarger, R.F. and Robins, B.D. *The Everyday Art of India.* New York, Dover, 1968.

Campbell, J. *The Masks of God.* 4 Volumes. New York, Viking Penguin 1962, Penguin 1976.

de Cardi, B. "Excavations at Bampur, a Third Millennium Settlement in Persian Baluchistan, 1966". *Anthropological Papers of the American Museum of Natural History* 51, Part 3, New York, (1971).

Carter, H. "An Ostracon Depicting a Red Jungle Fowl". *JEA* IX, (1923).

Casal, J. *Fouilles de Mundigak. Memoires de la Delegation*

Archeologique Francaise en Afghanistan, Paris, 1961.

―― *Fouilles d'Amri.* 2 vols. Paris, Klincksieck, 1964.

――"Fresh Digging at Amri". *PA*, I (1964).

Chandra, M. "Indian Costumes From Earliest Times to the first century BC". *Bhartiya Vidya* I (1939).

――"Indian Costume from first-fourth century AD" *JISOA* 8, Calcutta, (1940).

―― *Stone Sculpture in the Prince of Wales Museum.* Bombay, Prince of Wales Museum, 1974.

Chandra, P. *Stone Sculpture in the Allahabad Museum.* Poona, American Institute of Indian Studies, 1970.

Chattopadhyaya, K. *Carpets and Floor Coverings of India.* Bombay, 1969.

Childe, V.G. *New Light on the Most Ancient East.* London, Routledge & Kegan Paul, 1952.

Cohen, S.J. *The Unappreciated Dhurrie.* ed. David Black and Clive Loveless. London, David Black Oriental Carpets, 1982.

――"The Development of Indian Floor-Coverings and their Appearance in Miniature Paintings". Ph.d. thesis, *SOAS*, London (1986).

Collingwood, P. *The Techniques of Rug Weaving.* London, Faber, 1968; reprint, 1987.

Collon, D. *First Impressions: Cylinder Seals in the Ancient Near East.* London, British Museum, 1987.

Cook, J.M. *The Greeks in Ionia and the East.* London, Thames and Hudson, 1962.

Coomaraswamy, A.K. *Arts and Crafts of India and Ceylon.* Edinburgh, 1913.

――"Early Iconography II. Sri-Lakshmi". *Eastern Art I*, no.3 (Jan 1929).

――"Archaic Indian Terracottas". *Marg* VI (1952-53).

―― La Sculpture de *Barhut.* Paris, 1956.

―― *History of Indian and Indonesian Art.* New Delhi, 1972.

―― *Yakshas.* Washington, 1931; reprint, New Delhi, Munshiram Manoharlal, 1980.

Cowell, E.B. ed. *The Jataka, or Stories of the Buddha's Former Births.* Cambridge, C.U.P., 1895.

Craven, Roy C. *A Concise History of Indian Art.* London, Thames and Hudson, 1976.

Crawford, V. "Beside the Kara Su". *BMMA*, 22.

Crooke, W. *The Northwestern Provinces of India*, 1897, reprinted, London, 1972.

―― *Tribes and Castes of Northern India.* New Delhi,

―― *Popular Religion and Folklore of Northern India.* reprinted Delhi, 1968.

Crowfoot, G.M. "Textiles, Basketry, and Mats" in *A History of Technology*, eds. C. Singer, E.J. Holmyard & A.R. Hall. Oxford, Clarendon, 1954-58.

Cunningham, *A. Report for the Year* 1872-73, *ASI*, V. Calcutta (1875).

―― *The Stupa of Bharhut.* London, W.H. Allen, 1879.

Dales "New Investigations at Mohenjo-daro". *Archeology*, 18, 1965.

Dalley, S. "Ancient Assyrian Textiles and the Origins of Carpet Design". *Iran*, XXIX (1991).

Dani, A.H. "Excavations in the Gowal Valley". *AP*, 5 (1970-71).

――"Origins of Bronze Age Cultures in the Indus Basin". *Expedition*, 17.

Darling, M.L. *The Punjab Peasant in Prosperity and Debt.* London, O.U.P., 1925.

Datta, V.N. and Phadke, H.A. *History of Kurukshetra*

Kurukshetra, Vishal Publications, 1984.

Desai, K. *Iconography of Vishnu.* New Delhi, Abhinav, 1973.

Deshayes, J. "Ceramiques Peintes de Tureng Tepe". *Iran.* V (1967).

Dhamija, J. "Embroidery". *The India Magazine* (September, 1988).

Dikshit, K.N. "India: The Work of the Archeological Survey of India During the Year 1935-36". *Annual Bibliography of Indian Archaeology*, XI (1936).

Douie, J.M. *Punjab Settlement Manual.* Lahore, Punjab Govt., 1930.

Dowson, J. ed. *The History of India as Told by its own Historians, The Posthumous Papers of Sir H.M. Elliot.* 1871; reprinted, Calcutta, 1957.

―― *A Classical Dictionary of Hindu Mythology and Religion, Geography, History, and Literature.* fourth ed. London, Kegan Paul, Trench, Trubner, 1903.

Dunbabin, T.J. *The Greeks and their Eastern Neighbours.* London, S.P.H.S. (1957).

Dupree, L. "Deh Morasi Ghundai: A Chalcolithic Site in South-Central Afghanistan". *Anthropological Papers of the American Museum of Natural History* 50, Part 2, New York, 1963.

Eggeling, J. tr. *The Satapatha-Brahmana. The Sacred Books of the East.* ed. F. Max Muller Vol.41, Oxford, Clarendon, 1894; reprint, New Delhi, Motilal Banarsidas, 1989.

Eisen, G.A. *Ancient Oriental Cylinders and Other Seals with a Description of the Collection of Mrs. William H. Moore.* Chicago, University of Chicago Oriental Institute Publications, XLVII (1940).

Emery, I. *The Primary Structures of Fabrics.* Washington, D.C., 1966.

Enthoven, R.E. "The Folklore of Gujarat". supplement to *TIA*, XLVI (1917).

Erdmann, K. *Oriental Rugs and Carpets. A Survey of Seven Centuries.* London, Faber and Faber, 1970.

Fairservis, W.A., Jr. "Archeological Studies in the Seistan Basin of South-Western Afghanistan and Eastern Iran", *Anthropological Papers of the American Museum of Natural History.* 48, Part 1, New York (1961).
—— *The Roots of Indian Civilization.* London, Allen & Unwin, 1971.
——"Harappan Civilization According to its Writing". *South Asian Archaeology.* ed. B. Allchin, Cambridge, C.U.P. (1984).

Fergusson, J. *Tree and Serpent Worship.* London, India Museum 1873.

Forbes, R.J. *Studies in Ancient Technology.* Vol. IV, second edition, Leiden, 1964.

Foster, W. ed. *Early Travels in India.* 1583-1619. Oxford, O.U.P. 1921; Indian edition, Delhi, Chand & Co., 1968.

Franses, M. and Pinner, R. "Dhurries, the Traditional Tapestries of India". *Hali*, 4, No.3 (1982).

Frankfort, H. "*Early Studies of the Pottery of the Near East*". 1924.
——"The Indus Civilization and the Near East". *Annual Bibliography of Indian Archaeology.* 1932. VII, Leyden: Brill, 1934.
—— *Cylinder Seals.* London, 1939.
——"Ishtar at Troy". *JNES* VIII (1949).
—— *The Art and Architecture of the Ancient Orient.* Harmondsworth, Penguin, 1954; reprint, 1988.
—— *Memoires de la Mission Archeologique Francaise en Asie Centrale.* Paris, 1989.
—— *Fouilles de Shortughai. Recherches sur l'Asie Centrale Protohistorique,* 2 vols.

Frifelt K. & Sovensen P. eds. *South Asian Archaeology* 1985. Scandinavian Institute of Asian Studies, Papers No.4, London, Curzon, 1989.

Frumkin, G. *Archaeology in Soviet Central Asia.* Leiden, Brill, 1970.

Fuchs, S. *The Aboriginal Tribes of India.* New York, St. Martin's Press, 1973.

Gadd, C.J. *The Stones of Assyria.* London, Chatto and Windus, 1936.

Gajjar, I.N. *Ancient Indian Art and the West.* Bombay, Taraporevala, 1971.

Garbini, G. "The Stepped Pinnacle in Ancient Near East". *EW*, No. 9 (1958).

Gardner, P. *Coins of the Greek and Scythic Kings of Bactria and India in the British Museum.* London, Longmans, 1886.
—— *A History of Ancient Coinage* 700-300 BC. Oxford, Clarendon, 1918.

Geijer, A. *Oriental Textiles in Sweden.* Copenhagen, 1951.
—— *A History of Textile Art.* London, 1979.

Ghani, A. "Arms and Armour Motifs on Chaukandi Type Tombs". *PA.* 10-22 (1974-1986).

Ghirshman, R. *Fouilles de Sialk, pres' de Kashan.* 2 vols. Paris, 1938-9.
—— *Iran: Parthians and Sassanians.* tr., S. Gilbert & J. Emmons. London, Thames & Hudson, 1962.
—— *Persia: From the Origins to Alexander the Great.* tr., S. Gilbert and J. Emmons. London, Thames & Hudson, 1964.

Ghosh, A. ed. *Jaina Art and Architecture.* 3 vols. New Delhi, Bhartiya Jnanpith, 1974.

Ghosh, L. and Roy, D. *Ajanta and Ellora.* Bombay, IBH, 1986.

Gill, H.S. *Folk Art of the Punjab.* Patiala, Punjabi University, 1975.

—— *A Phulkari from Bhatinda.* Patiala. Punjabi University, 1977.

Gimbutas, M. *The Goddesses and Gods of Old Europe.* second ed. London, Thames & Hudson, 1982.
—— *The Language of the Goddess.* London, Thames & Hudson, 1989.

Goff, C. "Excavations at Baba Jan. 1968: Third Preliminary Report", *Iran* VIII (1970).
—"Excavations at Baba Jan: The Bronze Age Occupation", *Iran* XIV (1976).

Gorakshkar, S. ed. *Animals in Indian Art.* Bombay, Prince of Wales Museum, 1979.

Goswamy, B.N. *Essence of Indian Art.* Ahmedabad, Mapin, 1986.

Goswamy, B.N. and Grewal, J.S. *The Mughals and the Jogis of Jakhbar. HAS* Simla, Indian Institute of Advanced Studies, 1967.

Grabar, O. *The Formation of Islamic Art.* New Haven, 1973.

Gray, J. *Near Eastern Mythology.* London, Hamlyn, 1969; reprint, 1988.

Grewal, N. "Punja Durries of Punjab". *Swagat* (January, 1990).

Grey, C. *European Adventures of Northern India,* 1785-1849.1929; Reprint, Patiala, Language Dept., 1970.

Griffith, R.T.H. *The Hymns of the Rig Veda.* 2 vols. 1889; reprint, New Delhi, Munshiram Manoharlal, 1987.
—— *The Hymns of the Atharva-Veda.* 1895-96; reprint, New Delhi, Munshiram Manoharlal, 1985.

Guillaume, O. *Graeco-Bactrian and Indian Coins from Afghanistan.* tr., O. Bopearachchi. Delhi, O.U.P., 1991.

Gunter, A. "Representations of Urartian and Western Iranian Fortress Architecture in the Assyrian Reliefs". *Iran* XX (1982).

Gupta, S.P. *Archaeology of Soviet Central Asia and the Indian Borderlands.* Delhi, 1979.

—— ed., *Kushana Sculptures from Sanghol.* New Delhi, National Museum, 1985.

——"The Wine-Carrying Mother Goddess at Sanghol". *Archaeology and History, Essays in Memory of A. Ghosh.* ed. B.M. Pande & B.D. Chattopadhyaya. New Delhi 1987.

Gupte, B.A. "Notes on Female Tattoo Designs in India". *TIA* XXXI (1902).

——"Some Rock and Tomb Incised Drawings from Baluchisthan". *TIA* XXXIX (1910).

Hackin, J. *Nouvelles Recherches Archeologique a Begram.* Paris, Imprimerie Nationale. 1953-4.

Halim, A. *History of the Lodi Sultans of Delhi and Agra.* Delhi, 1974.

Hall, R. *Egyptian Textiles.* Princess Risborough, Shire, 1986.

Hamlyn, C. "The Early Second Millennium Ceramic Assemblage of Dinkha Tepe". *Iran* 12 (1974).

——"Dalma Tepe". *Iran* 13 (1975).

Handa, D. *Osian History, Archaeology, Art and Architecture.* Delhi, Sundeep Prakashan, 1984.

Handa, O.P. *Pahari Folk Art.* Bombay, Taraporevala, 1975.

Hansen, D.P. "New Votive Plaques from Nippur". *JNES* XXII (1963).

Hansman, J. and Stronach, D. "A Sasanian Repository at Shahr-i Qumis". *JRAS (1970).*

Hargreaves, H. and Seymour Sewell, R.B. "Potsherds from Prehistoric Sites in Baluchistan". *PA* 1 (1964).

—— *Excavations in Baluchistan, Sampur Mound, Mustung and Sohr Damb.* 1929; Reprinted New Delhi, 1981.

Harle, J.C. "An Early Indian Hero-Stone and a Possible Western Source". *JRAS.* (1970).

—— *Gupta Sculpture: Indian Sculpture of the fourth to the sixth centuries AD.* Oxford, Clarendon Press, 1974.

—— *The Art and Architecture of the Indian Subcontinent.* Harmondsworth, Penguin, 1986.

Harris, H.T. *A Monograph on the Carpet Industry of South India.* Madras, 1908.

Harris, N. *Rugs and Carpets of the Orient.* London, Hamlyn, 1977.

Hartner, W. "The Earliest History of the Constellations in the Near East and the Motif of the Lion-Bull Combat". *JNES* XXIV (1965).

Hendley, T.H. *Asian Carpets: 16th and 17th century Designs from the Jaipur Palaces.* London, 1905.

Henrickson, E.E. "An Updated Chronology of the Early and Middle Chalcolithic of the Central Zagros Highlands Western Iran". *Iran* XX111 (1985).

Henrickson, R.C. "A Regional Perspective on Godin 111 Cultural Developments in Central Western Iran". *Iran* XX (1986).

Hermann, G. "Lapis Lazuli: The Early Phases of its Trade", *Iraq* XXX (1968).

——"The Sculptures of Bahram II". *JRAS.* (1970).

Hershman, P. *Punjabi Kinship and Marriage.* Delhi, Hindustan Publishing Corporation, 1981.

Herzfeld, E.E. *Iran in the Ancient East.* London, O.U.P., 1941.

Hill, G.F. *Catalogue of the Greek Coins of Lycaonia, Isauria, and Cilicia.* London, British Museum, 1900.

Hitkari, S.S. *Phulkari. The Folk Art of Punjab.* New Delhi, 1980.

Hopkins, E.W. *The Religions of India.* Boston, Ginn, 1895.

Houghton B.A., ed. *Animals in Archaeology.* London, Barrie and Jenkins, 1972.

Housego, J. *Tribal Rugs.* London, Scorpion, 1978.

Hugel, C. *Travels in Kashmir and the Punjab.* tr. Major T.B. Jervis, London, 1845.

Hultzsch, E. ed. *Corpus Inscriptionum Indicarum I, Inscriptions of Ashoka.* Oxford, Clarendon Press, 1925.

Ibbetson, D. *Punjab Castes, Races Castes and Tribes of the People of Panjab.* 1916; reprinted, New Delhi, 1981.

Idris Siddiqi M. *Thatta.* Karachi, Department of Archaeology and Museums, 1979.

Ingholt, H. *Gandharan Art in Pakistan.* New York, Pantheon, 1957.

Irwin, J. and Schwartz, P.R. *Studies in Indo-European Textile History.* Calico Museum of Textiles, Ahmedabad, 1966. Reprints of articles first published in serial form in the *Journal of Indian Textile History.*

Irwin, J. and Brett, K.B. *Origins of Chintz.* London, Victoria and Albert Museum. London, H.M.S.O. Publication, 1970.

—— *Indian Painted and Printed Fabrics.* Ahmedabad, Calico Museum of Textiles, 1972.

Irwin, J. and Hall, M. *Indian Embroideries, Historic Textiles of India at the Calico Museum.* Vol. II. Ahmedabad, 1973.

Jacobson, J. ed. *Studies in the Archaeology of India and Pakistan.* New Delhi, 1986.

Jacobson, T. "Formative Tendencies in Sumerian Religion", *The Bible and the Ancient Near East,* ed. G.E. Wright. Cambridge, Mass, 1961.

James, E.O. *The Ancient Gods,* 1960.

Jarrige, J.F. "Nouvelles Recherches Archaeologique en Baluchistan:

Les Fouilles de Mehrgarh". *Colloques du C.N.R.S.* No. 567, Paris (1976).
——"Excavations at Mehrgarh-Naushero", *P.A.* 10-22 (1974-1986).
—— *Fouilles de Pirak.* 2 vols. Paris, 1989.

Jarrige J.F. and Lachevallier, M. "Excavations at Mehrgarh, Baluchistan. Their Significance in the Prehistorical Context of the Indo-Pakistan Borderlands". *South Asian Archaeology* IV (1977).

Johnstone, D.C. *Monograph on Woollen Manufactures of the Punjab.* Punjab, Punjab Government Press, 1886.

Jones, O. *The Grammar of Ornament.* Reprint London, 1988.

Joshi, J.P. "A Note on the Excavations at Bhagwanpura". *Puratattva*, 8.
——"Interlocking of Late Harappa Culture and Painted Grey Ware Culture in the Light of Recent Excavations". *ME* II (1978).
——"Settlement Patterns in Third, Second, and First Millennia India – With Special References to Recent Discoveries in Punjab". *Ratambhava Studies in Indology*, Ghaziabad, Acharya Udayvira Shastri, 1986.

Joshi, J.P. and Bala, M. "Life during the time of Late Harappan and PGW Culture". *JISOA.*

Joshi, L.M., and Singh, F., eds. *History of the Punjab. Vol.I. From Prehistoric Times to the Age of Ashoka.* Patiala, Punjabi University, 1976.

Kang, K.S. *Mural Paintings in 19th century Punjab.* PhD. Dissertation, Punjab University Chandigarh, 1978.
—— *Punjab Art and Culture.* Delhi, 1988.
——"Phulkari". *Advance* (May, 1989).

Kantor, H.J. "The Shoulder

Ornament of Near Eastern Lions". *JNES* VI (January-October, 1947).
—— H.J. "Achaemenid Jewelry in the Oriental Institute". *JNES* XVI (1957).
——"A Bronze Plaque with Relief Decoration From Tell Tainat". Oriental Institute Museum Notes, No.13. *JNES* XXI (1962).

Keall, E.J. Leveque, M. and Willson, N. "Qal'eh-I Yazdigird: Its Architectural Decorations". *Iran* XVIII (1980).

Kendrick, A.F. and Tattersall, C.E.C. *Hand-woven Carpets, Oriental and European.* London, 1922.

Kennedy, J.K. "The Early Commerce of Babylon with India 700-300 BC". *JRAS* (1898).

Khan, F.A. *The Indus Valley and Early Iran.* Karachi, Department of Archaeology and Museums, 1964.
——"Kot Diji". P.A. 2 (1965).

Khan, I. *The Punjab Under Imperialism* 1885-1947.

Khan, M.I. ed. *Archaeology of Sind.* Karachi, Department of Archaeology and Museums, 1986.

Khlopin, I.N. "The Manufacture of Pile Carpets in Bronze Age Central Asia". *Hali* 5, No.2 (1982).

Kircho, L.B. *The Origin of the Bronze Age in Southern Turkmenistan.*

Koch, E. *Shah Jehan and Orpheus.* Graz, 1988.

Kohl, P.L. "A Note on Chlorite Artifacts from Shahr-i-Sokhta". *EW* 27 (1977)
—— ed. *The Bronze Age Civilization of Central Asia. Recent Soviet Discoveries* New York, 1981.

Kohl, P.L. and Hestel, D.L. "Archaeological Reconnaissances in the Darreh Gaz Plain. A Short Report". *Iran* XV11 (1980).

Konieczny, M.G. *Textiles of Baluchistan.* London, British Museum, 1979.

Kozloff, A.P. ed. *Animals in Ancient Art From the Leo Mildenberg Collection.* Cleveland, Cleveland Museum of Art, 1981.

Konnur, B.B. trans. *Sri Suktam.* Bombay, Bhartiya Vidya Bhavan, 1987.

Kramrisch, S. "Kantha", *JISOA* VII (1939).
—— *The Hindu Temple.* Calcutta, University of Calcutta, 1946.
——"An Image of Aditi-Uttanapad". *AA* XIX (1956).

Kumar, A.S. "Naga Shawl". *Swagat* (November, 1992).

Kybalova, L. *Coptic Textiles.* London, 1967.

Lal B.B. "Perhaps the Earliest Ploughed Field So Far Excavated Anywhere in the World". *Puratattva*, No.4.
——"Kalibangan and the Indus Civilization". Agrawal and Chakrabarti, eds. *Essays in Indian Protohistory.* Delhi, 1979.

Lamberg-Karlovsky, C. "The Proto-Elamite Settlement at Tepe Yahya". *Iran* IX (1971).
——"Tepe Yahya". Reports in *Iran* VIII-XI London, (1971-4).
——"Tepe Yahya 1971: Mesopotamia and the Indo-Iranian Borderlands". *Iran* X (1972).

Lamberg-Karlovsky, C. and Sabloff, J. A. *Ancient Civilizations. The Near East and Mesoamerica.* California, 1979.

Lamberg-Karlovsky, C. and Tosi, M. "Shohr-i Sokhta and Tepe Tahya: Tracks on the Earliest History of the Iranian Plateau". *E.W.* 23 (1973).

Lamm, C.J. *Cotton in Medieval Textiles of the Near East.* Paris, 1937.

Landreau, A.N. and Pickering. *Bosporus to Samarkhand: Flat-woven Rugs.* Catalogue of exhibition of the Washington Textile Museum, Washington, 1969.

Lane-Poole, S. *Medieval India Under the Mohammedan Rule.* Delhi, 1980.

Latimer, C. *Monograph on Carpet Making in the Punjab.* 1905-6. Lahore, 1907.

Lawrence, H.M.L. *Adventures of an Officer in the Punjaub.* 2 vols. 1883; reprint, Patiala, Languages Department, Punjab, 1970.

Le Breton, L. "The Early Period at Susa: Mesopotamian Relations". *Iraq* XIX (1957).

Legrain, L. *Empreintes de Cachets Elamites. Mission en Susdiane,* Memoires de la Delegation en Perse XVI Paris, 1921.
⎯ *Ur Excavations,* Vol. X: *Seal Cylinders.* London, British Museum, 1951.

Leoshko, J. "The Case of the Two Witnesses to the Buddha's Enlightenment". *Marg.* XXXIX, no.4.

Lewis, O. and Barnouw, V. *Village Life in Northern India: Studies in a Delhi Village,* Urbana, University of Illinois, 1958.

Lloyd, S. and Sofar, F. "Tell Uqair: Excavations by the Iraq Government Directorate of Antiquities in 1940 and 1941". *JNES* II (1943).

Lloyd, S. *The Archaeology of Mesopotamia. From the Old Stone Age to the Persian Conquest.* London, Thames and Hudson Ltd., 1978.

Loud, G. *Khorsabad, Part I, Excavations in the Palace and at a City Gate.* Chicago, U.C.P., 1936.

MacDonell, A.A. *The Vedic Mythology.* Varanasi, Chowkhamba Vidyabhavan, 1961.

Mackay, E.J.H. *Further Excavations at Mohenjo-daro,* 1927-1931. Delhi, 1938.
⎯ *Chanhu-daro Excavations 1935-36,* New Haven, American Oriental Society. 1943.

Mackenzie, D.A. *The Migration of Symbols and Their Relations to Beliefs and Customs.* New York, Alfred Knopf, 1926.
⎯ *Myths of Crete and Pre-Hellenic Europe.* London, Gresham, no date.

Maclagan, E.D. "The Earliest English Visitors to the Punjab, 1585-1628". *JPHS* I No.2.

Macpherson, D. *History of European Commerce with India.* London, 1812.

Mallory, J.P. *In Search of the Indo-Europeans.* London, Thames and Hudson, 1989. reprinted 1991.

Mallowan, M.E.L. "Excavations at Tall Arpachiyah, 1933". *Iraq* II (1935).
⎯"The Excavations at Tall Chagar Bazar". *Iraq* III (1936).
⎯"Excavations at Brak and Chagar Bazar". *Iraq* IX (1947).
⎯ *Early Mesopotamia and Iran.* London, 1965.

Manchanda, Dr. O.P. *Ribbed Pottery: A Study of the Harappan Pottery.* Delhi, 1972.

Margabandhu, C. and Gaur, G.S. "Sanghol Excavations 1987: Some New Evidences". *Puratattva* 17, New Delhi (1986-87).

Marriot, McKim, *Village India Studies in the Little Community.* Chicago, University of Chicago Press (1955).

Marshack, A. *The Roots of Civilization: The Cognitive Beginnings of Man's First Art, Symbol and Notation.* New York, Mc-Graw Hill, 1972.

Marshall, J. ed. *Mohenjo-daro and the Indus Civilisation.* 3 vols. London, Probsthain, 1931.
⎯ *Taxila.* 3 vols. Cambridge, C.U.P., 1951.
⎯ *The Buddhist Art of Gandhara,* Cambridge: C.U.P., 1960.
⎯ *Exhibition of Gandhara Art of Pakistan.* Tokyo, 1984.

Marshall, J. and Foucher, A. *The Monuments of Sanchi.* Calcutta, 1940.

Martin, F.R. *A History of Oriental Carpets before 1800.* Vienna, 1908.

Mason, C. *Narrative of Various Journeys in Baluchistan, Afghanistan, and the Punjab.* 3 vols. London, 1842.

Masson, V.M. tr. Henry N. Michael *Altyn-Tepe,* Philadelphia, 1988.
⎯"The Urban Revolution in South Turkmenia". *Antiquity,* XLII (1968).

Masson V.M. and Sarianidi, V. *Central Asia. Turkmenia before the Achaeminids.* London, Thames and Hudson, 1972.

Matheson, S.A. *Persia: an Archeological Guide.* London, 1976.

Maxwell-Hyslop, K.R. *Western Asiatic Jewellery 3000-612 BC.* London, Methuen, 1974.

McCrindle, J.W. *Ancient India as described by Megasthenes and Arrian,* Calcutta, Chuckervertty, Chatterjee, 1926.

Mellaart, J. *The Neolithic of the Near East.* London, Thames and Hudson, 1965.
⎯ *Catal Hüyük: A Neolthic Town in Anatolia.* London, 1967.

Mellaart, J. Hirsch, U. and Balpinar, B. *The Goddess from Anatolia.* Adenau, 1989.

Ministere des Relations Exterieures, *Au Pays de Baal et d'Astarte: 10000 ans d'art en Syrie.* Paris, 1983-1984.

Ministry of Industries, Government of Pakistan. *Threadlines.* Pakistan, Karachi, 1987.

Mohamed, U.A. *Modern Kashi Earthenware Tiles and Vases In Imitation of the Ancient.* trans. John Fargus. Edinburgh, Museum of Science and Art.

Moorcroft, W. and Trebeck, G. *Travels in the Himalayan Provinces*

of Hindustan and the Punjab; in Ladakh and Kashmir; in Peshawar, Kabul, Kunduz and Bokhara. ed. H.H. Wilson. Calcutta, Asiatic Society, 1837; reprint, Patiala Dept. of Languages, 1970.
___ An Account of the Kashmir Shawl Industry. ed. H.H. Wilson. London, 1841.

Mohanty, B.C. Chandramouli, K.V.and Naik, H.D. Natural Dyeing Processes of India, Studies in Contemporary Textile Crafts of India. Ahmedabad, Calico Museum of Textiles, 1987.

Mohanti, B.C. and Mohanty, J.P. Block Printing and Dyeing of Bagru, Rajasthan, Studies in Contemporary Textile Crafts of India. Ahmedabad, Calico Museum of Textiles, 1983.

Moorey, P.R.S. Catalogue of the Ancient Persian Bronzes in the Ashmolean Museum. Oxford, Clarendon, 1971.

Mughal, R.M. The Decline of the Indus Civilization and the Late Harappan Period in the Indus Valley. LMB. III, No.2 (1990).

Mukherjee, B.N. Nana on Lion: A Study in Kushan Numismatic Art. Calcutta, Asiatic Society, 1969.

Mumtaz K.K. Architecture in Pakistan. Singapore, Mimar, 1985.

Mungkar, B. "Notes on Two Ancient Fertility Symbols". EW 28 (1978).

Munn Rankin, J.M. "Ancient Near Eastern Seals in the Fitzwilliam Museum". Iraq XXI (1959.)

Nabholz-Kartaschoff, M. Golden Sprays and Scarlet Flowers. Traditional Indian Textiles from the Museum of Ethnography, Basle, Switzerland. Kyoto, 1986.

National Museum of Art, Osaka. The Exhibition of Gandhara Art of Pakistan. 1984.

Nazim, M. The Life and Times of Sultan Mahmud of Ghazna. New Delhi, Oxford University Press, 1931.

Nehru L. Origins of the Gandharan Style. Delhi, O.U.P., 1989.

Neumayer, E. Prehistoric Indian Rock Paintings. Delhi, 1983.

Nissen, H.J. The Early History of the Ancient Near East 9000-2000 BC. Chicago and London, 1988.

Oates, J. Babylon. London and New York, 1979.

O'Flaherty, W.D. The Rig Veda. Harmondsworth, Penguin, 1981; reprint, 1983.

Okladnikov, A.P. Ancient Populations of Siberia and Its Cultures, Cambridge, Peabody Museum of Archaeology and Ethnology, 1959.

Oppenheim, A. L. "The Golden Garments of the Gods". JNES 8 (1949).

Pal, P. "A Pre-Kushan Buddha Image from Mathura". Marg XXXIX, no.4.

Pande, B.M. "The Neolithic in Kashmir: New Discoveries". The Anthropologist XVII No. 1 & 2 (1970).

Parker, B. "Excavations at Nimrud, 1949-1953: Seals and Seal Impressions". Iraq XVII (1955).

Parpola, A. "New Correspondences Between Harappan and Near Eastern Glyptic Art". South Asian Archaeology (1981) ed., B. Allchin, Cambridge, C.U.P., 1984.

Parrot, A. Le Temple D'Ishtar, tome I, Mission Archeologique de Mari. Paris, Geuthner, 1956.
___ Sumer. London, 1961.

Payne, H. Necrocorinthia. A Study of Corinthian Art in the Archaic Period. Oxford, Clarendon, 1931.

Payne, J.C. "Lapis Lazuli in Early Egypt". Iraq XXX (1968).

Perkins, A.L. The Comparative Archaeology of Early Mesopotamia. Chicago, U.C.P., 1957.

Petsopoulos, Y. Kilims, The Art of Tapestry Weaving in Anatolia, the Caucasus, and Persia. London, 1979.

Pinner, R. "Decorative Designs on Prehistoric Turkmen Ceramics". Hali 5 no.2 (1982).

Platts, J.T. A Dictionary of Urdu, Classical Hindi, and English. Delhi, Munshiram, Manoharlal, 1988.

Pope, A.U. Memoires de la Delegation en Perse XIII. Paris, Leroux, 1912.
___ Masterpieces of Persian Art. New York, Dryden, 1945.
___ A Survey of Persian Art. 6 Vols. London, O.U.P., 1938-39 & 1958.

Porada, E. "The Relative Chronology of Mesopotamia, Part I", in Chronologies in Old-World Archaeology, ed. R.W. Ehrich. Chicago, University of Chicago Press, (1965).
___ Ancient Iran: The Art of Pre-Islamic Times. London, Methuen, 1965.
___"Remarks on Seals found in the Gulf States". AA 33 (1971).

Possehl, G.L. Harappan Civilization. New Delhi, 1982.
___"Indian Archaeology, A Review: Guide to Excavated Sites, 1953-54 through 1984-85". Puratattva 18 New Delhi (1987-88).
___"Revolution in the Urban Revolution: The Emergence of Indus Urbanization", Annual Review of Anthropology, (1990).

Prakash, B. Political and Social Movements in Ancient Panjab. Delhi, 1964.

Prater, S.H. The Book of Indian Animals. Bombay, Bombay Natural History Society, 1948, reprint, 1980.

Pumpelly, R. Excavations in Turkestan I & II 1905, 1908.

Punia, D.S. "New Evidence of Pre-Kushan Sculpture from Gurgaon District (Haryana)". *EW* 31 (1981).

Punja, S. *An Illustrated Guide to Museums of India.* Hong Kong, The Guidebook Company, 1990.

Rao, S.R. *Lothal and the Indus Civilization.* New York, 1973.

Rasmussen, T. and Spivery, N., eds. *Looking at Greek Vases.* Cambridge, C.U.P., 1991.

Ratnagar, S. *The Westerly Trade of the Harappa Civilization.* Oxford, O.U.P., 1981.
— *Enquiries into the Political Organisation of Harappan Society.* Pune, Ravish, 1991.

Rawlinson, H.G. *Intercourse Between India and the Western World From the Earliest Times to the Fall of Rome.* Cambridge, C.U.P., 1916.

Ray, N. *Maurya and Post-Maurya Art.* Delhi, I.C.H.R., 1945.

Ray, S.K. "Folk-Art of Bengal: The Theriomorphs". *Roopa-Lekha* XXVIII (1958).
— *The Brata Art of Bengal.* Calcutta, Mukopadhyay, 1961.

Reath, N.A. and Sachs, E.B. *Persian Textiles and their Technique from the sixth to the 18th centuries.* New Haven, Yale University Press, 1937.

Rieftstahl, R.M. *Persian and Indian Textiles from the 16th to the early 19th century.* New York, 1923.

Roaf, M. "The Art of the Achaemenians". *The Arts of Persia* R.W. Ferrier, ed. New Haven, Yale University Press, 1989.

Robins, B. D. & Bussabarger, "Folk Images of Sanjhi Devi". *AA XXXVI* (1974).

Robinson, V.J. *Eastern Carpets.* London, 1893.

Rose, H.A. "A Version of Hir and Ranjha". *TIA* (1925).

— *A Glossary of the Tribes and Castes of the Punjab and the North-West Frontier Province.* 3 vols. Lahore, Govt Printing Press, 1919.

Rosenfield, J. *The Dynastic Arts of the Kushans.* Berkeley & Los Angeles, University of California, 1967.

Rosu, A. "Purnaghata et le symbolisme du lotus dans L'Inde". *Arts Asiatiques* VIII (1961).

Rudenko, S.I. *Frozen Tombs of Siberia, the Pazyryk Burials of Iron Age Horseman.* London, 1970.

Rye, O.S. and Evans, C. *Traditional Pottery Techniques of Pakistan; Field and Laboratory Studies.* Washington, Smithsonian Institution Press, 1976.

Saar, S.S. *Ancestors of Kashmir.* New Delhi, Lalit Art Publishers, 1992.

Sarianidi, V. "Southern Turkmenia and Northern Iran. Ties and Differences in Very Ancient Times". *EW* 21 (1971).

Santoni, M. "Potters and Pottery at Mehrgarh During the Third Millennium BC (Periods VI and VII)". *South Asian Archeology* (1985).

Sarkar, S.C. *Some Aspects of the Earliest Social History of India.* London, O.U.P., 1928.

Sarma, A. "Decline of Harappan Cultures: A Re-look". *EW* 27 (1977).

Sarre, F. *Ancient Oriental Carpets.* trans. by A.F. Kendrick, K.K. Oesterreich Museum fur Kunst und Industrie. Vienna, 1926-9.

Schmidt, E.F. *Excavations at Tepe Hissar, Damghan,* 1931-33. Philadelphia, 1937.

Schlinghoff, D. "Cotton Manufacture in Ancient India". *Journal of the Economic and Social History of the Orient.* 17 Part I (1974).

Schwartz, A. "Reel and Spinning Wheel". *CIBA Review* 59 (1947).

Schwartz, P.R. "French documents on Indian cotton painting": (i) The Beaulieu ms., ca. 1734, *JITH,* II 5 (1956), (ii) "New Light on Old Material", *JITH* III (1957). Appendix A. "The letters of Father Coeurdoux, 1742 & 1747. Appendix B. Anonymous Report, 1752. (iii) "The Roxburgh account of Indian Cotton painting, 1795". *JITH* IV (1959).

Sethna, K.D. *Karpasa in Prehistoric India. A Chronological and Cultural Clue.* New Delhi, 1986.

Sen, A. *Animal Motifs in Ancient Indian Art.* Calcutta, Mukhopadhyay, 1972.

Sharma, R.C. *Buddhist Art of Mathura.* Delhi, 1984.
— *Urban Decay in India.* New Delhi, 1987.

Sharma, Y.D. "Past Patterns in Living as Unfolded by Excavations at Rupar". *LK* Nos. 1-2 (1955-1956).

Shastri, A.M. *India as Seen in the Brahatsamhita of Varahamihira.* Delhi, Motilal Banarsidass, 1948.

Shastri, J.L. ed. *Ancient Indian Tradition and Mythology,* Delhi: Motilal Banarsidass, 1984, vol.27. *The Agni Purana,* tr. N. Gangadharan.

Shere, S.A., "Stone Disks found at Murtaziganj", *JBRS,* XXXVII, 1951.

Singh, G.B. and Narang, D.R. "Correct date of Birth of Guru Gobind Singh", *The Sikh Review* 40: 1 (January, 1992).

Singh, P. "The Ninth Delhi". Sir George Birdwood Memorial Lecture delivered to the Commonwealth Section of the Royal Society for the Encouragement of Arts, Manufactures and Commerce. RSA, 1971.

Singh R.P. *Rise of the Jat Power.* New Delhi, Harman Publishing House, 1988.

Sinor, D. ed. *The Cambridge History of Early Inner Asia.* Cambridge, C.U.P., 1990.

Sivaramamurti, C. *Birds and Animals in Indian Art.* New Delhi, National Museum, 1974.

Skelton, R. et al, eds. *Facets of Indian Art.* London, Victoria and Albert Museum, 1986.

Snead, S. *Animals in Four Worlds.* Chicago, University of Chicago Press, 1989.

Spear, P. *A History of India*, II. Hardmondsworth, Penguin Books, 1966.

Srinivasan, D.M. *Mathura: The Cultural Heritage.* Poona, American Institute of Indian Studies, 1989.

Srivastava, A.L. *Life In Sanchi Sculpture.* New Delhi, 1983.

Srivastava, V.C. *Sun-Worship in Ancient India.* Allahabad, Indological Publications, 1972.

Starr, R.F.S. *Nuzi.* Cambridge, Harvard University Press, 1937-39.
— *Indus Valley Painted Pottery.* Princeton, Princeton University Press, 1941.

Steel F.A. *Folklore of the Punjab. TIA* XI (1882).
— *Monograph on Silk Industry in the Punjab*, Punjab. Government Press, 1887.
— "Phulkari Work in the Punjab". *JIA.* II No.24 (October, 1888).

Stein, A. *An Archaeological Tour to Gedrosia.* Reprinted New Delhi, 1982.
— *Innermost Asia: detailed report of explorations in Central Asia, Kan-su, and E. Iran 3 vols.* Oxford, O.U.P., 1928; reprint, New Delhi, 1981.
— *Serindia Detailed Report of Explorations in Central Asia and Westernmost China.* 5 vols. Oxford, O.U.P., 1921.

Ancient Khotan: Detailed report of archaeological explorations in Chinese Turkestan. 2 vols. London, 1907; reprint, New Delhi, 1981.

Stronach, D. "Tepe Nush-i Jan". *Iran* XX11 (1974) X111 (1975).

Sumner, W. "Excavations at Tall-i Malyan 1971-72", *Iran* 12 (1974).

Swynnerton, C. *Romantic Tales from the Punjab.* 1903; reprinted Patiala, 1963.
— *Folk Tales from the Upper Indus.* reprinted, Islamabad: 1987.

Talwar, K. and Krishna, K. *Indian Pigment Paintings on Cloth*, Vol.III, Historic Textiles of India at the Calico Museum, Ahmedabad. Ahmedabad, Calico Museum of Textiles, 1979.

Tanavoli, P. *Lion Rugs: The Lion in the Art and Culture of Iran.* Basel, Wepf, 1985.

Tartakov, G.M. and Dahejia, V. "Sharing, Intrusion, and Influence: The Mahisasuramardini Imagery of the Calukyas and the Pallavas", *A.A.* XLV (1984).

Temple, R.C. The Legends of the Punjab. 3 vols. 1884; reprint, Patiala, Language Department, 1962.

Thakur, J.P. "Peacock: The National Bird of India". *Pavo* 1, no. 1 (March, 1963).

Thaper, B.K. "Kalibangan, a Harappan Metropolis Beyond the Indus Valley". *Expedition* 17 (1975).

Thapar, R. Asoka and the Decline of the Mauryas. Oxford, O.U.P., 1961.
— A History of India, Vol. I. Harmondsworth, Penguin Books, 1965.

The Wealth of India. Delhi, Council of Scientific and Industrial Research, 1948.

Tosi, M. "Excavations at Sahr-i Sokhta, a Chalcolithic Settlement in the Iranian Seistan. Preliminary Report on the First Campaign October-December, 1967". *EW, New Series 18.* (1968).

Trilling, J. "The Roman Heritage Textiles from Egypt and the Eastern Mediterranean 300 to 600 AD". *TMJ 21* (1982).

Tripathi, R.R. "New Clay Sealings from Kausambi". *JNSI* XXXIX (1977).

Vanden Berghe, L. *Archaeologie de l'Iran Ancien.* Leiden, 1959.

Van Der Waeden, B.L. "Babylonian Astronomy. The Thirty-six Stars". *JNES* VIII (1949).

Van Buren, E.D. *Clay Figurines of Babylon and Assyria, Yale Oriental Series-Researches Vol. XVI.* New Haven, Yale, 1930.

Van Rosevelt, A. "Coptic Textiles: An Introduction". *The Art of the Ancient Weaver.* Kelsey Museum of Archeology, Ann Arbor, The University of Michigan, 1980.

Varadarajan, L. "Silk in Northeastern and Eastern India: The Indigenous Tradition". *Modern Asian Studies 22, 3* (1988).

Vats, M.S. *Excavations at Harappa 1920-21 and 1933-34.* Delhi, Manager of Publications, 1940.

Victoria and Albert Museum, London and Mapin Publishing, Ahmedabad. *Indian Animals Daybook,* 1990.

Victoria and Albert Museum. *Indian Embroidery.* London, H.M.S.O., 1951.

Victoria and Albert Museum. *The Indian Heritage.* London, 1982.

Vogel, J.P. *Indian Serpent Lore or the Nagas in Hindu Legend and Art.* London, Probsthain, 1926.
— *La Sculpture de Mathura.* Paris & Brussels, Van Oest, 1930.

Von Mitterwallner, G. *Kusana Coins and Sculptures.* Mathura, The Government Museum, 1986.

Ward, W.H. *The Seal Cylinders of Western Asia*. Washington, Carnegie, 1910.

Weibel, A.C. *Two Thousand years of Textiles*. published for Detroit Institute of Arts, New York, 1952.

Welch, S.C. *Royal Persian Manuscripts*. London, Thames and Hudson, 1976.
— *Indian Art and Culture 1300-1900*. New York, Metropolitan Museum of Art, 1985.

Wheeler, M. *Charsada*. Cabridge, C.U.P., 1951.

Whitehead, H. *The Village Gods of South India*. Calcutta, Association Press, 1921.

Wiseman, D.J. *Cylinder Seals of Western Asia*. London, Batchworth Press, n.d.

Williams, D. *Greek Vases*. London, British Museum, 1990.

Wittkower, R. *Allegory and the Migration of Symbols*. London, 1977.

Woodford, S. *An Introduction to Greek Art*. London, Duckworth, 1986; reprint, 1989.

Woolley, L. *Ur Excavations, Vol. II: The Royal Cemetery*. London, British Museum, 1934.

Wright H.N. *Catalogue of the Coins in the Indian Museum Calcutta, Vol. III: Mughal Emperors of India*. Oxford, Clarendon, 1908.

Wulff, H.E. *The Traditional Crafts of Persia*. Cambridge, M.I.T. Press, 1966.

Zettler, R.L. "On the Chronological Range of Neo-Babylonian and Achaemenid Seals". *JNES 38* (1979).

Zimmer, H. *Myths and Symbols in Indian Art and Civilization*. Princeton: Princeton University Press, 1946; New York, Pantheon, 1962; Indian edition: New Delhi, 1990.

— *The Art of Indian Asia*. 2 vols. Princeton, Princeton University Press, 1955; Paperback edition, 1983.

Glossary

Asan	Small durrie on which one person sits
Atti	Skeins
Bagh	Handspun cotton wedding veil completely covered with hand embroidery
Belna	Small hand worked cotton gin
Bistra	Bedding roll consisting of durrie, *chattahee, khes* or *razai* and pillow
Bumbal	Decorative ropes of warp ends.
Burfi	Lozenge-shaped sweet
Buti	Small floral ornament
Chaddar	Cotton sheet
Chakla and Belan	Dough board and rolling pin
Charkha	Wooden spinning sheel
Charpoi	Indian bed with wooden frame and webbing base
Chattahee	Cotton sheet, often hand-embroidered
Chhatri	Umbrella
Devi	Goddess
Dikhawa	Formal display of dowry items at the time of wedding
Diye	Traditional earthenware oil lamp
Dubbe	Boxes
Dumroo	Narrow-waisted drum
Durrie	Indian flat-woven cotton rug for floor or bed
Equid	Member of the equidae family which includes horses and asses
Farshi	Large Indian cotton durrie woven for use on the floor

Gaddi	Mattress
Gadva	Metal milk vessel
Gelim	Iranian flat-woven woollen rug
Gharha	Globular pottery water jar
Guddi Guddian	Doll/Girls
Gungru	Small bells of brass
Gurudwara	Sikh Temple
Guttian	Small bundles of yarn with which the durrie is woven
Hatthi	Weaver's comb made of iron with wooden handle
Heddle	Bar along which alternate warps are held
Jalebi	Popular coiled sweet
Jali	Lattice
Janjeeri	Decorative "chain" woven at either end of a durrie to keep the wefts in place – weft twining
Jat	Farming community of northern India
Join	Point where two colours meet
Kakka/ Kakke	Children
Kana	Light wooden stick on which the cotton is rolled and made ready for spinning
Kantha	Necklace
Khadi	Handspun, handwoven cloth
Khes	Coarse, handspun cotton sheet
Khind	Soft quilted cotton mattress of Himachal Pradesh

Kilim	Turkish flat-woven woollen rug	*Shamiana*	Tent
Mandir	Hindu temple	*Shed and Counter-shed*	Alternate movement of warp threads
Marhi	Small shrines to Guru Guga	*Shed rod*	Rod used to change shed in Rajasthani loom
Mindian	Decorative plaits of warp ends	*Shed bar or board or lease rod*	Board used to change shed to countershed.
Moorha	Circular plaited grass mat bound with coloured cotton	*Shuttle*	Wooden yarn holder for weaving
Nuchla	Spun yarn	*Takla*	Spindle
Panakh	Jointed strip of wood/broad holder for keeping width constant	*Tallai*	Thin, padded mattress
		Tara	Bow with string for separating cotton fibres
Panja/ Punja	Elsewhere in India the name for Hatthi, weaver's comb, and for the durries woven in the technique	*Teran*	Wooden hand, or static, reel
		Tukri	Pieces
Patkari	Alum	*Vahana*	Animal mount of a deity
Phul	Flower	*Vedi*	Marriage altar
Phulkari	Handspun cotton wedding veil partially covered with hand embroidery	*Yakshi*	Supernatural beings who serve Kubera, god of Wealth
Phunde/ Phulwe	Pompoms meaning flowers		
Pirhi	Low wooden stool with webbing seat		
Punia	Loose rolls of cotton fibre from which yarn is spun		
Punkha	Fan		
Purna Kalasa	The vase of plenty, symbol of the bounty of nature and fullness of life		
Razai	Padded cotton quilt		
Rosette	Formalized representation of the open face of a flower		
Sandook	Dowry chest		
Sarak	Road		
Sarpanch	Village headman		